The Accounting Procedures Guidebook

Second Edition

Steven M. Bragg

Published by AccountingTools LLC, Centennial, Colorado.

For more information about AccountingTools® products, visit our Web site at www.accountingtools.com.

ISBN-13: 978-1-938910-26-5

Printed in the United States of America

Table of Contents

Preface

A business needs a set of well-designed procedures to ensure that its transactions are completed in a uniform manner. Otherwise, a company will experience inefficiencies and an increased incidence of fraud, and will spend an inordinate amount of time correcting transaction errors. The *Accounting Procedures Guidebook* rectifies these problems by walking you through dozens of accounting and operational procedures and forms. Applying these procedures makes it easier to manage, increases operational efficiencies, reduces errors, and enhances the level of control.

In Chapter 1, we discuss the need for accounting procedures, how to determine the correct number of procedures to develop, and how to create and distribute them. In Chapters 2 through 7, we cover the procedures needed for the sales cycle, from the initial receipt of orders through credit planning, shipping, billing, collections, and the receipt of cash. In Chapters 8 through 13, we describe the procedures needed for the procurement cycle, including purchasing, accounts payable, receiving, and several related topics. In Chapters 14 through 17, we address the same types of information for inventory, payroll, fixed assets, and treasury activities. Finally, Chapter 18 addresses the process flows for closing the books of a private company and a public company.

The answers to many questions about accounting procedures can be found in the following chapters, including:

- How do I format a procedure?
- How do I handle deviations from procedures?
- How do I handle a return merchandise authorization?
- What process should I follow for a credit examination?
- What controls should be placed on the shipping of goods?
- Which format should I use for a statement of account?
- Which controls should I include in a cash receipts procedure?
- How do I construct a purchasing procedure?
- What system is needed to manually process expense reports?
- How does the three-way matching process work in accounts payable?
- How do I conduct a physical inventory count?
- What is the procedure for processing payroll?

The Accounting Procedures Guidebook is designed for both professionals and students. Professionals can use it as a reference tool for creating and revising procedures and forms, while it provides students with an overview of the entire system of procedures. Given its complete coverage of the accounting procedures topic, *The Accounting Procedures Guidebook* may earn a permanent place on your book shelf.

Centennial, Colorado
January 2014

About the Author

Steven Bragg, CPA, has been the chief financial officer or controller of four companies, as well as a consulting manager at Ernst & Young. He received a master's degree in finance from Bentley College, an MBA from Babson College, and a Bachelor's degree in Economics from the University of Maine. He has been a two-time president of the Colorado Mountain Club, and is an avid alpine skier, mountain biker, and certified master diver. Mr. Bragg resides in Centennial, Colorado. He has written the following books:

Accountants' Guidebook	Credit & Collection Guidebook
Accounting Controls Guidebook	Financial Analysis
Accounting for Inventory	Fixed Asset Accounting
Accounting for Managers	GAAP Guidebook
Accounting Procedures Guidebook	IFRS Guidebook
Budgeting	Inventory Management
Business Ratios	Investor Relations Guidebook
CFO Guidebook	Lean Accounting Guidebook
Closing the Books	Mergers & Acquisitions
Corporate Cash Management	New Controller Guidebook
Cost Accounting Fundamentals	Payroll Management
Cost Management Guidebook	

On-Line Resources by Steven Bragg

Steven maintains the accountingtools.com web site, which contains continuing professional education courses, the Accounting Best Practices podcast, and hundreds of articles on accounting subjects.

The Accounting Procedures Guidebook is also available as a continuing professional education (CPE) course. You can purchase the course and take an on-line exam at:

www.accountingtools.com/cpe

Chapter 1
Overview of Accounting Procedures

Introduction

The intent of this book is to provide you with a large number of sample accounting procedures and forms. Before doing so, we will first lay the groundwork for a system of procedures. In this chapter, we discuss the nature of procedures, why we need them, and how many to develop (a crucial point), as well as how to construct and use them. By the end of this chapter, you should have developed an understanding of the work required to create, maintain, and enforce a system of procedures.

> **Related Podcast Episode:** Episode 161 of the Accounting Best Practices Podcast discusses when to write a procedure. You can listen to it at: **accounting-tools.com/podcasts** or **iTunes**

The Nature of a Procedure

A procedure documents a business transaction. As such, it lists the specific steps required to complete a transaction, and is very useful for enforcing a high degree of uniformity in how those steps are completed. A procedure frequently incorporates one or more controls, which are designed to mitigate the risk of various types of losses. In some cases, an entire procedure is intended to *be* a control. Procedures may also be used to instruct new employees in how a company does business. Thus, a procedure has three purposes:

- To encourage uniformity in the completion of business transactions
- To enforce the use of controls
- To train employees

From the perspective of the management team, the first purpose (uniformity) is the most important, since it leads to greater efficiency. However, an auditor or risk manager may be more concerned with the second purpose (control), since they have a great interest in mitigating any number of risks to which a business is subjected. Further, the human resources staff has a great interest in the third purpose (training), since it is involved in training new employees. Thus, there are multiple constituencies within a business that have a considerable interest in the construction and maintenance of a set of procedures.

We will expand upon the nature of the procedure in the next section, where we address the specific issues that procedures can remedy.

The Need for Procedures

Procedures are needed to ensure that a company is capable of completing its objectives. For example, the primary purpose of a consumer products company is to place reliable and well-constructed products in the hands of its customers. In order to sell goods to those customers, it must be able to complete the following tasks consistently, time after time:

- Log in a customer order
- Pick the goods from stock
- Assemble them into a complete order that is ready for shipment by the promised date
- Reliably issue an accurate invoice to the customer

A procedure is needed to give structure to these activities. For example, one procedure could instruct the order entry staff regarding how to record order information from a customer into a sales order (which is used to process an order within a company), which errors may arise and how to deal with them, and where to send copies of the sales order.

It is certainly possible for very experienced employees to handle these tasks without a formal procedure, because they have been with the company long enough to have learned how to deal with most situations through experience. However, such an approach relies upon the verbal transfer of information to more junior employees, which is an unreliable approach that gradually leads to the use of many variations on a single procedure.

Imagine a situation where there are no formal procedures in a company that operates multiple retail stores. Each store develops its own methods for handling business transactions. Each one will have different control problems, different forms, different levels of efficiency, and different types of errors. Someone trying to review the operations of all the stores would be overwhelmed by the cacophony of different methods.

You can see from this example that procedures are of great value in providing structure to a business – they define how a business *does* things. In more detail, we need procedures because:

- *Best practices*. When a business routinely examines its operations with the intent of creating procedures, the documentation process often brings to light questionable or inefficient practices. If brought to the attention of management, there may be an opportunity to use best practices to upgrade the company's processes to a more efficient and effective level.
- *Efficiency*. It is much easier for the accounting staff to process business transactions and issue financial statements when there is a regimented approach to dealing with each type of transaction.
- *Errors*. It takes far more time to correct any transaction error than it takes to complete the transaction correctly the first time. Therefore, error avoidance is an excellent reason to use procedures.

- *Computer systems.* An accounting or enterprise-wide system typically works in conjunction with a set of procedures. If there is not a consistent set of procedures surrounding the system, employees may have difficulty entering information, and may not know the sequence of events needed to process transactions through the system.
- *Controls.* When it becomes evident that there is a control weakness in a company, the system of procedures can be adjusted to correct the problem.
- *Handoffs.* Many processes involve handing off work to someone in a different department. Any handoff involves a considerable risk that work will not be transferred correctly, resulting in a transaction lapse that may ultimately impact a customer. A procedure states exactly how a handoff is to be completed, and so reduces the risk of a transaction lapse.
- *Governance.* In a business that has a top-down organizational structure, procedures are needed to ensure that the decisions made by management are carried out properly.
- *Roll out consistency.* It is vastly easier to roll out a business concept when every location uses exactly the same set of procedures.
- *Training.* Procedures can form the basis for employee training manuals that address the basic functions of a business.

The sheer volume of reasons presented here should make it clear that there is a resounding need for procedures. However, we do not need a set of procedures for *everything*, as discussed in the next section.

The Number of Procedures to Develop

Even a smaller business may have a large number of processes. How many of them really need to be documented in a formal procedure? If a business documents all of them, it may find that it has spent an inordinate amount of time and money on some procedures that are rarely used, and which must now be updated from time to time. To keep from making an excessive expenditure on procedure development, consider the following factors when deciding whether to create a procedure:

- *Auditor concern.* If the auditors have indicated that there are control problems in a particular area, you will almost certainly have to develop a procedure that incorporates any controls that they recommend. Otherwise, the issue will have an impact on the auditors' control assessment of the business, which may require them to employ additional audit procedures that increase the price of their audit. In short, an auditor finding essentially mandates the creation of a procedure.
- *Risk.* If there is no procedure, is there a risk that the company will suffer a monetary or reputational loss? If this loss is significant, a procedure is probably called for, even if the procedure will be rarely used. Conversely, a procedure may not be necessary if there is little underlying risk associated with it.

- *Transaction efficiency.* There may be multiple ways in which a business transaction can be completed, of which one is clearly more efficient. If so, create a procedure that directs employees to use the most efficient variation. If there is only one way to complete a transaction, there is less need for a procedure.
- *Transaction volume.* As a general rule, there should be a procedure for the 20% of all transactions that comprise 80% of the total transaction volume in which a business engages. These procedures cover most of the day-to-day activities of a business, and so can be of considerable assistance in defining the jobs of new employees, as well as for ensuring that the most fundamental activities are followed in a prescribed manner.

The last point, transaction volume, is a key determinant of the need for a procedure. There are many low-volume activities where it simply makes no sense to engage in any documentation activities at all. Instead, allow employees to follow their best judgment in deciding how to complete a lesser activity.

Once you have used these criteria to decide which transactions should be documented with a procedure, consider using the next section as a guide for their construction.

The Mechanics of Procedure Production

A typical company will operate with anywhere from several dozen to several hundred procedures. It is of some importance that procedures be produced in the same manner and be issued in the same format, to prevent confusion among employees that may (for example) find one procedure to be excessively detailed and another so general as to be utterly unworkable. The following steps are useful for attaining the appropriate level of consistency.

Procedure Production Steps

The following steps show the sequence of events needed to construct a new procedure. Some smaller procedures can be constructed using a compressed production process, but the full set of operations will be required in most cases.

1. *Determine need.* The most important question to address when producing a procedure is whether the procedure is needed at all. As described in the Number of Procedures to Develop section, there are many situations where a new procedure is not necessary or cost-effective. Consider requiring the approval of the controller or chief financial officer before initiating work on a new procedure.
2. *Define boundaries.* Determine where the procedure documentation is to begin and end, since it is possible that only a portion of a process requires a procedure.
3. *Conduct interviews.* Schedule and complete interviews with the people who are currently involved in the process being documented.

4. *Create draft.* Create a first draft of the procedure, using the company's standard procedure template, along with sample forms (if any) and a flowchart.

5. *Review by users.* Have all interviewed people review the procedure for accuracy. If someone wants to make a documentation change, ask the other interviewees about the change to see if it accurately represents the existing process.

6. *Reiterate.* Issue a new version of the procedure that incorporates the changes indicated by the interviewees. Have the interviewees review the document again. There may be several iterations of this step.

7. *Approve.* The series of reviews should result in an accurate procedure. Nonetheless, the approval of the department manager(s) impacted by the procedure should also be obtained, since they will be responsible for following it.

8. *Distribute.* A procedure is useless if it is not distributed to those people most in need of it, and in a timely manner. Consequently, develop a list of positions to which procedures should be distributed, and update it regularly. Procedures should be released to those employees indicated on the list as soon after approval as possible.

> **Tip:** It is much better to have a distribution list by employee title than by employee name, since normal employee turnover would soon render a name-based distribution list obsolete. Employee titles change less frequently, which makes a title-based distribution list less subject to updates.

Formatting Steps

The following bullet points are not really "steps" needed to format a procedure, since they can be used in any sequence. Instead, they show the general layout to be used for a procedure. The bullet points are listed in order as they would be found on a procedure, from the top to the bottom of a procedure document.

- *Procedure header block.* There should be a consistently-applied block of information at the beginning of each procedure that clearly identifies it. In a smaller organization, the procedure title is probably sufficient. In a larger organization, the following more detailed set of information might be required:
  - *Title.* The name of the procedure.
  - *Identification number.* A unique number that identifies the procedure. It may begin with a contraction of the name of the department in which it is primarily used, followed by a sequential number.
  - *Version number.* The number of the most recent version of the procedure. The release date (see next) can substitute for the version number.
  - *Release date.* The date on which the procedure was released for use. The version number can substitute for the release date.

- *Procedure summary*. A brief description of the procedure, and why it is used.
- *Procedure steps*. A clear description of the actions to be taken to complete each procedure step. Use a consistent outlining structure for all procedures that employs only a few levels of indentation.
- *Responsible party*. The person(s) responsible for completing each indicated step.
- *Control issues*. Control issues related to the procedure that an employee should be aware of.
- *Cross references*. If there are similar procedures, list them, as well as any unique identification numbers assigned to them.
- *Forms*. Any forms used in a procedure. Forms can be described in considerable detail, including brief descriptions of each field in a form, and sample forms that have already been completed. Many sample forms are shown in the following chapters.
- *Reports*. Any reports used in a procedure. A sample printout may be provided, along with a description of the information in each field on a report.
- *Flowchart*. A flowchart is extremely useful for giving a visual representation of how a procedure is supposed to operate. It usually makes references to any forms and reports used in a procedure. A case could be made for limiting their use to the more complicated procedures with many decision points, but we have found that some readers prefer them to a purely text-based procedure. Consequently, consider including one in most procedures.

> **Tip:** Flowcharts can be especially useful in a multi-lingual workplace or where employee turnover is high, since they present an easy-to-understand overview of a process.

Through the remaining chapters of this book, we present sample procedures in approximately the format recommended here. The primary exception is that we describe forms in separate sections at the beginning of each chapter, rather than integrating them into each procedure. The separate presentation prevents the duplication of forms, many of which are referenced in multiple procedures.

Procedure Design Tips

This section contains a number of design tips that can assist you in creating tightly-constructed procedures that present information in a clear and readily understandable manner. The points are:

- *Avoid excessive detail*. Some procedure writers have a tendency to wallow in extraordinary levels of detail, such as how to fill in each field on a computer screen. Instead, present a level of detail where only the key information needed to complete a procedure is stated. Otherwise, an employee will see a procedure that spans several dozen pages, and not even attempt to read it.

- *Streamline the header section.* Some procedures contain an abundance of material in the header section, detailing the background for the procedure, why it is needed, related policies, and so forth. This level of detail gets between the reader and the actual procedure that they need. Where possible, only include a brief description of the procedure, and dispense with any extra material.

- *Use the outline format.* A procedure written in paragraph format is too dense to follow, especially if it involves numerous steps. A better approach is to use the outline format, where each step is numbered and sub-steps are indented. For example:

    1. Complete matching of accounts payable documents.
        - Compare price on purchase order to price on supplier invoice.
        - Compare units received on receiving report to units on supplier invoice.

    2. If a unit variance of greater than 2% is found, complete these steps:
        - Contact the purchasing manager with the details of the variance.
        - Record the supplier invoice in the accounts payable module at a price adjusted for the amount of the units received.
        - Issue an adjustment letter to the supplier.

This approach clearly separates each step in a procedure, making it much easier to understand than a procedure written in a paragraph format.

- *Simplify flowcharts.* The intent of a flowchart is to clarify a procedure. Therefore, the flowchart should contain less information than the procedure, so that only the highlights of the basic process steps are revealed. This means stripping out minor steps and limiting the number of shapes used. It is generally sufficient to use only the following shapes:

Symbol	Discussion
	Process: This is the primary symbol used in a business process flowchart. State each step within a process box. It is possible that a simplified process flowchart may contain no other shapes.
	Decision: This is used when a decision will result in a different process flow. The decision symbol can be overused. Try to restrict its usage to no more than two per flowchart. Otherwise, the flowchart will appear overly complex. If more decision symbols are needed, consider

Symbol	Discussion
	subdividing a procedure into multiple procedures.
	Document: This symbol is particularly useful for showing where an input form is used to collect information for a process, though it can also represent a report generated by a process.
	Database: This symbol is used less frequently, and shows when information is extracted from or stored in a computer database. In most cases, the use of a database can be implied without cluttering up a flowchart with the symbol.

- *Number pages within each procedure.* If you are issuing procedures in a loose-leaf format (see the next section) or as separate files, state the page numbers on each procedure in the "Page 1 of 2" format, so that readers can see how many pages are supposed to be included in the procedure.

Whatever set of design concepts you choose to adopt, be sure to apply them consistently across the company's entire set of procedures. Rolling out a design revision can require a considerable amount of reformatting work, especially if a company has hundreds of procedures. This is a good reason why there tend to be few design changes that are implemented only at long intervals.

Dissemination of Procedures

Once procedures have been developed, how do you disseminate them throughout a business? The simplest approach is to assemble them into a single integrated document, and issue a replacement version of it at regular intervals. Each version should state the following information in the beginning of the document:

- All procedures that have been deleted
- All procedures that are entirely new
- Which procedures have been modified, and the reasons for the changes
- Any effective date for the procedural changes (usually as of the release date of the new version)

These notifications tell users if they should delve further into the document to clearly understand any updates, or if the changes have minimal impact on them.

But what if a company is a large one, with many procedures that span multiple volumes? In this situation, it may be cost-prohibitive to completely replace the entire set of procedures on a regular basis. If so, there are two approaches to incremental changes, which are:

- *Binder updates.* Issue procedures in loose-leaf format, with instructions to store them in three-ring binders. When a procedural update is issued, only those pages pertaining to the change are distributed, with a cover page stating which existing pages should be eliminated and/or replaced with the new version. This approach mandates the specific identification of each page with a procedure identification number and revision date.

> **Tip:** Buy slant-ring binders, rather than circular ring binders. The slant-ring version holds more pages, and pages are less likely to jam when the binder is opened.

- *Central storage with notification.* Store all procedures in a server that is accessible by all authorized employees. Then issue an e-mail, stating which pages have changed and the file number on the server to be accessed if employees wish to print those pages. This approach minimizes the distribution of excess documentation, since employees will only print those documents that they intend to use.

> **Tip:** A variation on the central storage concept is to post the procedures manual on a central file server, and encourage employees to use it instead of retaining a private copy. If you use this approach, be sure to continue to issue notifications of procedural changes, so that employees will know if they need to look up a procedure modification on the file server.

An alternative approach is to simply post all procedures on the company's intranet site, so that the information can be accessed as needed by employees. The singular benefit of this approach is that incremental changes can be made with no need to push printed documents out into the workplace. However, employees must also be informed of any procedural changes and sent a link to the page where these updates are listed; otherwise, there is no way for employees to know that procedures have been altered.

> **Tip:** When the procedures manual is posted on-line, consider adding a help feature that explains the more arcane terms, as well as a link back to the procedure developer, in case users want to notify the developer of an error in a procedure.

A special issue regarding the dissemination of procedures is the new employee. The human resources staff should have an action item on its new employee checklist, notifying the person in charge of distributing procedures that a new employee has started work. This notification includes the job title of the new employee and the person's inter-office mailing address and e-mail address, so that a copy of the relevant procedures can be sent to the employee.

> **Tip:** If management wants to reinforce the importance of procedures with new employees, schedule a training session for new hires, during which procedures are distributed and their importance discussed.

Retrieval of Procedures

When employees leave the company, it is possible that other employees will take their old procedures manuals. Since updates to these manuals had previously been directed to the departed employees, it is quite likely that the old manuals will no longer be updated. This can result in employee activities that deviate from the latest version of the procedures manual. To prevent these old manuals from proliferating within the company, include a step in the employee termination process to retrieval old procedures manuals.

Procedural Updates

Procedures should be released on a schedule that coincides with changes in the underlying processes that they document. This means that some procedures may not change for years, while others may be updated every few months. There will be a greater need for updates when a company is implementing best practices, has just discovered control problems, or is involved in an acquisition. In all three cases, processes will likely be changed, and written procedures must be altered along with them.

Thus, there may be no fixed schedule to follow in updating procedures. Instead, maintain close contact with the department managers who are responsible for processes, since they can provide information about prospective process updates. Also, talk to the internal audit manager regularly about the results of internal audits, which may uncover undocumented process changes. At a minimum, schedule an annual meeting with each process owner or department manager, to briefly discuss each existing procedure to see if any updates are required.

When updating a procedure, it may be sufficient to simply adjust the one or two parts of the document that have been altered, along with the accompanying adjustments to forms and flowcharts. However, if it becomes apparent that a number of alterations have been made, it is better to have the process users review the entire procedure to ensure that the document still accurately reflects how the process works. Without these reviews, a number of inconsistencies will eventually creep into procedures, which increases the impression among employees that the procedures can no longer be relied upon.

> **Tip:** Minor procedural updates can be handled with a notification and replacement e-mail or mailing. However, consider the introduction of a new procedure or the complete replacement of an existing one to be similar to a product launch, with a correspondingly greater level of marketing within the company; doing so improves the probability that it will be perused in detail and followed.

Enforcement of Procedures

A company can develop a flood of procedures, but they are completely useless if employees do not follow them. It is especially difficult to enforce the use of procedures in environments where procedures are updated in a halfhearted manner, and especially where management has displayed little interest in them. The following activities can be of use in improving the situation, and are divided into "carrot" and "stick" methods:

"Carrot" Activities

The following four activities are designed to proactively assist employees with up-to-date procedures that are closely tied to the needs of a business:

- *Link to systems development staff.* Build a working relationship between the procedures development staff and those employees tasked with making alterations to the company's systems. With this connection in place, the procedure developers will be made aware of any system alterations being contemplated, and so can issue procedural revisions at the same time that the changes are implemented.
- *Link to auditors.* If the internal or external auditors review the company's systems and find control problems, the procedures development staff should be aware of the nature of those problems, so that they can develop procedural remedies.
- *Issue rapid updates.* Create a system that issues procedural updates on a regular basis. Doing so gives employees the impression that management is willing to keep employees up-to-date with the latest changes in company operations.
- *Conduct training.* Provide training as needed regarding procedural changes, especially where an entirely new procedure is being installed. This is especially useful for new employees who are least familiar with the company's systems.

"Stick" Activities

The following four activities are designed to bring compliance failures to the attention of management, which may lead to problems for those people with a long history of not following procedures. The activities are:

- *Report on procedural failures.* The controller will probably become aware of instances where procedural breakdowns caused any number of problems. These issues should be documented and issued to the management team. The chief executive officer should enforce remediation of each failure with follow-up actions to ensure that targeted improvements were implemented.
- *Request internal audits.* Request that the internal audit staff engage in an ongoing series of reviews to determine the extent to which employees are following procedures (or not). If there is no internal audit staff, consider hiring a systems analysis consultant for this work on an ongoing basis. The result of these reviews should be a report that is sent to the management team, pointing out areas of noncompliance with procedures.
- *Create audit committee.* Have the board of directors create an audit committee, comprised of board members, which reviews the results of any audits by

internal and external auditors. This group can pressure the chief executive officer to enforce greater compliance with the company's official set of procedures.

- *Integrate into evaluations.* Convince the chief executive officer and human resources manager to include procedural compliance in the periodic reviews of employees. Serious non-compliance could even be grounds for dismissal from the company.

Adopting the preceding list of activities still requires the active approval and support of the management team, which is not always forthcoming. However, management is more likely to lend its support, if only grudgingly, if the outside auditors point out control breaches. Further, a robust system of controls (and therefore procedures) is an important certification that company management makes to its shareholders when a business is publicly held; in this case, complying with the rules for a public company will require managers to implement the preceding set of activities.

Deviations from Procedures

Since we have just addressed the enforcement of procedures, it is also worth discussing when to *allow* deviations from procedures. An extensive set of procedures can be considered a straitjacket that is imposed on employees in order to force them to do business in a certain way. An excessively strong level of enforcement leaves little room for employee creativity, explorations of alternative methods, or responses to unusual situations. For example, a retail establishment might consider empowering its customer service staff to respond to customer complaints in any way they believe will most satisfy customers, rather than following a rigid procedure. This type of deviation might even be encouraged, as long as it meets a company objective, such as achieving greater customer satisfaction.

However, deviations from stated procedures are not practical or safe in many situations. For example, the procedure for creating a wire transfer should be rigidly enforced, since there is a high risk of loss if someone circumvents the approvals that are normally built into this procedure. Similarly, a fast food chain with many stores needs to have a food preparation procedure that is absolutely identical across all of its restaurants, so that food preparation can be achieved in the most efficient manner possible.

In short, most organizations will find that there are a small number of procedures that can be considered advisory, rather than mandatory. In most cases, however, it is better to roll out changes in a carefully planned and tested manner, which does not allow for any ad hoc deviations. The manner in which a business is operated will dictate which procedures will fall into each of these categories.

The Procedure Writer

Who should write accounting procedures? The person best suited for the task has the following characteristics:
- Multi-year experience with accounting and other business processes
- In-depth knowledge of accounting
- In-depth knowledge of controls
- Excellent writing skills
- Excellent interpersonal skills, especially in regard to interviewing process users
- Ability to complete projects in a timely manner

The preceding list reveals that handing off the procedure-writing task to a new college graduate is probably not a good idea, since this person has no hands-on experience with systems. Instead, consider assigning the job to a person who has been working for the company for several years. It will probably be necessary for the person to have a college degree in accounting, since the position requires such a broad knowledge of processes and controls.

Tip: To make the procedure writing position more attractive to candidates, make it a requirement for anyone wanting to work as an assistant controller with the company. Procedure writing is excellent training for the assistant controller position, since it imparts a broad knowledge of company operations.

The Need for Policies

A policy is a broad guideline that typically restricts certain actions within a business. For example, a policy may state that:
- An employee cannot be reimbursed through petty cash for a parking violation; or
- The treasury department can only invest excess funds in overnight repurchase agreements; or
- Dry cleaning expenses will not be reimbursed.

The examples shown here, and most company policies, tend to be of a negative nature, where they restrict company actions.

We find that companies have a strong tendency to aggregate all of their policies into a policy section within the corporate policies and procedures manual. We also find that employees have an equally strong tendency to avoid this section of the manual, concentrating instead on just those procedures pertaining to them. Consequently, we do not present a separate set of policies in this book. Instead, policies should be so tightly integrated into procedures that they are, in effect, invisible to employees. We feel that this approach results in better employee compliance with company policies. Thus, we prefer to think of the documentation of a company's business transactions as its *procedures* manual, rather than its *policies and procedures* manual.

Subsequent Chapters

The remainder of this book describes the procedures and related forms and controls that are needed for an accounting system and the other portions of a business that interact with the accounting department (such as the treasury function). You will likely need to alter these procedures to some extent to fit into the customized operations that most businesses have. Nonetheless, they should form a reasonable starting point for the construction of a comprehensive set of procedures for most small to midsized businesses.

As you review the remainder of this book and compare recommended procedures to what is currently in place, the recommended version may suggest alterations to your existing systems that will improve them. With this prospect in mind, we had included dozens of best practices tips in boxes throughout the text that discuss enhancements to the basic procedures. Thus, you can use the following chapters to either create entirely new procedures or to enhance existing ones.

Chapter 2
Order Entry Procedures

Introduction

Order entry is an area in which customer orders are examined, translated into the format used by a company to process orders, and eventually sent on to other parts of the company for credit checks and fulfillment.

In this chapter, we provide examples of the forms resulting from or used in the order entry process and then move on to the various order entry procedures. We provide separate procedures for:

- Order entry (manual system)
- Order entry (integrated system)
- Return merchandise authorization grants

Procedural improvement tips are provided throughout the text, as well as flowcharts showing a streamlined view of each procedure.

Forms: Sales Order Form

The sales order form is used to translate a customer order into a standardized format for internal use by a business. The form should always be assigned a unique identification number, so that it can be tracked. If the company pays commissions, there should also be a space on the form to state the name of the person who is being credited with the sale. A sample format follows.

The sample form includes a considerable amount of payment information, which is only needed if the order entry staff is also responsible for accepting payments from customers. In situations where customers are always invoiced, there is no need for this information on the sales order form.

If multiple copies of a sales order are to be issued, it may not be wise to include credit card information on the sales order, since this information will be spread throughout the company. An alternative is to use a stamp on just the order entry department's copy of the sales order, on which are noted the credit card payment details.

Sample Sales Order Form

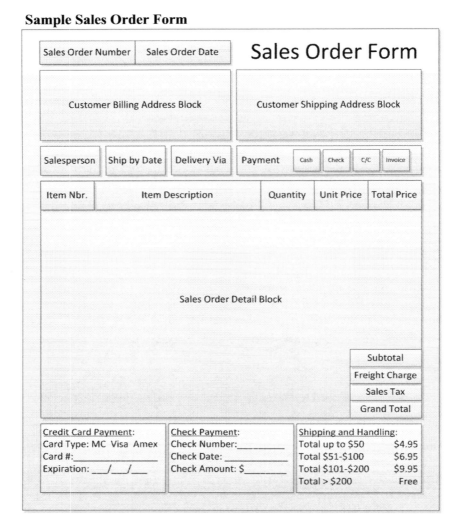

Forms: Return Merchandise Authorization

The return merchandise authorization (RMA) form is the authorization document issued by the order entry staff and used by the receiving department to accept back goods originally shipped to a customer. It should state the RMA date, as well as a notice that the RMA is only valid for a certain number of days from that date. Setting a date limitation curtails the liability of the company. There is no need to include the price of the goods being returned, since that information will be compiled later by the billing clerk who creates a credit memo for the customer. A sample RMA follows.

Sample Return Merchandise Authorization

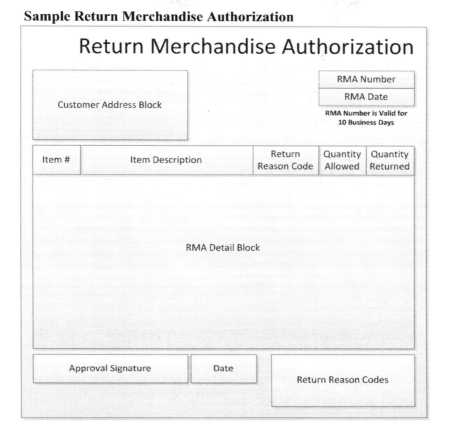

The Order Entry Procedure (Manual System)

This section describes the steps to be followed when the order entry staff manually records customer orders and distributes this information to a variety of other departments within the company for further processing. The procedural steps noted here should also apply when the computer system used by the order entry department is not linked to the systems used by other departments, necessitating the manual transfer of information to the other departments. The order entry procedure for a manual system is outlined below:

1. **Review customer purchase orders.** Scan each purchase order received from a customer for obvious errors, such as a missing "ship to" address, item description, or quantity. Contact the customer if any items require correction. This may result in the issuance of a replacement purchase order.
   Responsible party: Order entry staff
   Control issues: If the company has had problems with unauthorized customer orders, have the order entry staff verify that each purchase order received has been signed. Also, if an order includes unusual terms, have it reviewed by the company's legal staff prior to accepting the order.

> **Tip:** If it is necessary for the customer to issue a replacement purchase order, keep the old copy in a tickler file, and use it as a reminder to contact the customer for a replacement. When the new purchase order arrives, shred the old version, so it is not mistaken for the new version.

2. **Verify customer purchase order** (optional). If a customer issues a purchase order and the amount is sufficiently large, contact the customer to verify that the purchase order is valid and was properly authorized.
   Responsible party: Order entry staff
   Control issues: This step is rarely used, but may be necessary when profit margins are so slim that the company cannot afford to fulfill large orders that may be revoked by customers.

> **Tip:** Consider verifying the first few orders from a new customer until they have established a track record of reliably placing orders and paying in a timely manner. Thereafter, only verify orders if they exceed a certain predetermined amount.

3. **Check product availability** (optional). If the purchase order is for goods (rather than services), go to the warehouse and verify that the requested goods are available for sale. If not, go to the production planning staff (for manufactured goods) or purchasing staff (for purchased goods) and verify when the goods will be available for shipment. If a prolonged backorder period is anticipated, contact the customer with this information and suggest an alternative product.
   Responsible party: Order entry staff

4. **Create a sales order.** Write the customer's order onto a sales order form. A manually-generated sales order should have a unique identification number, so that it can be tracked as orders move through the company. If there is no customer purchase order, this may be the first step in the order entry process.
   Responsible party: Order entry staff
   Control issues: If a sales order is for a sufficiently large amount, it may make sense to have a second person review the order to ensure that it was correctly entered, with appropriate pricing and discounts.

> **Tip:** In a completely manual order entry system, it may make sense to maintain a sales order log, in which are stated the unique identifying number, customer name, and order total associated with each sales order. This log is useful for tracking the existence of sales orders, as well as for comparing recorded revenue levels to the revenues indicated by sales orders.

5. **Process payment information** (optional). In cases where customers are required to pay for their orders up-front, the order entry staff accepts checks and

forwards them to the accounting department, or takes down credit card information and processes the payment transactions themselves.

Responsible party: Order entry staff

Control issues: If the order entry staff is handling checks, it may be necessary to summarize all checks in a daily batch and match them against the related sales orders, to ensure that all payments are appropriately indicated on the sales orders.

> **Tip:** An alternative transaction flow is to route sales orders with attached credit card information to the accounting staff, which processes the payments. However, this approach is less efficient, since any credit card processing failures must then be routed back to the order entry staff for resolution, which delays the sales cycle.

6. **Issue sales order copies.** Issue the following copies of the sales order:
   - *Customer.* This copy is intended for verification purposes, so the customer will contact the company if there is an error on the sales order. However, this copy is not needed if shipment of the goods is expected to be immediate.
   - *Accounting department.* This copy goes to the billing staff within the accounting department, which stores it in a sales order file. Once the shipping department notifies the billing staff that a shipment has been sent, it uses the sales order as the basis for a customer invoice.
   - *Credit department.* This copy is used as the basis for a credit review. If approved, the credit staff stamps the document as approved and sends a copy to the shipping department, which represents authorization for shipment.
   - *To file.* This copy is retained by the order entry staff.

Responsible party: Order entry staff

Control issues: It is important for the order entry staff to retain a copy of each sales order, from which it can provide replacements if other departments lose their copies. Thus, the order entry department should be considered the central repository for sales orders.

> **Tip:** Even if a customer prepays, it is best to route all sales orders through the credit department, since this results in a streamlined and easily understandable process flow. The alternative is to bypass the credit department for small orders and send these orders directly to the shipping department.

The following exhibit shows a streamlined view of the order entry procedure for a manual system, not including the option to verify customer purchase orders.

Order Entry Process Flow (Manual System)

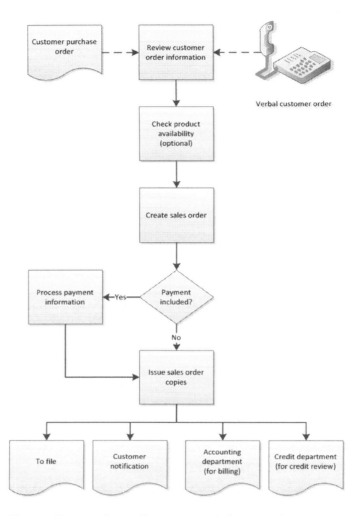

The Order Entry Procedure (Integrated System)

The number of order entry steps is reduced when a company's computer systems are fully integrated, since there is no need to distribute paper copies of the sales order. In the following procedure, we note the reduced procedural steps, referring back to the preceding procedure for those steps that are the same as those used for a manual order entry system.

1. **Review customer purchase orders.** It is still necessary to review customer purchase orders for errors, irrespective of the level of computer system integration. This step matches the one shown earlier for a manual order entry procedure.

2. **Verify customer purchase order** (optional). If a customer order is large enough, it is always prudent to contact the customer to verify the order. This step matches the one shown earlier for a manual order entry procedure.

3. **Create a sales order.** Enter the customer's order into an online sales order form. An integral part of this entry is that the system automatically checks for product availability. The order entry staff can use this information to persuade customers to order alternative products if something is not in stock. There is no need to manually maintain a sales order log, since the system can generate a log on demand.
   Responsible party: Order entry staff
   Control issues: If there is a history of order entry errors, consider having the system route larger orders to the order entry supervisor for review and approval.

   > **Tip:** Be sure to maintain a high level of inventory record accuracy, or else the system may indicate that items are available for sale when that is not really the case.

4. **Process payment information** (optional). If customers must pay for their orders in advance, the payment processing step is the same as was noted earlier for the manual order entry procedure.

5. **Release sales order.** Once the order entry staff is satisfied that it has correctly entered all information related to a customer order, it releases the sales order into the order processing system. The system then sends an e-mail notification to the customer, as well as notifying the accounting and credit departments that the sales order is now available in the system. No paper copies are distributed.
   Responsible party: Order entry staff

   > **Tip:** There is no need for the order entry staff to print and store copies of sales orders, since this information can be called up as needed from the order entry database.

The following exhibit shows a streamlined view of the order entry procedure for an integrated system, not including the customer order verification step.

Order Entry Process Flow (Integrated System)

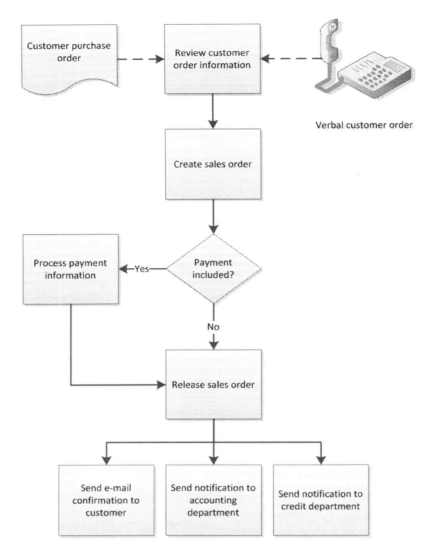

The Granting of Return Merchandise Authorizations

When a customer wants to return goods, the order entry staff reviews its request and grants a return merchandise authorization (RMA) if the request is valid. The RMA number associated with the authorization is required by the receiving staff to accept the return of goods. The procedure for granting an RMA is outlined below; it is an abbreviated version of the RMA procedure shown in the Receiving Procedures chapter.

1. **Issue RMA number.** When a customer wants to return goods that it purchased from the company, it contacts the order entry staff. The order entry staff determines the reason for the return; if valid, it issues a return merchandise authorization number to the customer. The customer is instructed to write the RMA number on the outside of the package to be returned. The use of RMA numbers is quite important in some industries, where retailers and wholesalers would otherwise return all unsold goods to a company.
   Responsible party: Order entry staff
   Control issues: Any RMA number should be valid only for a certain period of time. Otherwise, the company may be forced to accrue an expense for goods that may never be returned.

2. **Forward copy to receiving.** The order entry staff maintains a master log of all RMA numbers issued, and also sends a notification to the receiving department for each new issuance, detailing exactly which items are allowed in each return shipment.
   Responsible party: Order entry staff and receiving staff

3. **Match against RMA.** When a delivery of returned goods arrives at the receiving dock, the receiving staff matches the RMA number posted on the delivery to their file of outstanding return merchandise authorizations. If there is no corresponding RMA number in their file, they reject the delivery.
   Responsible party: Receiving staff
   Control issues: In practice, the receiving staff is unlikely to reject a delivery without first contacting the order entry department to see if there is an RMA on file that never reached the receiving department.

4. **Notify of receipt.** The receiving staff creates three copies of an RMA receipt notification. One copy goes to the order entry staff, which uses the notification to flag an RMA number in its master log as having been fulfilled. Another copy goes to the billing department, which uses it as the basis for generating a credit memo to the customer. The receiving department retains the original and staples it to the RMA (if the RMA is a separate document). If the full amount of the RMA has not yet been received, the documents are returned to the file of open authorizations. If the full amount *has* been received, the documents are stored in a file of completed return merchandise authorizations.
   Responsible party: Receiving staff
   Control issues: This step has a built-in control, which is that customers will complain to the accounting department if they do not receive a credit memo for returned goods.

> **Tip:** The entire process of notifying various parties of the presence or fulfillment of return merchandise authorizations is much easier if the information is stored in a central database. In such a computerized system, the order entry staff creates the initial RMA record, the receiving staff updates it with the quantity of received goods, and the system notifies the billing department to issue a credit memo.

The following exhibit shows a streamlined view of the procedure for granting return merchandise authorizations.

RMA Granting Process Flow

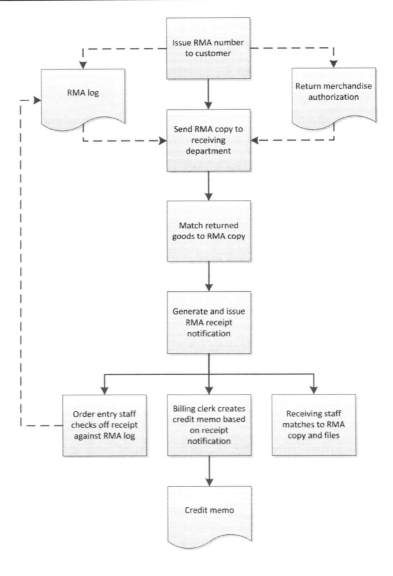

Summary

The order entry staff is responsible for converting a disorderly flow of customer orders into a standardized set of order records that contain all of the information needed by the production and purchasing departments to fulfill orders. This conversion process can only be achieved through the implementation of an order entry procedure to which employees closely adhere. Otherwise, downstream departments will have to continually deal with customer orders that are incorrect or incomplete. Thus, the order entry area is an excellent place in which to require a comprehensive system of procedures.

Chapter 3
Credit Procedures

Introduction

Credit management is an area in which a company attempts to ensure that all customer orders being fulfilled on credit are capable of eventually being paid. This requires an order processing flow that forces sales orders through the credit department, where they can be examined for creditworthiness in accordance with various credit rules.

In this chapter, we provide examples of the forms resulting from or used in the credit process, and then move on to the various credit-related procedures. We provide separate procedures for:

- Credit examination (manual system)
- Credit examination (integrated system)

Procedural improvement tips are provided throughout the text, as well as flowcharts showing a streamlined view of each procedure.

Forms: Sales Order Form

The sales order form is used to translate a customer order into a standardized format for internal use by a business. The form should always be assigned a unique identification number, so that it can be tracked. If the company pays commissions, there should also be a space on the form to state the name of the person who is being credited with the sale. A sample format follows.

The sample form includes a considerable amount of payment information, which is only needed if the order entry staff is also responsible for accepting payments from customers. In situations where customers are always invoiced, there is no need for this information on the sales order form.

If multiple copies of a sales order are to be issued, it may not be wise to include credit card information on the form, since this information will be spread throughout the company. An alternative is to use a stamp on just the order entry department's copy of the sales order, on which are noted the credit card payment details.

Sample Sales Order Form

Sales Order Number	Sales Order Date	Sales Order Form

Customer Billing Address Block	Customer Shipping Address Block

Salesperson	Ship by Date	Delivery Via	Payment	Cash	Check	C/C	Invoice

Item Nbr.	Item Description	Quantity	Unit Price	Total Price

Sales Order Detail Block

Subtotal	
Freight Charge	
Sales Tax	
Grand Total	

Credit Card Payment:	Check Payment:	Shipping and Handling:	
Card Type: MC Visa Amex	Check Number:_____	Total up to $50	$4.95
Card #:_____	Check Date: _____	Total $51-$100	$6.95
Expiration: ___/___/___	Check Amount: $_____	Total $101-$200	$9.95
		Total > $200	Free

Forms: Credit Application

The credit department routinely issues a credit application to those customers wanting to set up credit with the company. The following sample credit application is designed to require a sufficient amount of information for the credit staff to render a well-informed decision regarding the amount of credit (if any) to grant to an applicant.

The credit application form may also include a field in the "For Company Use" section, in which the credit staff can insert the payment terms negotiated with a customer. The form may also include a number of legal clauses, such as an agreement to reimburse the company for collection fees, personal guarantees, and permission for the company to obtain payment by ACH debit. These clauses are typically included on the back of the credit application.

27

Sample Credit Application

Credit Application

Customer Address Block	Date Started	For Company Use
	Business Type	Credit Amount
	Incorporation State	Date
	Corporate Parent	Approved By

Customer Financial Information

Last Year Sales	Current Cash	Current Debt Level
Last Year Profits/Losses	Current Working Capital	Current Retained Earnings

☐ Financial Statements Attached

References

Supplier Reference #1	Contact Information
Supplier Reference #2	Contact Information
Supplier Reference #3	Contact Information

Bank Reference	Checking Account Number
	Savings Account Number

I authorize the above suppliers and bank to release credit information to the Company for its evaluation of this credit application.

Customer Officer: [signature]	Date

The Credit Examination Procedure (Manual System)

The credit department may receive paper copies of sales orders from the order entry department, documenting each order requested by a customer. In this manual environment, the receipt of a sales order triggers a manual review process where the credit staff can block sales orders from reaching the shipping department unless it forwards an approved copy of the sales order to the shipping manager. The credit examination procedure for a manual system is outlined below. A primary assumption of this procedure is that a *new* customer is placing an order; the procedure also shows alternative steps for returning customers (for which a separate flowchart is shown at the end of this procedure).

1. **Receive sales order.** The order entry department sends a copy of each sales order to the credit department. If the customer is a new one, the credit manager

assigns it to a credit staff person. A sales order from an existing customer will likely be given to the credit person already assigned to that customer.
Responsible party: Credit manager

> **Tip:** It may be possible to grant a small default amount of credit to new customers. By doing so, the credit staff can reserve its analysis time for larger credit requests.

2. **Issue credit application.** If the customer is a new one or has not done business with the company for a considerable period of time, send them a credit application and request that it be completed and returned directly to the credit department.
Responsible party: Credit staff

3. **Collect and review credit application.** Upon receipt of a completed sales order, examine it to ensure that all fields have been completed, and contact the customer for more information if some fields are incomplete. Then collect the following information, if necessary:
   - Credit report
   - Customer financial statements
   - Contacts with customer credit references, including information about average and maximum credit granted, as well as slow payments, discounts taken, and bad debt situations
   - Contacts with bank references concerning the existence of bank accounts, the size range of account balances, and how long the customer has done business with each bank
   - Any previous ordering, payment, bad debt, and dispute history with the company

   Responsible party: Credit staff

> **Tip:** If a sales order is for a small amount, it may not be necessary to collect some of this information. In particular, it may not be cost-effective to obtain a credit report for a small order, nor may some customers be willing to forward their financial statements.

> **Tip:** It can take some time to assemble the information needed for a credit application, which may drive an impatient customer to a competitor. To keep the credit review process from being prolonged, the credit staff should review the status of all unapproved sales orders every day.

4. **Assign credit level.** Based on the collected information and the company's algorithm for granting credit, determine a credit amount that the company is willing to grant to the customer. The following are all valid approaches to granting credit:

- Assign a minimum credit amount in all cases; or
- Assign credit based on the item being ordered (where higher credit levels are allowed for items being cleared from stock); or
- Assign credit based on estimated annual sales volume with the customer; or
- Assign credit based on the credit score listed in a third party's credit report; or
- Assign credit based on a decision table developed from the company's overall credit experience; or
- Assign credit based on an in-house credit granting algorithm

It may also be possible to adjust the credit level if a customer is willing to sign a personal guarantee.
Responsible party: Credit staff

5. **Hold order** (optional). If the sales order is from an existing customer and there is an existing unpaid and unresolved invoice from the customer for more than $\_\_\_$, place a hold on the sales order. Contact the customer and inform them that the order will be kept on hold until such time as the outstanding invoice has been paid.
    Responsible party: Credit staff

> **Tip:** Always inform the sales manager before placing a hold on a sales order. The customer will probably contact the sales manager once it learns of the hold, so the sales manager should be prepared in advance for this call.

6. **Obtain credit insurance** (optional). If the company uses credit insurance, forward the relevant customer information to the insurer to see if it will insure the credit risk. The result may alter the amount of credit that the credit staff is willing to grant.
    Responsible party: Credit staff

> **Tip:** It may be possible to bill the customer for the cost of the credit insurance.

7. **Verify remaining credit** (optional). A sales order may have been forwarded from the order entry department for an existing customer who already has been granted credit. In this situation, the credit staff compares the remaining amount of available credit to the amount of the sales order, and approves the order if there is sufficient credit for the order. If not, the credit staff considers a one-time increase in the credit level in order to accept the order, or contacts the customer to arrange for an alternative payment arrangement.
    Responsible party: Credit staff
    Control issues: The credit manager should review and approve larger one-time credit extensions.

8. **Approve sales order.** If the credit staff approves the credit level needed for a sales order, it stamps the sales order as approved, signs the form, and forwards a copy to the shipping department for fulfillment. It also retains a copy.
   Responsible party: Credit staff
   Control issues: It may be necessary to maintain control over the credit approval stamp, since someone could use it to fraudulently mark a sales order as having been approved.

> **Tip:** If the customer has agreed to bear the cost of credit insurance, notify the billing department of the additional amount to be billed to the customer.

9. **File credit documentation.** Create a file for the customer and store all information in it that was collected as part of the credit examination process. This information is useful for future reference, either during periodic reviews or when a customer requests a change in credit level.
   Responsible party: Credit staff

> **Tip:** If there are many customers, it may make sense to use a standard methodology to create a unique customer index number for filing purposes. Doing so will reduce the risk that multiple files will be created for the same customer.

The following exhibit shows a streamlined view of the credit procedure for a manual system, excluding most optional steps, and assuming that sales orders are being processed only for new customers.

Credit Process Flow (Manual System for New Customers)

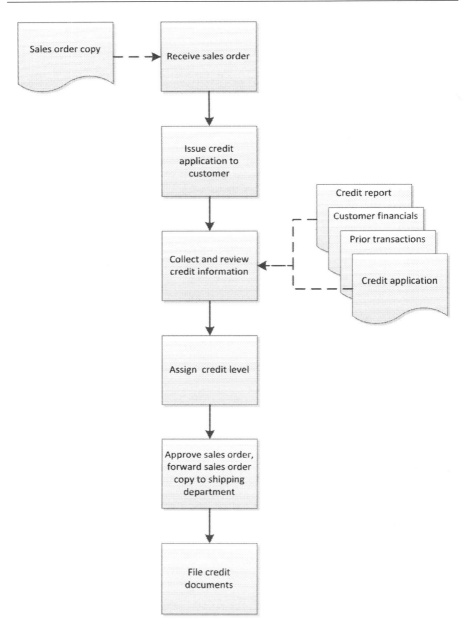

The following exhibit shows a streamlined view of the credit procedure for a manual system, excluding most optional steps, and assuming that sales orders are being processed only for existing customers. In this case, the procedure can be considerably shortened if there is a sufficient amount of unused credit already available to accommodate a sales order.

Credit Process Flow (Manual System for Existing Customers)

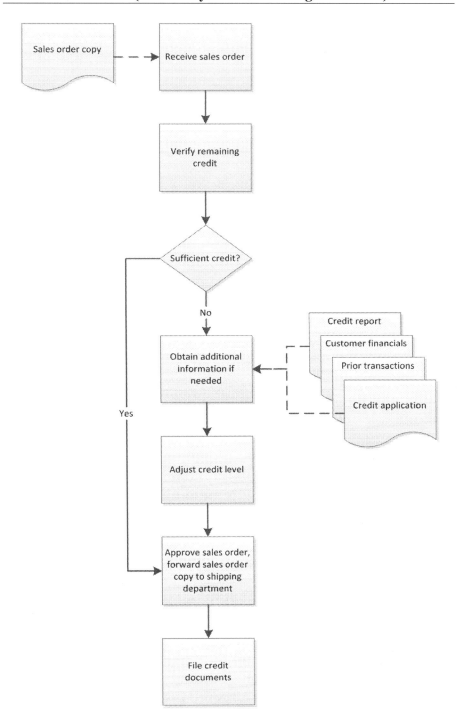

The Credit Examination Procedure (Integrated System)

When the credit department has on-line access to a company-wide integrated computer system, the credit examination process can be streamlined to a considerable extent, particularly in regard to the receipt and forwarding of sales orders. The credit examination procedure for an integrated system is outlined below. A primary assumption of this procedure is that a *new* customer is placing an order; the procedure also shows alternative steps for returning customers (which are listed in a separate flowchart at the end of this procedure).

1. **Receive sales order.** The computer system notifies the credit department that a new sales order is now available for viewing. If the customer is a new one, the credit manager assigns it to a credit staff person. A sales order from an existing customer will likely be forwarded automatically to the credit person already assigned to that customer.
   Responsible party: Credit manager

   > **Tip:** Prior to credit analysis, the system should automatically place a hold designation on all sales orders. This keeps sales orders from being accidentally fulfilled.

2. **Issue credit application.** This step is similar to the one shown earlier for the manual system, with two changes. First, the computer system will notify the credit staff that a sales order is ready for its review, rather than the forwarding of a sales order document that is required in a manual system. Second, the company could direct customers to an on-line credit application form that they can complete, and which is routed directly to the credit department for review. This tends to accelerate the credit review process flow.
   Responsible party: None, since these activities are automated

3. **Collect and review credit application.** This is the same step described in the preceding procedure.

4. **Assign credit level.** This is the same step described in the preceding procedure. In addition, it may be possible to automate the process of granting credit for smaller amounts, with the system forwarding its initial credit grants to the staff for approval, or only for larger credit amounts. Also, once a credit level has been determined for a customer, the credit staff enters that amount into the customer master file in the computer system. Once this information has been loaded, the system will automatically approve future sales orders as long as there is sufficient credit available.
   Responsible party: Credit staff
   Control issues: Consider periodically reviewing the credit levels loaded into the customer master file to see how recently they have been updated. This review can spot instances where the credit staff forgot to update the credit limit field.

> **Tip:** The system can automatically monitor the time required to complete the credit review process, and bring excessively delayed sales orders to the attention of the credit manager.

5. **Hold order** (optional). This is the same step described in the preceding procedure. In addition, the system could be designed to automatically place a hold on the indicated types of sales orders and issue related notifications to the credit staff and sales manager.

6. **Obtain credit insurance** (optional). This is the same step described in the preceding procedure.

7. **Verify remaining credit** (optional). This is the same step described in the preceding procedure, except that the system can be set to automatically forward any unusually large credit increases to the credit manager for review.
   Responsible party: Credit manager

8. **Approve sales order.** If the credit staff approves the credit level needed for a sales order, it flags the sales order record as being approved. The system then notifies the shipping department that the sales order is available for fulfillment. There is no need to print a copy of the sales order, since the record is available in the computer system.
   Responsible party: Credit staff

9. **File credit documentation.** This is the same step described in the preceding procedure. In addition, the credit staff may have to create a record for the customer in the customer master file in the computer system.
   Responsible party: Credit staff

> **Tip:** Consider scanning all of the credit-related information described for this step in the preceding procedure and storing the digitized records in the computer system. This makes the credit information more readily available to the credit staff, while also allowing you to eliminate the paper records or at least shift them to off-site storage.

The following exhibit shows a streamlined view of the credit procedure for an integrated system, excluding most optional steps, and assuming that sales orders are being processed for new customers.

Credit Process Flow (Integrated System for New Customers)

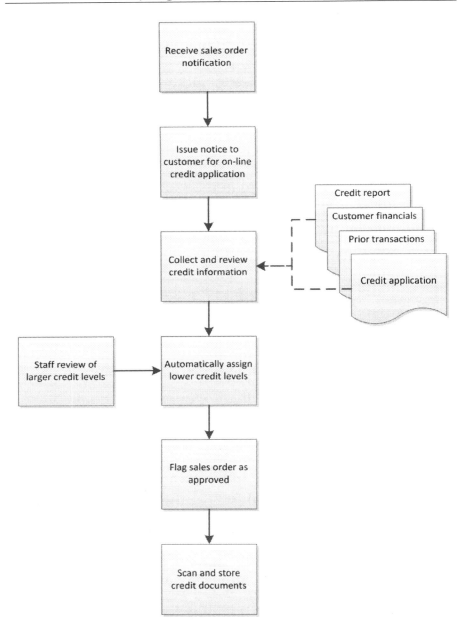

The following exhibit shows a streamlined view of the credit procedure for an integrated system, excluding most optional steps, and assuming that sales orders are being processed for existing customers. In this case, the procedure can be considerably shortened if there is a sufficient amount of unused credit already available to accommodate a sales order.

Credit Process Flow (Integrated System for Existing Customers)

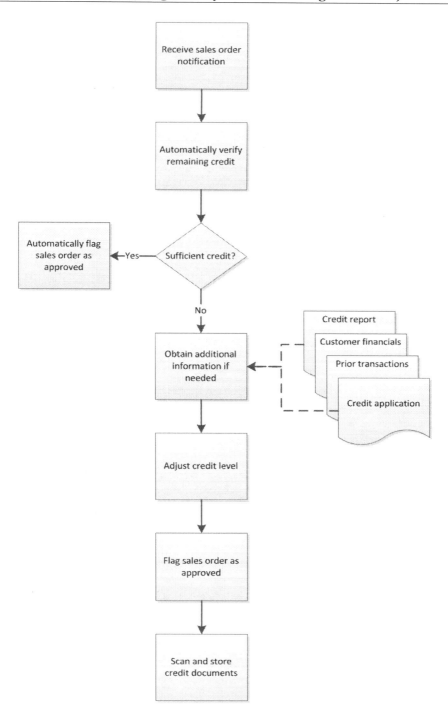

Summary

In many organizations, the credit examination process is considered an annoyance that interferes with the timely shipping of products to customers. Though there is some truth to this perception, the credit department also plays a crucial role – that of reducing the risk of incurring crippling bad debts. Thus, there is certainly a need for the credit function. By paying proper attention to streamlining the credit examination procedure, it is possible to reduce the perceived annoyance level. Possible options are to give the credit department on-line access to sales orders and other credit documents, as well as by automating the credit granting process for the more pedestrian customer orders. These changes will increase the speed of the credit examination process, while focusing the attention of the credit department on the more high-risk customer orders.

Chapter 4
Shipping Procedures

Introduction

The shipping function is responsible for picking items from stock, shipping goods to customers, and then forwarding the applicable shipping documentation to the accounting department for billing purposes.

In this chapter, we provide examples of the forms resulting from or used in the shipping process, and then move on to the various shipping-related procedures. We provide separate procedures for:

- Shipping (manual system)
- Shipping (integrated system)
- Drop shipping

Procedural improvement tips are provided throughout the text, as well as flowcharts showing a streamlined view of each procedure.

Forms: Sales Order Form

The sales order form is used to translate a customer order into a standardized format for internal use by a business. It is created by the order entry staff. If the credit department approves a sufficient amount of credit to ship the goods described in a sales order, it designates the sales order as approved and forwards a copy to the shipping department, which uses it to initiate a shipment. A sample format follows.

Sample Sales Order Form

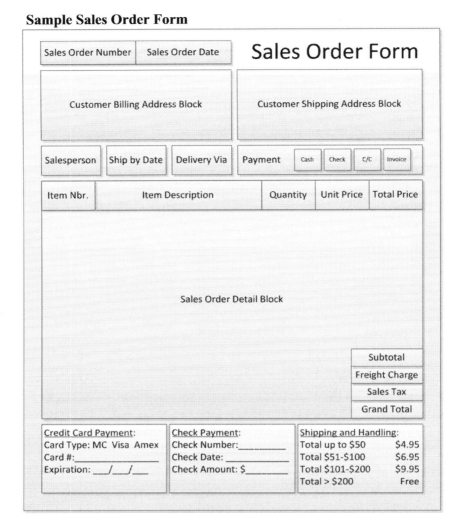

Forms: Pick List

The pick list is used by stock pickers to pick goods from inventory, to be shipped to customers. Each pick list is given a unique number for tracking purposes. It also states the location where items should be found in storage, and the identification number of each item. A stock picker enters in the "picked quantity" field the amount of goods actually picked. If it is less than the amount stated in the "units to pick" column, the difference is back ordered. A sample pick list format follows:

Sample Pick List

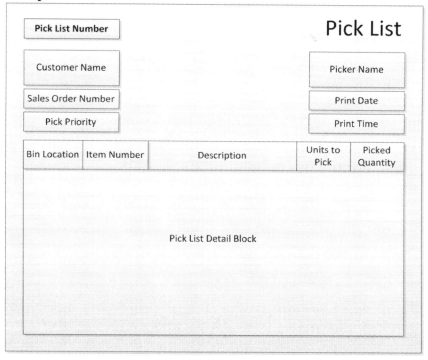

Forms: Packing Slip

A packing slip describes the contents of a delivery of goods to a customer. It is usually attached to the outside of a shipment, so that the receiving staff at the customer can easily access it. The packing slip identifies each item delivered, as well as the quantity shipped, and may also note any items that are still on backorder. The document should also refer to the order number under which the customer originally ordered the goods. A sample packing slip format follows.

Sample Packing Slip

The Shipping Procedure (Manual System)

In many organizations, the shipping department is not linked to the computer systems resident in other departments. This situation requires the use of paper-based notifications of customer orders to the department, as well as a considerable amount of subsequent paperwork to document the picking and shipment of each order. The shipping procedure for a manual system is outlined below.

1. **Verify sales order.** When a sales order arrives in the shipping department, review it to verify that it is authorized for shipment. This means that there is either a credit authorization stamp on it, or the amount to be shipped is of such a small dollar amount that it bypasses the credit department as per the company's credit policy. If the sales order is not authorized for shipment, send it to the credit manager.
   Responsible party: Shipping manager
   Control issues: Having an unauthorized sales order arrive in the shipping department is a serious breach in company procedures, so it may make sense to also notify the controller and/or internal audit manager of the issue.

2. **Issue picking document.** Make a copy of the sales order and forward it to a stock picker. Note on the retained version of the sales order the name of the stock picker to whom a copy was given. This person picks the goods listed on the sales order and brings them to the shipping area. If not all items were on hand, the picker notes this on his copy of the sales order. The stock picker gives the marked-up copy of the sales order to the shipping manager, who matches it to his copy of the document.
Responsible party: Stock picker
Control issues: The shipping manager should run a daily verification of all sales orders for which the picking version has not yet been returned, and follow up with the stock pickers assigned to these sales orders.

Tip: It is also possible to copy all picking information from the sales order to a separate pick list. However, there is some risk in a manual environment that the information will be transcribed incorrectly, leading to an incorrect pick.

---

3. **Issue backorder notification** (optional). If some items listed on the sales order were not in stock, ensure that they are clearly noted on the sales order, and send a copy back to the order entry department (a separate backorder form may also be used). The order entry staff may want to contact the customer about the shipping delay, and may attempt to persuade the customer to buy an alternative product. Another copy should go to the materials management staff, who schedule the backordered goods to be produced or procured. The shipping manager should retain a copy of the sales order in a backorders file, and periodically have the stock pickers review the inventory to see if the indicated items have arrived.
Responsible party: Shipping manager
Control issues: It is possible for items on backlog to be lost in an entirely manual system. One way to spot missing items is for the billing clerk to note on his or her copy of the sales order any items not yet invoiced, and periodically consult with the shipping manager regarding these missing items.

4. **Prepare goods for shipment.** Package the goods for shipment, and prepare shipping information based on the "ship to" address listed on the sales order. Contact the shipper to arrange a pickup.
Responsible party: Shipping staff
Control issues: If there is a history of incorrect inventory picks, it might be reasonable to have someone other than the inventory picker compare the picked items to the sales order prior to shipment.

5. **Complete shipping documents and ship.** Complete the bill of lading document. Verify that it matches the contents of the shipment. Then sign the document and have the shipper sign it, as well. Retain a copy of the bill of lading. Also print a packing slip, detailing the contents of the shipment. Affix a copy to the outside of the shipment, and retain a copy.

Responsible party: Shipping staff
Control issues: A copy of the bill of lading should always be retained, so that the company can prove that goods were shipped, as well as the date of shipment.

6. **Complete shipping log**. Use the information on the bills of lading or packing slip to complete the shipping log. This log is a summary of all shipments made, sorted by date.
   Responsible party: Shipping manager
   Control issues: To ensure that the shipping log is complete, periodically match it to the bills of lading retained by the department, and update it for any bills not listed in the log.

7. **Remove from inventory records.** Remove the shipped items from the inventory records for finished goods.
   Responsible party: Shipping staff
   Control issues: If this step is missed or completed improperly, it can be a major cause of inventory record inaccuracies, so use periodic inventory counts to verify inventory levels. Also, assign inventory record-keeping to a well-trained person, and prohibit all other employees from accessing the inventory records.

8. **Forward shipping documents**. Send a copy of the bill of lading or packing slip to the billing clerk. It may make sense to send the bills of lading, packing slips, and the daily shipping log together as a batch for an entire day of shipping activity, so that the billing clerk can compare the detail documents to the shipping log. If the company bills its customers for shipping charges incurred, note the type of shipping used for each delivery. This information initiates the preparation of a customer invoice.
   Responsible party: Shipping manager
   Control issues: From an accounting perspective, this is the most critical part of the shipping process, since unforwarded documents will prevent invoices from being generated. An easy control is to have the billing clerk go to the shipping department to request these documents if they do not arrive by a specific time each day.

> **Tip:** Require the shipping department to forward shipping documents to the billing clerk at least twice a day, so that the company can issue invoices as soon after shipments as possible. This practice tends to improve the speed with which customers pay their invoices.

9. **File documents**. Attach the bill of lading to the sales order, and file it by date within the shipping department. Also retain the original shipping log within the shipping department. This information may be accessed by auditors to verify that shipments were made, and may also be useful to the billing clerk for investigations of customer invoices.
   Responsible party: Shipping manager

Control issues: Consider storing this information in a locked cabinet, since it can be quite useful for investigative purposes at a later date.

The following exhibit shows a streamlined view of the shipping procedure for a manual system.

Shipping Process Flow (Manual System)

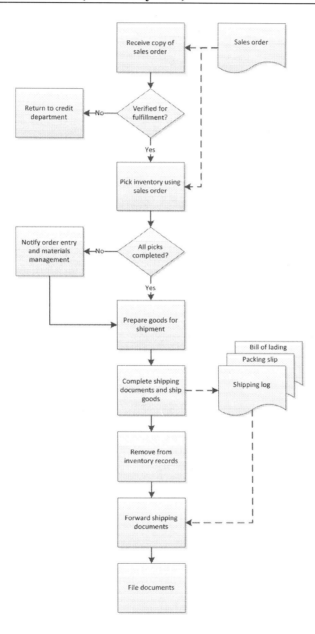

The Shipping Procedure (Integrated System)

When the computer systems used by the shipping staff are integrated into those of the rest of a company, there are opportunities for a considerable reduction in the amount of paperwork required to pick goods from stock and ship them to customers. In the following procedure, we include many of the steps described in the preceding procedure, but also note how the integrated system eliminates some or all manual intervention in certain steps.

1. **Issue pick list.** The shipping manager prints a pick list from the computer system for the customer order and forwards it to a stock picker. Note in the computer system the name of the stock picker to whom the picking task was assigned. This person picks the goods listed on the pick list and brings them to the shipping area. If not all items were on hand, the picker notes this on the pick list. The stock picker gives the marked-up copy of the pick list to the shipping manager, who enters the picking information in the computer system.
   Responsible party: Stock picker and shipping manager
   Control issues: The shipping manager should be able to run a report that shows the status of all assigned pick lists, and follow up with the stock pickers regarding the status of each customer order.

   > **Tip:** It is also possible to route picking information directly to hand-held computers used by the stock pickers. This approach is more efficient than using pick lists, and also removes inventory from bin locations in the accounting records, making the inventory records more up-to-date.

2. **Issue backorder notification.** This differs significantly from the step shown in the preceding procedure. In an integrated computer environment, the system flags all backordered items and makes the information available to all departments that can use the information. Thus, no paper-based notifications are required.
   Control issues: There is much less risk that a backordered item will be lost in an integrated system, unless the shipping manager mistakenly records an unavailable item as having been shipped. If so, this error may still be spotted because the supposed shipment of an unavailable item should relieve inventory, resulting in a negative quantity on hand.

3. **Prepare goods for shipment.** This is the same step noted in the preceding procedure.

4. **Complete shipping documents and ship.** Print the bill of lading and packing list. These documents should be automatically populated by the computer system. As was the case in the preceding procedure, it is still necessary to sign the bill of lading and have the shipper sign it. It is also still necessary to retain a copy of this document, since it now includes signatures attesting to the ship-

ment. Finally, affix the packing slip to the outside of the shipment. It is not necessary to retain a printed copy of the packing slip, if this information is accessible through the computer system. This step should include flagging the shipped items in the computer system as having been shipped.

Responsible party: Shipping staff

Control issues: A copy of the signed bill of lading should always be retained, so that the company can prove that goods were shipped, as well as the date of shipment.

5. **Complete shipping log.** There is no longer a need to manually prepare a shipping log, as was the case in the preceding procedure, since the computer system can compile this information from the shipping documents.

6. **Remove from inventory records.** The system should automatically remove shipped items from the inventory records as soon as the shipment is flagged in the system as having been shipped.

7. **Forward shipping documents.** The system should automatically make shipping information available to the billing clerk as soon as the shipping staff has flagged the shipped items as having been shipped. There is no need to send any shipping documents to the billing clerk.

8. **File documents.** It is still necessary to file the shipping department's copy of the bill of lading, since it contains the signature of the shipper who has taken responsibility for the shipped goods. File it by date.

Responsible party: Shipping manager

Control issues: Consider storing bills of lading in a locked cabinet, since this information can be quite useful for proving the transfer of goods to the shipper, as well as the dates on which goods were shipped.

Note that there was no sales order verification step in this procedure, as there was for the preceding procedure. The reason is that the computer system will automatically block all sales orders from reaching the shipping department until they have either been approved by the credit department or are automatically authorized under the company's sales order authorization rules.

The following exhibit shows a streamlined view of the shipping procedure for an integrated system.

Shipping Process Flow (Integrated System)

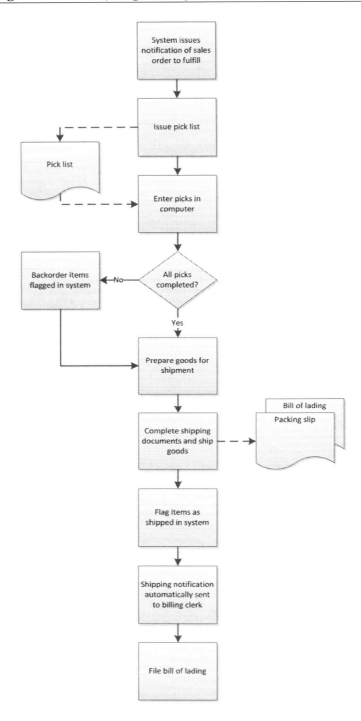

The Drop Shipping Procedure

Drop shipping is a working capital reduction technique where a company has its suppliers ship goods directly to its customers, with no need to stockpile inventory on the company premises. The drop shipping procedure is outlined below.

1. **Forward sales order.** Upon receipt of a sales order from the order entry department, the shipping manager ascertains whether the order contains any items that are to be fulfilled directly by a supplier. If so, transmit a copy of the sales order to the supplier, with the items to be fulfilled noted on the form.
   Responsible party: Shipping manager
   Control issues: Consider contacting the supplier to ensure that any transmitted sales orders were received.

> **Tip:** If a company maintains no inventory at all, the order entry staff (rather than the shipping manager) sends the sales order to the supplier.

All shipping steps used in drop shipping are identical to those described in the preceding two procedures, except that they are completed by the shipping department of the supplier.

2. **Forward shipping documents.** The supplier sends a copy of the bill of lading or packing slip to the company's billing clerk. This information initiates the preparation of a customer invoice.
   Responsible party: Shipping manager of supplier
   Control issues: There is a considerable risk that shipping information will not reach the billing clerk, especially since the shipping notification is being transmitted from another entity, which increases the risk of transmission failure. To mitigate this risk, the billing clerk should routinely contact all suppliers to whom sales orders were sent, and inquire about the shipping status of all open sales orders.

No exhibit is provided for the drop shipping procedure, due to its brevity.

Summary

The shipping function is a key part of the revenue-generating activities of a business, and so must be accomplished with a minimum of mistakes. Otherwise, revenue cannot be recognized, and there will be a considerable risk of customer dissatisfaction. Mistake reduction can be achieved through adherence to the small number of procedures outlined in this chapter. Given the critical need for a mistake-free shipping process, this is an area in which a company should consider monitoring shipping errors on an ongoing basis and correcting the underlying reasons for them.

Chapter 5
Customer Billing Procedures

Introduction

One of the most fundamental and critical accounting procedures is billing customers. If you do not correctly create and record customer invoices, you will have incorrect revenue and receivable records, and will also have trouble collecting from customers. Thus, the following procedures are particularly careful in describing the billing process.

We begin with examples of the forms resulting from the billing process, and move on to the basic billing procedure. There are significant additional steps required if you have a manual bookkeeping system; those steps are itemized separately. There are several types of billing situations, so we provide separate procedures for:

- Billing
- Credit memos
- Statements of account

As usual, procedural improvement tips are provided throughout the text, as well as flowcharts showing a streamlined view of each procedure.

Forms: The Invoice

Accounting software always contains a standard invoice template, which most businesses use with only minor adjustments to bill their customers. The typical invoice contains the following information:

- *Header section.* Itemizes the billing address of the seller and customer, as well as the invoice number, invoice date, and payment due date. There may also be space for the name of the salesperson (if any), which is used for contact information and calculating salesperson commissions.
- *Billing detail block.* Lists each item sold to the customer, including the description, unit price, quantity, and extended price.
- *Summary section.* This is an extension of the billing detail block, in which all items sold are summarized. A freight charge and sales tax may be added, to arrive at a total invoice amount.

You may want to make several modifications to the template to reduce the time required to receive payments from customers, as well as to reduce the number of customer payment errors. Consider implementing the adjustments in the following table:

Invoice Format Changes

Credit card contact information	If customers want to pay with a credit card, include a telephone number to call to pay by this means.
Early payment discount	State the exact amount of the early payment discount and the exact date by which the customer must pay in order to qualify for the discount.
General contact information	If customers have a question about the invoice, there should be a contact information block that states the telephone number and e-mail address they should contact.
Payment due date	Rather than entering payment terms on the invoice (such as "net 30"), state the exact date on which payment is due. This should be stated prominently.

The goal in creating an invoice format is to present the minimum amount of information to the customer in order to prevent confusion, while presenting the required information as clearly as possible. The following sample invoice template incorporates the invoice format changes that we just addressed.

Sample Enhanced Invoice Template

Forms: The Credit Memo

There should be an approval form that explains the need for a credit memo and the amount being requested. The form should also specify whether the credit memo will be a standard one that is issued to the customer, or an internal one that is not issued. If possible, the form also states the number of the invoice that is to be offset by the credit, which is used to reduce the invoice amount in the aged accounts receivable report. A sample credit memo approval form is shown below.

Sample Credit Memo Approval Form

Credit Memo Approval Form

| Customer Name | Credit Memo ☐ |
| Customer Number | Internal Credit Memo ☐ |

Credit Amount Requested	Reason for Request
Invoice to Offset (if any)	
	Supervisor Approval Block

There are several varieties of credit memo, each one serving a different purpose. They are:

- *Specific credit.* A credit may be granted for a specific product return, price adjustment, or other reason related to the contents of an invoice. If so, the customer may be waiting for a detailed credit memo that it will refer to in its payment of an invoice. This type of credit memo calls for a format that states specifically what happened. It must contain a unique identifying number, which the customer can reference when it uses the credit as a deduction from a payment. The credit should also contain a field for a reason code, as well as the number of units returned. In all other respects, other than payment information and freight charges, the credit memo format is same as the invoice format. A sample credit memo template follows.

Sample Credit Memo Template

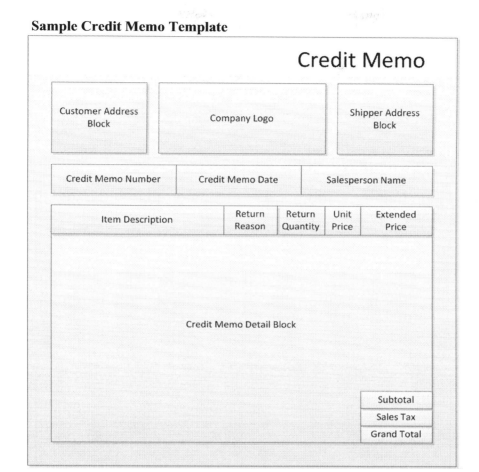

- *Internal credit memo.* Whenever the company writes off an account balance due to customer nonpayment, it should still create a credit memo, but it does not mail the document to the customer. Otherwise, the customer may use the credit to offset some other payment. Many accounting systems provide for an internal credit memo, along with a separate form that clearly states the nature of the transaction. In this case, the key point is that the form state that it is an internal credit memo, and that it is not to be mailed to the customer. A sample template follows.

Sample Internal Credit Memo Template

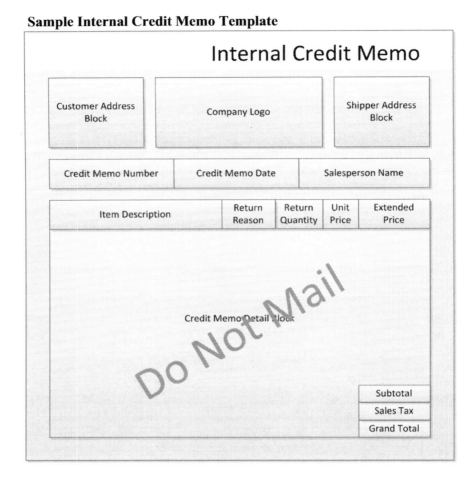

- *General statement.* One option is to periodically send a letter to customers, informing them of a credit balance on their account. This approach may seem counterintuitive, since it can result in a reduction of the amount of cash paid by customers. However, they may also make new purchases in order to use up their credits, which can *increase* profits. A sample general statement of credit follows.

Sample General Statement of Credit

CREDIT BALANCE NOTICE

Customer name
Customer address
Customer address

Dear _____ :

Our accounting records as of [date] indicate that you have a credit with [company name] of $____. You may use this credit as a deduction from the future purchases of goods and services from the company. If you believe that this credit is in error, please contact us at [contact information].

[Add the following block of text with caution, since it will not lead to additional sales]

If there are no pending orders with us or you do not anticipate additional orders in the near future, we can issue you a refund instead. Please contact us at [contact information] to request a refund.

Thank you for your business!

Forms: The Statement of Account

The statement of account is intended to summarize all open invoices remaining as of the statement date. It is also quite useful to include any customer payments that have not yet been assigned to an invoice, since this may prompt a contact from the customer, informing the accounting staff of how to assign a payment. Further, consider including time buckets at the bottom of the statement, showing whether any invoices are overdue for payment; customers can glance at these time buckets to see if any invoices are overdue, and will then be more likely to delve into the statement in greater detail. Finally, the statement should be constructed to have a tear-away section that can be used as a remittance advice, so that customers can pay directly from the statement. A sample statement of account template follows.

Sample Statement of Account Template

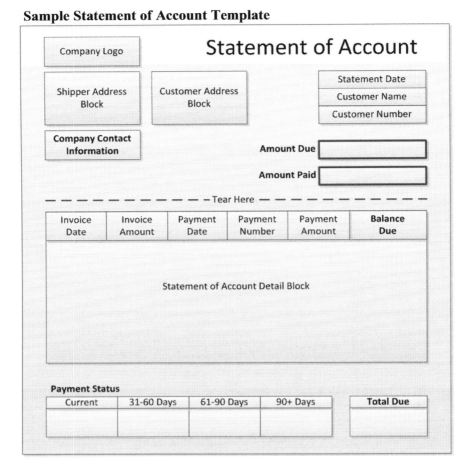

The Billing Procedure

The general process flow for creating a customer invoice is that a packet of information arrives from the shipping department, which the billing clerk verifies and converts into an invoice. There are numerous other steps involved before the shipping department ever sends this information to the billing clerk, including order entry, credit approval, production scheduling, and shipment.

The billing procedure should be followed every day. Customers are supposed to enter the invoice date in their computer systems when logging in supplier invoices, so that the computer pays each invoice after the correct number of days, as listed in the payment terms on the invoice. However, many data entry employees do not go to the trouble of entering this date, and instead use the default date, which is the current day. Invoices entered in this manner will be paid later. Thus, you need to process invoices as soon as possible in order to be paid as soon as possible.

The detailed billing procedure, including responsibilities and basic controls, follows:

1. **Access shipping documents.** In a fully computerized system, this will be a screen in the accounting system. In a manual system, this is a document sent from the shipping department that states what has been shipped to a customer. It is frequently a copy of the bill of lading or packing slip.
   Responsible party: Billing clerk
   Control issues: The person shipping goods cannot be the same person who creates the invoice. Otherwise, an employee could ship goods to a company that he controls and then modify the invoice to contain fewer items shipped or lower prices than normal.

2. **Access the customer order.** In a computerized system, one can access an on-line form that itemizes all customer order items shipped. You then verify that you want to print an invoice for all flagged items. If there is no automated linkage from the shipping department to the accounting software, locate the sales order, of which a copy should have been sent from the customer service department to the accounting department when each customer originally placed an order.
   Responsible party: Billing clerk
   Control issues: In a non-computerized system, it is possible to lose customer sales orders. The order entry staff should always store a backup copy of each sales order, which is usually stapled to any customer purchase order that it may also have received. These documents are usually filed by customer name. If the order entry staff wants to keep two copies of the sales order, pre-number the forms and file the second copy by number. Though probably overkill, this later approach reduces the risk of a lost sales order.

3. **Verify prices** (optional). In a computerized system, the customer service staff should have already verified pricing when they created the sales order, so there is nothing more to be done. When customer orders are placed manually, compare the prices listed on the sales order to the standard price list, and flag any items that vary from the standard rates. There should not be too many prices on orders that contain non-standard prices. If there are, consider periodically compiling these orders to see if certain salespeople are allowing nonstandard pricing, or if the marketing department is running undocumented discounts, and so forth.
   Responsible party: Billing clerk
   Control issues: There can be significant control problems with pricing when the marketing department is constantly running promotions at varying discount rates. The simplest control is to restrict the number of promotions. If that is not possible, ensure that both the order entry and accounting departments are on the mailing list for all special promotions, and give the marketing department immediate feedback if it does not rigidly adhere to this distribution.

> **Tip:** A company may change its official price list at regular intervals, such as once a year. If so, it is quite possible that a customer may have placed an order when earlier prices were in effect. In such cases, match prices to the price list that was in effect on the date when the order was placed. In addition, consider having a policy to give customers whichever price is lower – the old one or the new price. This may call for some invoice adjustments, but it can create customer goodwill, especially if there is a prominent note on the invoice that explains the reason for the price reduction.

4. **Calculate shipping.** This can be a time-consuming part of invoicing, because not all forms of shipping charges are easily automated in a computerized system. Here are several examples of shipping calculations:
   - *Customer pickup.* The customer comes to the company to retrieve his order. This needs to be established at the time of order placement, and either flagged in the computer system or stamped on the order.
   - *Price based.* This is typically an increasing price that is based on the price of the order, not its cubic volume or shipping weight. Many order-taking systems contain this feature.
   - *Promotional rate.* This is usually free shipping if customers order by a certain date or in an amount greater than a set order size.
   - *Prepaid.* If the initial customer order states that shipping is prepaid, do not charge any freight on the invoice.

   Responsible party: Billing clerk

   Control issues: Unusual shipping requests, such as overnight delivery to a distant location, can cause losses, since these charges may be inordinately high, and the company may underbill the customer for them. If so, either require the customer to pay the delivery company itself, or forbid such deliveries, or forbid them only when the company is uncertain of the full amount of the shipping charge that it will eventually be billed by the transportation firm.

> **Tip:** If you want to have a fairly automated invoicing process, standardize the shipping calculation as much as possible, with very few variations from the standard calculation. The simplest approach is to offer free shipping. The next simplest is to use a standard shipping charge based on the total size of the order – this involves a simple table lookup, and is easy for a computer system to accomplish. From the standpoint of simplicity, a customer-specific shipping rate is a bad idea, since it usually calls for a manual override of the computer-generated shipping rate.

5. **Charge sales tax.** Charge the sales tax rate for the government entity in which the customer is receiving the goods. This tax rate should be included in the accounting software, so the software automatically applies it. If you are creating invoices by hand, keep the sales tax information in a summary sheet for easy reference.

Responsible party: Billing clerk

Control issues: The sales tax code is usually set up in a separate file in the accounting software, which in turn is referenced in the customer master file for each individual customer. If the sales tax code is incorrect, or the customer master file incorrectly references the wrong sales tax code, you will either collect sales taxes for the wrong government entity, or in the wrong amount. This problem can be difficult to spot. One option is to have a second person cross-check all changes to computer records involving sales taxes. Another possibility is to have an internal auditor review these records periodically.

> **Tip:** Governments usually mail out updates to their sales tax rates near the end of each calendar year. Have the person in charge of the mail route all of these notifications to you, so that you can update them in the computer system.

6. **Print invoice**. If you are using a pre-printed invoice form, make sure that it is positioned properly in the printer, conduct a test print if necessary, and print the invoice. If the computer requires you to print invoices in batch mode, print all of the invoices that you have selected.
Responsible party: Billing clerk

> **Tip:** Consider using a color printer, so that you can use colors to highlight specific fields on an invoice, such as the amount of an early payment discount or the due date of an invoice.

7. **Burst invoice** (optional). If the company is using multi-part forms, burst the copies apart. If it is a two-part form, you usually file the extra copy by customer name. If it is a three-part form, you typically file the third copy by invoice number. These extra copies are useful for cross-referencing information at a later date, if there is a need to research an invoice.
Responsible party: Billing clerk

> **Tip:** The impact printers used to create multi-part invoices are far more likely to jam than laser printers, so consider moving away from this form of printing.

7. **Proofread the invoice** (optional). If an invoice is unusually complex or is for a large amount, consider having someone else proofread it. There should be no unnecessary delays caused by customer protests at an inaccurate billing, so proofreading may be prudent. The original billing clerk should not conduct this review, since the person who creates a document is less likely to see errors.
Responsible party: Second billing clerk

> **Tip:** Do not use proofreading for routine invoices, since these items rarely contain errors, and proofreading can delay invoice delivery.

8. **Mail invoice**. Stuff the completed invoices into mailing envelopes, and stamp each envelope with an "Address Correction Requested" stamp, so that the post office will notify the company if a customer changes its address.
Responsible party: Billing clerk
Control issues: As noted in this procedure step, it is important to keep track of customer addresses, since the billing staff may inadvertently mail an invoice to an old address. To avoid this, have the mail room staff forward all change of address forms received from customers to the accounting department.

> **Tip:** It may be necessary to use different types of mailing to get an invoice into the hands of the correct person at a customer. For example, you may need to use registered mail if customers continually claim that they never receive invoices. Other customers prefer e-mail delivery, or that you enter the invoice into an electronic invoicing portal. In order to be reminded about which mailing method to use, create a code in the customer master file that indicates a specific form of delivery, and have this code appear in a unique box somewhere on the invoice.

9. **File invoice copy** (optional). If there is an extra copy of an invoice, file it in the customer's file, along with the sales order and customer purchase order (if any), and the proof of shipment. It is better to use a fastener file folder for storing invoices, so that they can be affixed to the folder securely. This reduces the risk of losing documents, and keeps the invoices in order by date. If you created another copy, file it by invoice number in a separate binder.
Responsible party: Accounting clerk (does not have to be the billing clerk)
Control issues: It is not uncommon to lose invoices simply by filing them under the wrong customer name. This has become a relatively minor control issue, since the accounting staff can still access electronic records of invoices through the computer system. However, if you use the computer as the primary method of access to accounting records, keep records available in the computer for several preceding years – do not archive them for as long as possible.

> **Tip:** Do you need to print or file a copy of an invoice at all? As long as the backup method for the accounting system is first-rate, you can always print an invoice at a later date if needed. An alternative is to print the invoice and then scan it into an electronic document management system, along with all other documents related to the invoice, such as evidence of shipment and the customer's original order. This results in an easy source of all information about an order, which can be accessed from any computer terminal, and is very useful for the customer service staff, which may have to respond to customer queries.

10. **Retain extra sales order copy** (optional). If the sales order has not been entirely fulfilled, make a copy of it, circle the remaining items that have not yet been shipped, and store it in a pending file. This is eventually matched to the shipping documents for the backordered items when they are shipped.

Responsible party: Billing clerk

Control issues: Review the sales orders for backordered items periodically, and investigate those that are quite old. This can serve as a useful reminder for the order entry staff, who can follow up with customers to see if they want to buy alternative products.

The following exhibit shows a streamlined view of the standard billing procedure, including a few of the more common optional steps. This process flow assumes that a computer system exists that links the order entry, shipping, and accounting departments. See the next section for an alternative system that assumes the complete absence of computers from the process flow.

Standard Billing Process Flow

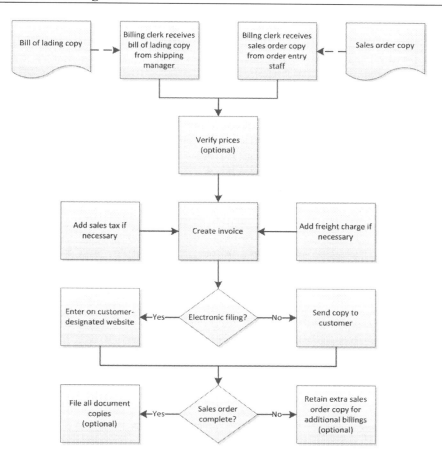

Additional Manual Billing Steps

There are a number of additional steps involved in the billing procedure if systems are entirely manual. These steps involve the accumulation of documents from other parts of the company that pertain to billing, and manually recording the transaction in the accounting records. These steps are:

1. **Receive and match sales order and bill of lading.** The event that triggers the billing procedure is when the shipping department sends a bill of lading and marked-up copy of the sales order to the accounting department. The bill of lading indicates that the products have shipped, and the shipping staff will have indicated on the customer order the specific line items that have shipped. These line items are the source information for constructing an invoice, as was described in the last section. If either of these documents is missing, contact the shipping department for the missing copy.
   Responsibility: A designated person in the shipping department forwards the documents to the accounting department. The billing clerk is responsible for receiving and matching this information.
   Control issues: If the shipping department does not send shipment information to the billing clerk, this clerk is not even aware that an invoice should be created, which can be a major control issue. To mitigate this risk, periodically compare the list of invoices issued to the shipping log, to see if there are any items on the log that have not been billed.

   > **Tip:** For the purposes of manually creating an invoice, do *not* use any sales orders received from the order entry department. Instead, use the copy that you receive from the shipping department. The reason is that not all of the line items on the original order may have shipped, and the shipping staff will have checked off those that shipped. If you were to use the copy from the order entry department, you might over-bill the customer for items that have been backordered.

2. **Notify credit department of a missing credit approval stamp** (optional). In a manual system, the sales order is routed from the order entry department to the credit department, which affixes a credit approval stamp to the sales order if it deems the customer to have adequate credit, and then forwards the document to the shipping department for processing. If there is no credit stamp, this means that the paperwork flow has broken down, and something was shipped to a customer who may not be able to pay for it. If the process is so iron-clad that this problem never arises, this added step is optional.
   Responsibility: Billing clerk

3. **Prenumber invoices.** Always use prenumbered invoices. This means that each invoice has its own unique invoice number. This is important when customers send in their payments, because the remittance advices that usually accompany these payments list the invoice number that they are paying. If there is no

invoice number, and there are multiple unpaid invoices from a customer, the accounting staff can only guess at what they are paying.
Responsibility: Billing clerk

4. **Record the sale**. Use the second copy of the invoice to create a journal entry in the sales journal or general ledger. The entry will likely be in this format:

	Debit	Credit
Accounts receivable	xxx	
Sales		xxx
Sales taxes payable		xxx

Responsibility: Billing clerk
Control issues: It is very important to ensure that all customer billings are recorded properly; otherwise, you will not know which billings have not yet been paid, and will also not have an accurate sales figure. Accordingly, have someone other than the billing clerk periodically compare all copies of invoices generated to the sales journal or general ledger, and document all differences found.

The following exhibit shows a streamlined view of the manual billing procedure. This process flow assumes that no computer is used at any point in the process to record information – instead, the system relies entirely upon records and notifications that are on paper.

Manual Billing Process Flow

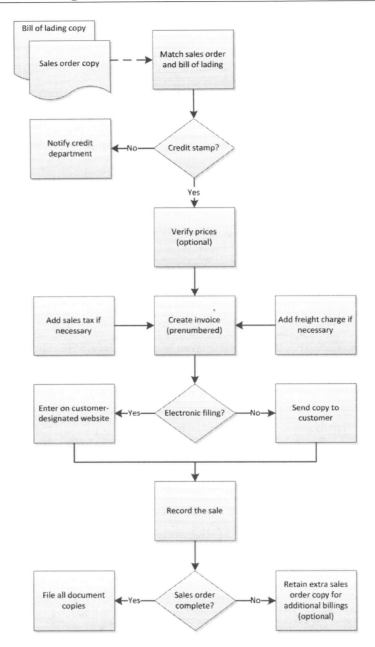

Variations on the Billing Procedure

There are several variations on how the billing procedure can be structured. They are:

- *Billing for services – funding cap.* If you are billing a customer for services performed, there is probably a maximum limit on the amount that you are allowed to bill the customer. If so, include a step early in the process to determine the amount of funding that is still available under the contract. If there is no remaining funding, there is no reason to create an invoice, since the customer will not pay you. However, the discovery that there is not sufficient funding available may trigger one or more of the following additional steps:
  o *Apply for funding expansion.* The customer may be willing to pay for more services, so contact the customer to see if it will issue an add-on to the contract to increase the amount of available funding.
  o *Contact the billing person.* The person who billed the additional services needs to know that there is no additional funding available, and so should no longer provide any additional services until further notice. This can be a simple e-mail notification.
  o *Shut down the job.* If there was a job number assigned to the project in the timekeeping system, shut it down so that no one else can charge hours to the project.
- *Billing for services – month-end billings.* If you are billing customers on an ongoing basis for work performed (as is frequently the case for consulting firms), the triggering event for invoice creation is the end of the month. If so, notify the staff to record their billable hours, which may call for one or more of the following additional steps:
  o *Early notification.* Several days prior to the end of the billing period, issue a blanket message to all employees who bill customers for their time, reminding them to update their billable hours in the reporting system.
  o *Period-end notification.* As soon as the billing period closes, issue a blanket message to all employees who bill customers for their time, reminding them to update their billable hours in the reporting system.
  o *Follow-up notification.* There will always be difficulty in getting some employees to update their time records, which interferes with the creation of invoices on a timely basis. If so, create a procedure step to notify these people very frequently, and also to issue a list of chronically late people to a manager, for further action.

> **Tip:** It is strongly advisable to install either an Internet-based timekeeping system or one that can be accessed through the company's computer system. This system can be accessed regularly to see who has not recorded his or her billable hours yet. Doing so creates a much faster feedback loop for dilatory employees than a paper-based timekeeping system.

- *Drop shipping.* You are using drop shipping when suppliers ship goods directly to your customers, so that the goods never pass through your warehouse. Since the usual trigger to create an invoice is the shipment of goods from the company's own warehouse, the following procedure step is needed to replace the triggering event:

- o *Match supplier shipping notice to sales order*. Require suppliers to issue a shipping notice for all shipments made to your customers, and create an invoice once this notice is received. You can also conduct a periodic investigation of open sales orders to see if any supplier shipping notices were never received.

- *Evaluated receipts billing*. A small number of companies do not want you to send them an invoice at all; instead, they pay based on the prices listed in the purchase order they sent to the company, multiplied by the quantities of goods they have received from it. If you have this situation, it is best to not create an exception to the standard billing procedure. Instead, print the invoice as usual, but do not send it to the customer. Then add the following step to the billing procedure:

- o *Match payments to customer purchase order number*. The customer is identifying the transaction based on its purchase order number, so you should, too. Record this number in the accounting system, and have it appear somewhere on the company invoice as a reference number. Then match the purchase order number listed on the deposit advice that accompanies the customer's payment to the same purchase order number in your records. This method can be used to investigate any unpaid amounts.

- *Entering invoices in electronic payment platforms*. Some customers have linked their accounting systems to Internet portals, and require you to enter invoices to them into these portals. There is a risk in doing so, because the entry may not be successful, and the company ends up waiting for the customer to pay the invoice when the customer does not have the invoice in its computer system. To prevent this problem, consider either of the following additional steps:

- o *Print notice of completion*. If you successfully enter an invoice, the Internet portal should create a notice stating that you have successfully completed the entry. If so, print this confirmation, and later match all confirmations to invoices to verify that all entries have been made.
- o *Track e-mail notifications*. Some Internal portals will issue a message when the customer has approved an invoice, or when payment has been scheduled. For large invoices, it may make sense to track invoice submissions on a calendar, and then predict when these subsequent notifications should arrive. If you do not receive a notice by the expected date, contact the customer to verify that the invoice is in their system.

> **Tip:** Perhaps the biggest problem with entering invoices in an Internet portal is forgetting to make any entry at all. It is useful to create a list of all customers who require invoice entry into an electronic payment platform and the related Internet address, and then make a note to review this list on the monthly calendar of activities.

- *Invoicing on customer premises.* In some situations, it may be necessary to create an invoice at the customer site, because you do not know the exact amount of the invoice until that time. This situation arises in various services industries, such as building maintenance and locksmith work, where the company's employee evaluates the situation on-site, provides services and possibly materials, and compiles an invoice on the spot. In such cases, consider these additional steps:
    - *Track invoice numbers.* Before employees leave on their service calls, give them a block of consecutively numbered invoices to use. When they return with copies of all invoices generated during the day, a consecutive string of invoice numbers should have been used. If there is a missing invoice, it may be because the customer paid in cash, and your employee destroyed the invoice to hide his theft of the cash.
    - *Match customer schedule to invoices.* You should be able to match an invoice copy to every customer that each company employee was scheduled to visit during their service calls. If there is a customer on the schedule for which there is no invoice, contact the customer and ask for a copy of the invoice.

- *Issuing invoices by electronic data interchange (EDI).* The company may have set up a formalized issuance of invoices to some customers using EDI, which involves the electronic transmission of invoices in a strictly-defined format. Upon receipt, the customer's computer system automatically incorporates these invoices into its accounting software (though some customers may do this manually). If EDI is used for invoice transmission, consider adding the following steps to the billing procedure:
    - *Print transmission document (optional).* Some companies do not have a fully integrated EDI system, sometimes because only a few larger customers insist that they use it. In these cases, the billing clerk may manually enter the invoice into the EDI software. If so, print whatever document is provided by the EDI software, indicating the text of the message, and whether it was successfully sent, and then file this document with the invoice. Then schedule a periodic comparison of invoices to transmission documents to ensure that invoice EDI documents were sent to all customers who require this form of transmission.
    - *Match acknowledgment of receipt to invoice (optional).* The customer's computer system should send an acknowledgment message

back, whenever it receives an EDI invoice. Match these acknowledgments to the invoices sent, and make inquiries regarding any invoices for which there are no acknowledgments.

These two additions to the billing procedure are only useful if you are manually keypunching invoices into an EDI system. Fully integrated EDI systems are designed to operate automatically, and so will issue a notification of any missing acknowledgments.

The Credit Memo Procedure

A credit memo is a document issued by the seller of goods or services to a buyer, reducing the amount that the buyer owes to the seller under the terms of an earlier invoice. It may be used because of a returned item, to deal with a customer complaint, or for some type of allowance granted the customer, such as a retroactive price reduction that is based on the annual total amount ordered by the customer. The detailed procedure, including responsibilities and basic controls, follows:

> **Tip:** Consider scheduling a review of the accounts receivable aging report at the end of each month, and issue credit memos for all open accounts receivable that are caused by small unpaid residual balances. This cleans up the aging report, and usually results in a minimal additional bad debt expense.

1. **Create credit approval form**. On a credit approval form, state the customer name, the invoice for which a credit is requested, the amount of the credit, and the reason for it.
   Responsible party: Collections clerk
   Control issues: This step is needed in preparation for obtaining approval for the credit, as noted in the next step. The primary intent of this step is to create documentation for *why* a credit is being issued.

> **Tip:** The majority of credit memos are issued for very small amounts, such as for eliminating outstanding receivable balances of a few pennies. In these cases, it is not cost-effective to create a credit approval form. Instead, allow the collections clerk to process credits for small amounts without any documentation.

2. **Obtain supervisor approval**. Have someone other than the collections clerk who is requesting the credit approve the request. This is usually someone in a supervisory position. The supervisor then forwards the form to the billing clerk.
   Responsible party: Supervisor
   Control issues: This step is needed to prevent the collections clerk from colluding with other accounting staff to fraudulently intercept cash paid to

the company by customers, and issue credit memos to hide the missing funds.

3. **Issue credit memo**. The billing clerk examines the approval form to ensure that it has been properly approved, and then issues a credit memo based on the information in the credit approval form. This is a normal credit memo for most transactions, but it may be an internal credit memo in situations where the customer is not supposed to be aware of the credit (see the Forms: The Credit Memo section).
    Responsible party: Billing clerk
    Control issues: The controller could review a report of all credit memos created during the past month, to see if any are of an unusual size or are worthy of investigation in some other way.

4. **Offset against invoice**. Immediately after issuing the credit memo, the billing clerk offsets it against the relevant invoice (if any) in the accounting system. This is needed to reduce any confusion by the collections staff re-garding which invoices are still outstanding.
    Responsible party: Billing clerk

> **Tip:** On at least a monthly basis, have an accounting staff person review the accounts receivable aging report for stray credits, and report back to the controller regarding how to resolve these items. Otherwise, there may be confusion between the company and its customers regarding which invoices have been paid (or not).

5. **Send copy to customer**. The billing clerk files one copy of the credit memo and sends another copy to the customer. However, if the credit memo was created in order to offset an invoice due to nonpayment by the customer, no copy is sent to the customer. This non-delivery keeps the customer from using the credit against some other invoice.
    Responsible party: Billing clerk

The following flowchart shows the basic process flow for the generation and distribution of both types of credit memos.

Credit Memo Process Flow

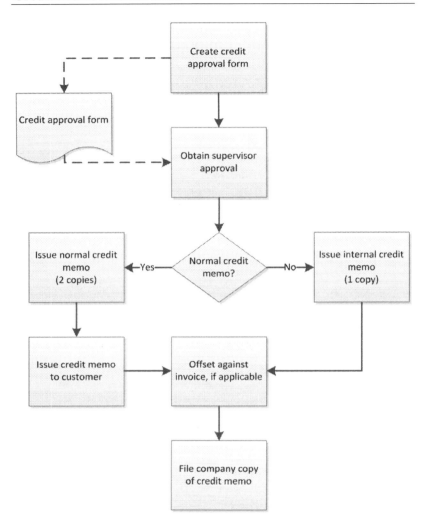

The Statement of Account Procedure

The primary reason for issuing a statement of account is to remind customers about any unpaid invoices. A secondary reason is that the statement acts as a control that can spot fraud being perpetrated within the company by the billings clerk. There are several types of fraud schemes under which the billings clerk can alter invoices in order to hide the theft of cash from the company. If someone other than the billings clerk issues month-end statements to customers, customers may spot these billing irregularities on the statements and contact the company with their concerns. Of course, if you issue statements for this second reason, be sure to list someone other than the billing clerk on the statement, so that any inquires are directed away from the position that could be engaged in fraud. The detailed procedure, including responsibilities and basic controls, follows:

1. **Review aged receivables report** (optional). Print the aged accounts receivables report and review it for any clearly incorrect information. It is best to rectify any issues found prior to sending statements to customers.
Responsible party: Not the billing clerk

2. **Print and mail statements**. Print the statements of account for all customers. It may be possible to set the printing program to skip statements for customers with very small balances, since it may not be worth the cost of mailing these statements to customers.
Responsible party: Not the billing clerk
Control issues: It is particularly important not to include the billing clerk in this step, since any fraud being perpetrated by the clerk can be hidden if this person can intercept and destroy statements before they reach customers.

3. **Investigate issues**. If customers contact the company with concerns about the information on their statements, they are routed to a more senior person than the billing clerk, who investigates their concerns.
Responsible party: Not the billing clerk
Control issues: As noted in the preceding step, someone other than the billing clerk should handle any issues arising from the statements of account.

Summary

There are several key issues to consider when using billing procedures. The first is speed of execution. Customers will not initiate their payment systems to send cash until the company sends them an invoice, so invoices must be created as soon after the delivery of products or services as possible. Second, if there is no fully integrated computer system for the order entry, shipping, and accounting functions, there are a number of extra processing steps that can introduce errors into invoices and the accounting records. Thus, full systems integration and a high degree of billing automation are worthy enhancements to the billing procedure.

Statement of Account Process Flow

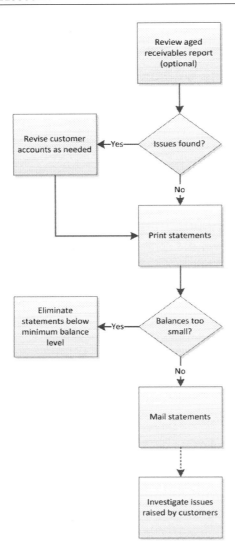

Chapter 6
Collection Procedures

Introduction

Once customer invoices have been issued, it is entirely possible that customers will not pay some of them by the agreed-upon payment dates. There are a large number of possible reasons for this, including lost invoices, late deliveries, incorrect shipments, and so forth. It is the job of the collections department to uncover and resolve these issues, hopefully resulting in the collection of overdue payments within a reasonable period of time.

In this chapter, we provide examples of the forms used in the collection process, and then move on to the various collection procedures. We provide separate procedures for:

- Collections
- Credit memo request
- Allowance for doubtful accounts calculation

As usual, procedural improvement tips are provided throughout the text, as well as flowcharts showing a streamlined view of each procedure.

Forms: The Credit Memo Approval Form

There should be an approval form that explains the need for a credit memo and the amount being requested. The form specifies whether the credit memo will be a standard one that is issued to the customer, or an internal one that is not issued. If possible, the form should also state the number of the invoice that is to be offset by the credit, which is used to reduce the invoice amount in the aged accounts receivable report. A sample credit memo approval form is shown on the next page.

This form is discussed further in the Customer Billing Procedures chapter.

The Collection Procedure

The collections staff may deal with an enormous number of overdue invoices. If so, the collection manager needs a procedure for dealing with customers in a standardized manner to resolve payment issues. The detailed collection procedure, including responsibilities and basic controls, is listed below. However, the process flow noted here only generally represents the stages of interaction with a customer. These steps might be shuffled, supplemented, or eliminated, depending on the payment status of each invoice.

Sample Credit Memo Approval Form

> **Tip:** The following procedure assumes the presence of a large number of overdue invoices. In some businesses, there may instead be a small number of large invoices, each of which requires a considerable amount of personalized attention. In this latter case, it may be considerably less necessary to impose a formalized collection procedure on the collections staff.

1. **Assign overdue invoices** (optional). When an invoice becomes overdue for payment, assign it to a collections person for collection activities.
   Responsible party: Collection manager
   Control issues: The collection manager should maintain a list of which collections staff are assigned to each invoice or customer.

> **Tip:** In a well-run collections department, all customers are already assigned to specific collections staff. Doing so allows the collections staff to build familiarity with certain customers. In this situation, assigning specific invoices to collections personnel is not required.

2. **Verify allowed deductions** (optional). A customer may submit a form detailing a deduction claim under the company's marketing plan. If so, verify the claim with the marketing manager and match it against deductions taken by the customer. If a deduction can be traced to the allowed deduction, submit a credit memo approval form to offset the amount of the deduction.
   Responsible party: Collections staff

Control issues: Have the marketing manager sign the customer's deduction form to authorize it, and attach the form to the credit memo approval form. This provides evidence of the reason for the credit.

> **Tip:** This can be an area of considerable dispute, since customers tend to have a broad interpretation of what can be deducted under a marketing plan. It is best to involve the marketing director in disputes. Also, consider advising the marketing director on definitions of allowable deductions before a marketing plan is released to customers.

3. **Issue dunning letters.** Use the accounting software to print dunning letters at fixed intervals, with each one pointing out overdue invoices to customers. Review the letters and extract any for which other collection activities are already in progress. Mail the other dunning letters to customers.
   Responsible party: Collections staff

> **Tip:** If the accounting system has this feature, e-mail the dunning letters rather than mailing them. Doing so eliminates the delay caused by mail float.

4. **Initiate direct contact.** If there are still overdue invoices outstanding, call customers to discuss the reasons for lack of payment. Following each call, record the details of the call, including the date, person contacted, reasons given for late payment, and promises to pay.
   Responsible party: Collections staff
   Control issues: The collection manager should review the documentation of customer contacts on a regular basis, to see if there are any potentially large collection issues that require accelerated action.

> **Tip:** Where possible, use a collections management system that is integrated into the accounts receivable file. Doing so not only increases the efficiency of the department, but also consolidates all collection notes in one place for review by the collection manager.

5. **Settle payment arrangements** (optional). If it is necessary to accept a longer payment period, document the terms of the payments to be made, as well as any interest to be paid and any personal guarantees of payment.
   Responsible party: Collections staff
   Control issues: The collection manager should approve all special payment arrangements.

6. **Adjust credit limit** (optional). At this point, the collections staff should have sufficient information about the financial condition of a customer to recommend to the credit staff if a reduction or termination of a customer's credit limit is in

order. The credit staff is responsible for changing a credit limit – the collections staff only provides information.
Responsible party: Collections staff and credit staff

7. **Monitor payments under settlement arrangements** (optional). If there are special payment plans, compare scheduled payment dates to the dates on which payments are actually received, and contact customers as soon as it appears that they will miss a scheduled payment date. This level of monitoring is required to keep customers from delaying their payments.
Responsible party: Collections staff
Control issues: This monitoring function can be given to a clerk who specializes in monitoring payments. Otherwise, the collections staff may forget to do so, resulting is a greater risk of customer default.

8. **Refer to collection agency.** Once all other in-house collection techniques have been attempted, shift invoices to a collection agency. At this point, the customer should certainly be placed on a credit hold list.
Responsible party: Collection staff
Control issues: The collection manager should approve the transfer of all invoices to a collection agency, since doing so will result in the payment of large fees if the invoices are eventually collected.

> **Tip:** Notify the sales manager before sending an invoice to a collection agency, since the vigorous collection methods employed by these agencies will likely have a deleterious effect on relations with the customer.

9. **Sue the customer** (optional). If all other alternatives have failed, meet with the company's legal staff to determine whether the company has a sufficient case against a customer to win a judgment against it in court. Also, the customer should have sufficient assets available to pay any judgment against it. If these issues appear favorable, authorize the legal staff to proceed with a lawsuit.
Responsible party: Collection staff, collection manager, legal staff

> **Tip:** From a practical perspective, it rarely makes sense to sue a customer. If they refuse to pay, it is typically because they are in significant financial difficulties, and so would not be able to pay a judgment against them.

10. **Write off remaining balance.** If all collection techniques have failed, complete a credit memo approval form in the amount of the invoice(s) to be written off.
Responsible party: Collection staff
Control issues: The collection manager should approve all larger credit memo approval forms. An approval is not necessary for smaller, incidental write-offs.

> **Tip:** When an invoice is written off, this means that the amount of credit granted to the customer in the customer master file will now appear to be available for use again, which could lead to the inadvertent sale of more goods to the customer. To prevent this, set the available credit balance to zero, and also configure the customer's record to require that all future business be conducted on cash-in-advance terms.

11. **Conduct post mortem.** If there was a specific problem with the company's systems that caused a bad debt to occur, call a meeting of those people most closely related to the problem to discuss a solution. Assign responsibility for action items, document the meeting, and schedule follow-up meetings as necessary.
Responsible party: Collection manager
Control issues: The controller or collection manager monitor assigned tasks to ensure that the underlying problem is resolved.

The following exhibit shows a streamlined view of the collection procedure, not including a number of optional steps. The flowchart shows the most likely collection activities that apply to the majority of situations.

The Credit Memo Request Procedure

The collections staff may find it necessary to request that the amount of a customer invoice be reduced or eliminated, usually because it will not be collected. The following procedure shows how a credit memo is requested.

> **Tip:** Schedule a review of the accounts receivable aging report at the end of each month, and issue credit memos for all open accounts receivable that represent small unpaid residual balances. This cleans up the aging report, and usually results in a minimal additional bad debt expense.

1. **Create credit approval form.** On a credit approval form, state the customer name, the invoice for which a credit is requested, the amount of the credit, and the reason for it.
Responsible party: Collections staff
Control issues: This step is needed in preparation for obtaining approval for the credit, as noted in the next step. The primary intent of this step is to create documentation for *why* a credit is being issued.

> **Tip:** The majority of credit memos are issued for very small amounts, such as for eliminating outstanding receivable balances of a few pennies. In these cases, it is not cost-effective to create a credit approval form. Instead, allow the collections staff to process credits for small amounts without any documentation.

Collection Process Flow

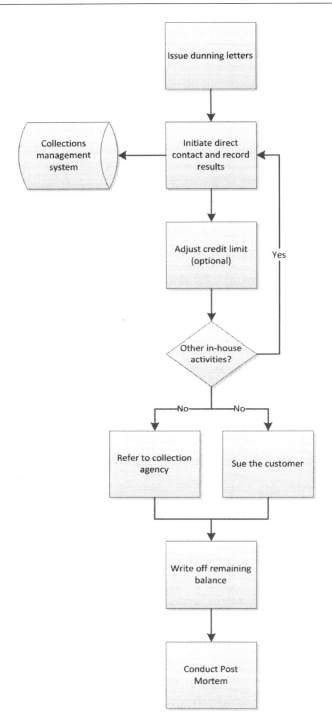

2. **Obtain supervisor approval**. Have someone other than the collections clerk who is requesting a credit approve the request. This is usually someone in a supervisory position. The supervisor then forwards the form to the billing clerk.
   Responsible party: Collection manager
   Control issues: This step is needed to prevent the collections clerk from colluding with other accounting staff to fraudulently intercept cash paid to the company by customers, and issue credit memos to hide the missing funds.

> **Tip:** It may be useful to require the approval of a higher-level person, such as the CFO, for the elimination of really large invoices, if only to bring these invoices to their attention.

The credit memo request is then processed by the billing clerk, as outlined in the Credit Memo Procedure section in the Customer Billing Procedures chapter.

Given the brevity of this procedure, no flowchart of the process flow is provided.

The Allowance for Doubtful Accounts Calculation Procedure

The collections staff is responsible for calculating the allowance for doubtful accounts, since it is best able to judge which invoices are at the greatest risk of not being paid. This allowance is a reserve for bad debts that may arise from existing accounts receivable. The procedure for calculating the allowance for doubtful accounts, including responsibilities and basic controls, follows:

1. **Clear out offsetting balances.** Review the accounts receivable aging report for any unapplied credits. Research such credits to see if they can be applied to open accounts receivable. This step is needed to ensure that no reserve is created for older invoices against which credits have already been created.
   Responsible party: Billing clerk

2. **Calculate theoretical reserve.** Print an accounts receivable aging report. Multiply the amount of receivables in each 30 day time bucket on the report by the historical bad debt percentage applicable to that time bucket. Summarize the total amount of theoretical bad debts. In addition, override the percentage calculation and include the full amount of any invoices where:
   - The customer has declared bankruptcy
   - The company is suing the customer for payment
   - The company has sent the invoice to a collection agency
   - Other information exists that indicates a high probability of failure to pay

> **Tip:** Verify that the aging report used for this calculation includes *all* invoices. This is not a minor point, since many businesses issue a large number of invoices at the very end of a reporting period, which might be excluded from an aging report that was run too soon.

Responsible party: Collections staff
Control issues: The collection manager should verify the amount of this calculation.

> **Tip:** There are multiple methods available for calculating the theoretical amount of the allowance for doubtful accounts. For example, it can be based on the risk level assigned to each customer, or on risk of nonpayment associated with specific invoices, or an overall historical percentage for the entire amount of accounts receivable.

> **Tip:** Update the historical bad debt percentage on at least a quarterly basis. Otherwise, using an old percentage when economic conditions are changing rapidly may result in an incorrect theoretical reserve.

3. **Adjust actual reserve.** Forward the approved calculation of the allowance for doubtful accounts to the general ledger accountant. This person adjusts the booked balance of the reserve to match the calculated balance, and includes the calculation in the accompanying journal entry documentation.
   Responsible party: General ledger accountant
   Control issues: The period-end closing procedure should include a task to update the allowance for doubtful accounts, which makes it more likely that the reserve will be adjusted regularly.

The following exhibit shows a streamlined view of the calculation procedure.

Allowance for Doubtful Accounts Calculation Process Flow

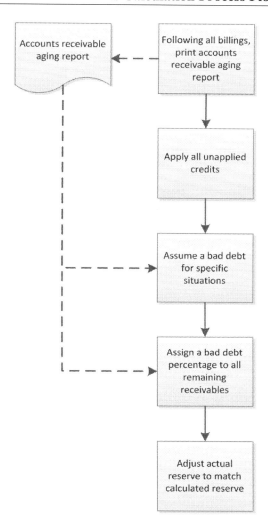

Summary

Collections is an area in which the risk of loss increases rapidly with the passage of time. This means that a strong system of procedures should be in place to ensure that overdue invoices are closely monitored. However, a practiced collections person should be allowed to depart from the standard collections routine if his or her experience indicates that a different approach is warranted. In such cases, the standard collection procedure may be more applicable for trainee collections personnel.

A large number of overdue invoices may not be the fault of the collections staff. The real issue may lie in some other part of the business, such as faulty product designs, late deliveries, or improper packaging that causes damage in transit.

Consequently, a key part of the collections procedure is an analysis of why customers are not paying their invoices on time, rather than timely contact with customers regarding overdue amounts.

Chapter 7
Cash Receipts Procedures

Introduction

Cash receipts is an area in which poorly-designed procedures can lead to the loss of cash, as well as errors in the application of that cash to customer receivables. Investigating lost or misapplied cash is extremely time-consuming, so it is of some importance to install robust procedures in this area.

In this chapter, we provide examples of the forms resulting from or used in the cash receipts process, and move on to the various cash receipts procedures. There are several types of cash receipt situations, so we provide separate procedures for:

- Process cash receipts
- Process check receipts
- Process credit card receipts
- Process lock box receipts
- Remote deposit capture

As usual, procedural improvement tips are provided throughout the text, as well as flowcharts showing a streamlined view of each procedure.

Forms: Sales Receipt

The sales receipt is used in low-volume sales environments where it is uneconomical or impractical to use cash registers. The following form is prenumbered in order to spot instances where a sales clerk might pocket both a customer's cash payment and the company copy of the form. The form also contains space to record credit card and check information. The sales receipt is always prepared in duplicate, so that the customer and the company both have copies.

Sample Sales Receipt

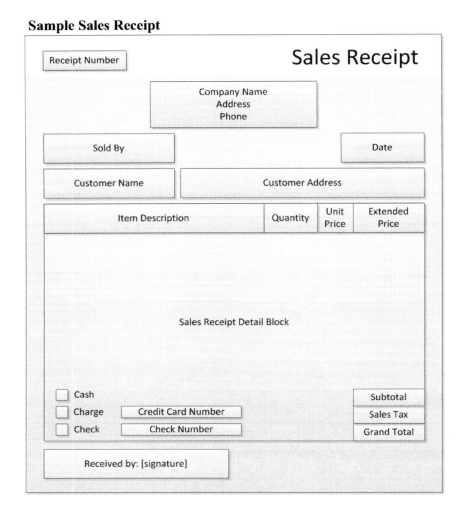

Forms: Mailroom Check Receipts List

The mailroom staff enters all cash and checks received through the mail on the following mailroom check receipts list. It is used as a control point to ensure that a party other than the cashier is compiling cash receipts, thereby making it more difficult for the cashier to abscond with funds without being noticed.

Sample Mailroom Check Receipts List

Mailroom Check Receipts List

		Receipts Date	

Paying Party	Check Number	Cash ?	Amount
		☐	
		☐	
		☐	
		☐	
		☐	
		☐	
		☐	
			Total Receipts

Received by cashier: [signature]	Prepared by: [signature]

The Cash Receipts Processing Procedure

The task of handling cash is considerably different from doing so for checks, since cash is not only much more subject to theft, but also does not require application against open accounts receivable – instead, it is typically recorded as part of an immediate sale. The procedure for cash receipts processing is outlined below:

1. **Accept and record cash.** If the business is paid by a customer in cash, record the payment in a cash register. If there is no cash register (as may be the case in a low-volume sales environment), the sales clerk instead fills out a two-part sales receipt, gives a copy to the customer, and retains the other copy.
   Responsible party: Sales clerk
   Control issues: Give each customer a receipt, since the recipient might examine the receipt to see if the amount recorded matches what they paid.

2. **Match receipts to cash.** Compare the amount of cash received to either the cash register receipt total or the total of all sales receipt copies, and investigate any differences. Complete a reconciliation form for any differences found.
Responsible party: Manager
Control issues: If sales receipts are used, prenumber them and subsequently see if there are any missing numbers. This indicates that a sales clerk issued a sales receipt to a customer, and pocketed both the store copy and the associated amount of cash.

3. **Aggregate and post receipt information.** Summarize the information in the cash register and post this information to the general ledger as a sale and cash receipt. If the cash register is linked to the company's accounting system and is tracking individual sales, then sales are being recorded automatically, as is the reduction of goods in the inventory records. If sales clerks are manually completing sales receipts, summarize the information in the sales receipts and record the sales and any related inventory reductions in the general ledger.
Responsible party: Accounting clerk
Control issues: Only record sales in the amount of the cash receipts verified in the preceding step.

4. **Deposit cash.** Prepare a bank deposit slip, retain a copy, and enclose the original slip along with all cash in a locked container for transport to the bank. After counting the cash, the bank issues a receipt stating the amount it has received.
Responsible party: Cashier and courier
Control issues: It may be useful to have a second person verify the amount stated on the deposit slip. Otherwise, the cashier could take some cash, overstate the amount on the deposit slip, and blame the courier when the bank receipt is for a lower amount than what is stated on the deposit slip.

5. **Match to deposit slip.** Compare the copy of the deposit slip to the bank receipt, and investigate any differences. A variation is to compare the cash receipts journal to the bank receipt.
Responsible party: Not the cashier or courier
Control issues: If there is a difference between the amounts stated on the deposit slip and the bank receipt, the persons responsible for preparing the deposit slip and transporting the cash to the bank should not be involved in the reconciliation, since they have an interest in the outcome.

The following exhibit shows a streamlined view of the cash receipts processing procedure.

Cash Receipts Process Flow

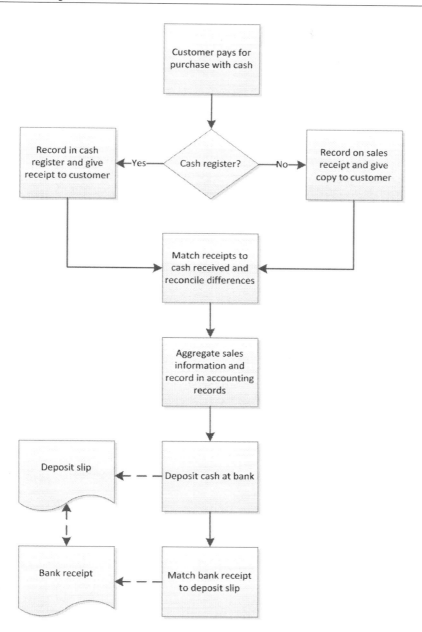

The Check Receipts Processing Procedure

The task of processing checks is loaded with controls. They are needed to ensure that checks are recorded correctly, deposited promptly, and not stolen anywhere in the process. The procedure for check receipts processing is outlined below:

1. **Record checks and cash.** When the daily mail delivery arrives, record all received checks and cash on the mailroom check receipts list (see the Forms: Mailroom Check Receipts List section for an example). For each check received, state on the form the name of the paying party, the check number, and the amount paid. If the receipt was in cash, state the name of the paying party, check the "cash?" box, and the amount paid. Once all line items have been completed, enter the grand total in the "total receipts" field at the bottom of the form. Sign the form, and state the date on which the checks and cash were received. Also, stamp "for deposit only" and the company's bank account number on every check received; this makes it more difficult for someone to extract a check and deposit it into some other bank account.
Responsible party: Mailroom staff
Control issues: Where possible, have two people record incoming checks and cash. Otherwise, someone could easily abscond with any payments received before they have been recorded in the company's accounting system.

2. **Forward payments.** Insert all checks, cash, and a copy of the mailroom check receipt list into a secure interoffice mail pouch. Have it hand-delivered to the cashier in the accounting department. The cashier matches all items in the pouch to the mailroom check receipt list, initials a copy of the list, and returns the copy by interoffice mail to the mailroom. The mailroom staff then files the initialed copy by date.
Responsible party: Mailroom staff, mail courier, and cashier
Control issues: These steps ensure that the payments are securely shifted to the cashier, and that the cashier officially acknowledges receipt of the funds. Responsibility for the funds has now shifted to the cashier.

> **Tip:** There may need to be an additional reconciliation step if the cashier finds that the checks and cash in the mail pouch do not match the amount listed on the mailroom check receipt list.

3. **Apply cash to invoices.** Access the accounting software, call up the unpaid invoices for the relevant customer, and apply the cash to the invoices indicated on the remittance advice that accompanies each payment from the customer. If there is no indication of which invoice is to be credited, record the payment either in a separate suspense account, or as unapplied but within the account of the customer from whom it came.
Responsible party: Cashier
Control issues: It is of some importance to apply cash to open accounts receivable at once, thereby reducing the amount of receivables that the collections staff should pursue. Once all cash received for the day has been applied, another control possibility is to print the cash receipts journal for the day, compare it to the mailroom check receipts list, and reconcile any differences.

4. **Record other cash** (optional). Some cash or checks will occasionally arrive that are not related to unpaid accounts receivable. For example, there may be a prepayment by a customer, or the return of a deposit. In these cases, record the receipt in the accounting system, along with proper documentation of the reason for the payment.

   Responsible party: Cashier

   Control issues: The controller may want to review the treatment of these payments, to ensure that they have been properly recorded within the correct account.

5. **Deposit cash.** Record all checks and cash on a deposit slip. Compare the total on the deposit slip to the amount stated on the mailroom check receipts list, and reconcile any differences. Then store the checks and cash in a locked pouch and transport it to the bank.

   Responsible party: Cashier and additional reviewer (see the following control issue)

   Control issues: An extra level of control is to have a second person compare the total on the deposit slip to the total on the mailroom check receipts list, which prevents the cashier from absconding with funds. This second person should not report to the cashier.

> **Tip:** Cash application should be completed on the same day of cash receipt, if only to ensure that no cash is held on the premises overnight. If it is not possible to apply cash to receivables that fast, make photocopies of the receipts that were not applied, so that cash can still be deposited at once.

6. **Match to bank receipt.** Upon receipt of the checks and cash, the bank issues a receipt for it. Someone other than the cashier compares this receipt to the amount on the deposit slip, and reconciles any differences.

   Responsible party: Accounting clerk

   Control issues: This step is used to prevent the theft of cash while in transit to the bank. Since the person transporting the cash is also returning with the receipt, it is quite possible that this person will deliberately lose the receipt. A missing receipt is therefore a possible indicator of fraud.

The following exhibit shows a streamlined view of the check receipts processing procedure.

Check Receipts Process Flow

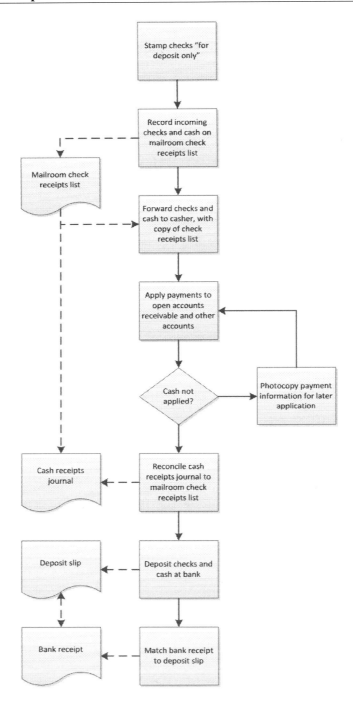

The Process Credit Card Receipts Procedure

The task of collecting credit card information is completely automated in on-line web stores. However, many companies still process credit card information manually for other types of sales. The following procedure is designed for the latter situation, where we assume that card information is manually entered by the company into an on-line processing site.

1. **Collect information.** When a customer pays by credit card, it is entirely possible that the sales clerk or order entry clerk will take down the information incorrectly. To mitigate this problem, record not only the information needed for the credit card payment, but also the contact information for the customer, in case it is necessary to verify or replace credit card information.
   Responsible party: Sales clerk or order entry clerk
   Control issues: Since credit card information is essentially cash for the company, treat the information like cash – lock up all sales receipts on which credit card information is recorded. However, unlike cash, shred the receipts once they are no longer needed (have exceeded the company's record retention period), so that no one can access the credit card information.

   > **Tip:** The format of the sales receipt form can be expanded to include contact information for any customer paying with a credit card.

2. **Enter card information.** Access the credit card processing site on the Internet and enter the credit card information. If the entry is rejected, contact the customer to verify the card information, or ask for a replacement card. If a replacement card is needed, enter the updated information on the sales receipt. When the information is eventually accepted by the site, print a receipt and staple it to the sales receipt.
   Responsible party: Accounting clerk
   Control issues: Printing a receipt is critical, since it proves that the credit card payment was processed. Thus, a reasonable internal audit task would be to review sales receipts for proof of data entry into an online credit card processing site.

3. **Record the sale.** Enter the sales receipt into the accounting system as a sale (this may involve creating an invoice, or it may be a journal entry). If the system provides for a credit card sale designation, flag that designation when making the entry. Then stamp the sales receipt as having been recorded.
   Responsible party: Accounting clerk
   Control issues: If the accounting system assigns a unique number to the transaction, enter it on the sales receipt. This creates a method for tracing credit card documentation into the accounting database.

Tip: It may be tempting to date credit card sales forward in time, so that they more closely correspond with the date when the cash from these sales actually arrives in the company's bank account. However, doing so essentially converts these sales to the cash basis of accounting, which is not acceptable if the company wants to have its financial statements audited under one of the major accounting frameworks. Thus, always record credit card sales as of the date of the sale.

4. **Issue receipt to customer** (optional). If customers pay by phone or e-mail, send them a receipt, which they will probably need when they reconcile their company credit card statements at the end of the month.
   Responsible party: Accounting clerk
   Control issues: Be sure to mail this receipt to the person named on the credit card, not the person who placed the order. Doing so ensures that the person responsible for the credit card is made aware of the payment.

5. **Verify the transaction.** Before filing sales receipts for credit card transactions, verify that the cash related to them has been posted to the company's bank account, and that they were posted to the accounting system.
   Responsible party: Accounting clerk
   Control issues: These verification steps can be included on the sales receipt stamp. The following form shows how the stamp might be structured.

Sample Sales Receipt with Accounting Stamp

6. **File documents.** File the company's copy of the sales receipt, as well as the attached credit card processing receipt, in the accounting records by customer name. If an invoice was printed as part of the sale, file all three documents together.

Responsible party: Accounting clerk

Control issues: The person filing these documents should first examine them to ensure that each one has been stamped to indicate that it was recorded in the accounting system.

The following exhibit shows a streamlined view of the credit card receipts processing procedure, including the optional step of issuing a receipt to the customer.

Credit Card Receipts Process Flow

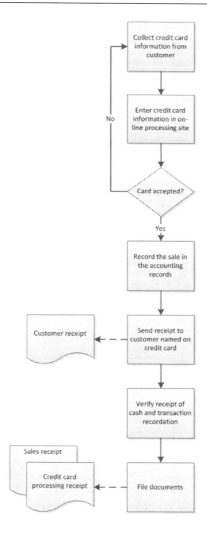

The Process Lockbox Receipts Procedure

When a company arranges to have customers send their payments directly to a lockbox at a bank, this substantially reduces the number of controls that would otherwise clutter the cash receipts procedure. The reason is that the cash never enters the company premises, so there is no risk of theft; instead, the focus of the procedure is on the proper recordation of the receipts forwarded by the bank. The procedure for lockbox receipts processing is outlined below:

1. **Bank processes receipts.** When payments arrive at the lockbox, bank employees immediately deposit the payments into the company's bank account. They also scan copies of the checks and any associated remittance advices, and store the digital images on-line, where the company can access them.
   Responsible party: Bank staff

   > **Tip:** It can be quite a chore to convince customers to route their payments to a lockbox. Schedule several reminder messages to customers, as well as a number of follow-up phone calls, and even then there will still probably be a few intransigent customers who persist in mailing their payments to the company. If so, have the mailroom staff immediately mail these payments to the lockbox. Doing so eliminates the need for in-house cash controls.

2. **Record payments.** The cashier accesses the bank's website each day to view the images of scanned payments from the preceding day. The cashier uses this information to apply the payments to open accounts receivable.
   Responsible party: Cashier
   Control issues: The cashier prints the cash receipts journal immediately after applying cash to verify that the total applied matches the total received by the bank.

   > **Tip:** In those cases where it is unclear where to apply cash, the cashier records it in a suspense account, and also prints out the images of the related receipts from the bank's website. The cashier retains these printed payment images in a folder until they can be properly applied.

Given the abbreviated nature of this procedure, we have not included a process flow for it.

The Remote Deposit Capture Procedure

Remote deposit capture involves scanning checks into a format that is uploaded to the bank as a deposit. This approach replaces the traditional method of using a courier to transport deposits to the bank, which modifies the back end of the cash receipts process. In the following procedure, we assume the normal receipt of checks on the front end of the process, with remote deposit capture inserted on the back end:

1. **Record checks.** This is the same step used in the earlier check receipts processing procedure. Even though the checks will not be deposited in the traditional sense, you still need to stamp the checks "for deposit only," along with the company's bank account number. The stamp is still needed to make it more difficult for someone to extract a check and deposit it into some other bank account.

2. **Forward payments.** This is the same step used in the earlier check receipts processing procedure.

3. **Apply cash to invoices.** This is the same step used in the earlier check receipts processing procedure.

4. **Record other cash.** This is the same step used in the earlier check receipts processing procedure.

5. **Deposit cash.** This is the procedural step at which remote deposit capture diverges from normal check receipts processing. Run all checks through the check scanner, and review the scans to ensure that they are of acceptable quality to be deposited. Then forward the electronic deposit to the bank and print the deposit receipt.
   Responsible party: Cashier
   Control issues: It is easy to forget to scan checks, so include it on the daily work schedule for the cashier. Also, the following step should be handled by someone other than the cashier, which can help to detect unscanned checks.

6. **Match to bank receipt.** Compare the deposit receipt to the cash receipts journal for the day's receipts, and reconcile any differences. This step is used not only to ensure that no checks were removed from the deposit, but also to ensure that the cashier did not forget to engage in the daily remote deposit capture activity.
   Responsible party: Accounting clerk other than the cashier
   Control issues: File the deposit receipt, as evidence that the deposit was properly transmitted to the bank.

7. **Destroy scanned checks.** Retain all scanned checks in a locked location for 15 business days and then destroy them, either by shredding or perforation. This step is needed to keep them from being incorrectly included in a normal physical deposit to the bank.
   Responsible party: Accounting clerk
   Control issues: To be absolutely certain of the document destruction, make someone responsible for it, have them sign a document destruction certificate

when the shredding or perforation is complete, and have the internal audit staff periodically examine the check destruction process.

The following exhibit shows a streamlined view of the remote deposit capture procedure, including all check receipts steps required prior to the use of remote deposit capture.

Remote Deposit Capture Process Flow

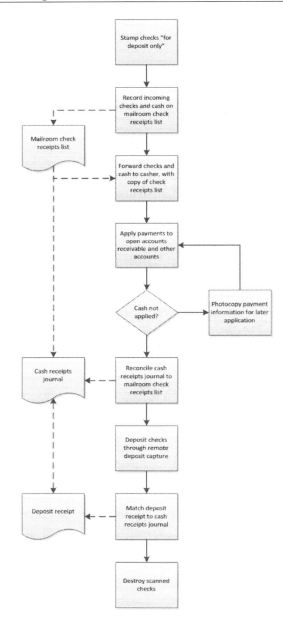

Summary

The nature of a business will drive the design of its cash receipts procedures. For example, an on-line store runs all of its customer payments through a credit card processor, and so has no cash receipts in the traditional sense. At the other extreme, a casino deals with enormous quantities of cash, and so requires superlative cash handling procedures that any other business would find overwhelmingly burdensome. Given the range of possible situations, the procedures outlined here may require extensive modification to meet the specific needs of a business. Given the risk of theft and errors in this area, it may make sense to consult with the company's auditors or bring in a controls consultant to examine the company's operations and decide upon how the procedures in this chapter should be tailored to meet the needs of the business.

Chapter 8
Purchasing Procedures

Introduction

Purchasing is an extremely important area in which to have a well-defined set of procedures, given the large amount of cash outflows associated with it. This chapter covers the classic approach to purchasing, which involves the use of purchase requisitions, purchase orders, and (sometimes) a bidding process. Because of the labor-intensive nature of these tasks, a large part of the purchasing activities have shifted to the use of procurement cards, which are addressed in the following chapter.

In this chapter, we provide examples of the forms resulting from or used in the purchasing process, and then move on to the various purchasing procedures. We provide separate procedures for:

- Purchase requisitions
- Purchasing (with a variation involving the use of blanket purchase orders)
- Bidding

As usual, procedural improvement tips are provided throughout the text, as well as flowcharts showing a streamlined view of each procedure.

Forms: Purchase Requisition

The purchase requisition is used by all company departments to request that the purchasing department acquire goods and services. The form is designed to give the purchasing staff extremely specific information about what is being ordered, including the suggested supplier, the catalog number used by the supplier for the item being ordered, and the price offered by that supplier. The form also includes space for a due date for each line item, which allows the requesting department to set different due dates for different items in the form. There is also space for a charge code for each line item, which keeps the purchasing staff from having to guess at where each purchase should be charged. Finally, the form contains a number of spaces for approval signatures, depending on the expense level of the item(s) being ordered. The budget approval signature is designed to ensure that there are sufficient funds in the budget to pay for the items being ordered.

Sample Purchase Requisition

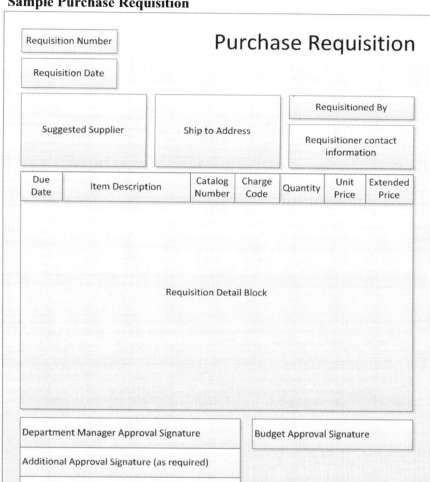

A variation on this form is to eliminate the budget approval signature and replace it with a budget approval initials block for each line item. This alternative approach may be useful when the items being ordered are to be charged to different accounts, each of which has a separate budget. This approach is not necessary as long as the department manager is only verifying purchases against the grand total amount of the department budget, rather than for individual expense line items.

Another variation on the requisition form is to require the requesting person to supply bidder information for at least three bidders. This information is usually contained within a series of blocks near the top or bottom of the form, and reduces the work load of the purchasing staff when bidding is required. However, this format assumes that all of the items listed on the requisition can be obtained from the three bidders, which may not be the case. Also, the requesting party is not necessarily the most knowledgeable person for selecting prospective bidders.

Forms: Purchase Order

The purchase order is the primary document used by the purchasing department to order goods and services. A sample purchase order is shown below. It should specify a considerable amount of information in order to avoid confusion with the supplier. In addition to the usual itemization of items to be purchased and their price, the following sample purchase order also states the due date, both freight and payment terms, and even a phone number to call to confirm receipt of the order.

Sample Purchase Order

Several other variations on the purchase order form are possible. For example, if a company routinely issues adjustments to its purchase orders, it can include a revision number field below the purchase order number. Another possibility is to include a page number, for those situations where a purchase order spans multiple pages. Yet another option is to include a cumulative total dollar amount for the purchase order that includes all revisions; this may be used to see if the revised purchase order total has increased to the point where an additional authorization is required.

Forms: Blanket Purchase Order Release

When a business issues a blanket purchase order, it is setting aside funding for multiple purchases from a supplier over a period of time. The blanket purchase order release form is used to order specific goods and services within the funding block set aside in the blanket purchase order. In the following sample release form, we see that it is quite similar to a standard purchase order form. However, standard contract terms (such as payment terms) are removed, with a reference back to the blanket purchase order, where the contract terms are located. Also, the release references the blanket order upon which it is based.

Sample Blanket Purchase Order Release

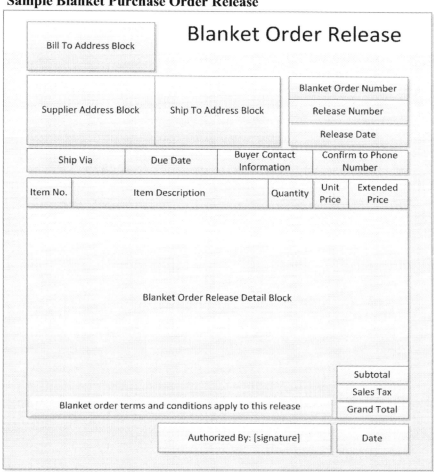

The Purchase Requisition Procedure

There should be a formal process for ordering materials and services. Otherwise, there is no control over the amounts spent, and the purchasing department will be buried with purchase requests. To mitigate these issues, many companies require their employees to fill out purchase requisitions. A purchase requisition form details exactly what someone wants to buy, shows the purchasing staff where the indicated items might be bought, and requires at least one approval signature. Thus, it can be a useful tool for organizing the flow of purchasing requests into the purchasing department. The procedure for processing purchase requisitions is outlined below:

1. **Complete requisition form.** Obtain a two-part purchase requisition form and fill in the following information:
    *   Item or service to obtain
    *   Required delivery date
    *   Shipping address
    *   Account number to be charged
    *   Recommended supplier and supplier part number

    Responsible party: Any employee
    Control issues: It may be useful to use prenumbered purchase requisitions, so that the purchasing department can keep track of which requisitions are still open. This control is not needed in a computerized system, where the software assigns a unique number to each requisition.

2. **Obtain approval.** At a minimum, obtain the approval of the department manager, who signs the requisition. If the request is for a more expensive item, obtain additional approval signatures as per the company authorization table (see the next procedure).
    Responsible party: Person completing the requisition
    Control issues: It may be useful for the purchasing department to periodically route back to the department managers a listing of the requisitions that they have purportedly signed, which can be used to detect fraudulent requisitions. However, this can be a time-consuming control activity.

> **Tip:** Include a field in the requisition form where the requesting person verifies that there is sufficient funding left in the budget for the requested item. Otherwise, there is a risk (especially towards the end of the budget year) that items will be inadvertently purchased for which there are no funds available.

3. **Forward to purchasing.** The requesting person should retain one copy of the requisition and forward the other copy to the purchasing department.
    Responsible party: Person completing the requisition

Control issues: The purchasing department could send an acknowledging e-mail back to the requester, stating that they have received the requisition. However, given the extra work involved, this extra control is rarely used.

4. **Match to purchase order** (optional). If the purchasing department sends back a copy of the purchase order that was created from the requisition, compare it to the requisition to ensure that the correct items have been ordered. If not, contact the purchasing staff to have the purchase order revised or replaced.
    Responsible party: Person completing the requisition

The following exhibit shows a streamlined view of the purchase requisition procedure, including the optional matching step.

Purchase Requisition Process Flow

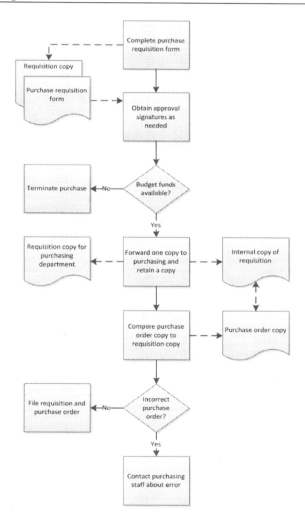

The Purchasing Procedure

The classic approach to ordered goods and services is the purchase order. It is a formal approach to buying that involves the issuance of a legal document, the purchase order, to a supplier. The purchase order identifies the items being ordered, as well as the price and other conditions under which a company is willing to make a purchase. Though the issuance of purchase orders is usually well-controlled, it also requires a considerable amount of time to complete. For this reason, it is generally restricted to more expensive purchases. The purchasing procedure is outlined below:

1. **Obtain pricing**. When the purchasing staff receives a purchase requisition, it needs to ascertain pricing in order to determine the level of authorization needed by the requesting party.
    Responsible party: Purchasing staff
    Control issues: It is very time-consuming to obtain multiple prices for the items listed on every purchase requisition, so the purchasing manager should set rules for allowing purchases from a small number of designated suppliers, with multiple bids only needed for larger purchases.

2. **Match against authorization table.** Once the purchasing staff has obtained preliminary pricing estimates, compare the amounts requested to the company's authorization table. If the requesting person represents sufficient authorization to approve the purchase, proceed with the ordering process. If not, retain a copy of the purchase requisition and send the original to the person whose approval is required. An example of an authorization table follows.

Sample Purchase Authorization Table

	Department Manager	Division Manager	Chief Operating Officer	Chief Executive Officer	Board of Directors
<$25,000	✓				
$25,000-100,000	✓	✓			
$100,001-250,000	✓	✓	✓		
$250,001-1,000,000	✓	✓	✓	✓	
$1,000,000+	✓	✓	✓	✓	✓

Responsible party: Purchasing staff
Control issues: The purchasing staff should routinely review its copies of unapproved purchase requisitions, and follow up with approvers regarding their status.

Tip: It may be more efficient for the purchasing department to shift this task onto the requesting person, so that all purchase requisitions contain the required approvals. However, this approach may not work if the requesting person is not sure of the prices of items being requested.

---

3. **Obtain additional documentation** (optional). If the item being requested exceeds the company's capitalization limit, send the purchase requisition back to the requesting person with a request to complete a capital request form (see the Fixed Asset Procedures chapter for more information).
Responsible party: Purchasing staff
Control issues: This step essentially terminates the purchasing process, so there is no need to retain a copy of the purchase requisition.

4. **Prepare purchase order.** Complete a purchase order, based on the information in the purchase requisition or bid results (see the following procedure). Depending on the size of the order, it may be necessary for the purchasing manager to approve and sign the purchase order. Retain a copy of the purchase order in a pending file, stapled to the department's copy of the purchase requisition, and send the original to the supplier. Additional copies go to the receiving department and accounts payable staff. Though not necessary, another copy could be sent to the person who submitted the requisition, as evidence that the order was placed. If the purchasing system is computerized, only a single copy is printed and sent to the supplier.
Responsible party: Purchasing staff
Control issues: If purchase orders are prepared manually, have them prenumbered, track all numbers used, and store unused purchase orders in a secure location. This is needed to keep someone from removing a purchase order and using it to order goods or services that have not been authorized.

5. **Obtain legal review** (optional). If the purchase order contains terms and conditions that are not the standard ones normally used in purchase orders, route the document to the legal staff for review.
Responsible party: Corporate counsel
Control issues: It can be difficult to determine what constitutes a reasonable exception from the normal terms and conditions, which would require legal review. Also, a legal review slows down the purchasing process. For both reasons, the purchasing staff may be reluctant to obtain a review. This issue can be detected after-the-fact with a periodic investigation by the internal audit team.

> **Tip:** You can avoid a legal review for recurring contracts whose terms were approved by corporate counsel in an earlier version, but only if the terms and conditions have not subsequently changed.

6. **Monitor change orders** (optional). If change orders are issued, keep track of the resulting change in the cumulative total authorized to be spent. If the cumulative total exceeds the original authorization level noted in the authorization table, obtain the higher authorization level needed for the new expenditure level.
Responsible party: Purchasing staff

Control issues: This step requires a considerable amount of monitoring, which the purchasing staff will be reluctant to do. It can be made easier by modifying the purchase order form to include a field for the cumulative dollar total, which the purchasing staff updates for each successive change order.

7. **Monitor purchase acknowledgments** (optional). For the more important items being purchased, it may make sense to ensure that purchase orders have been received by suppliers and acknowledged. This can be a simple phone call to the supplier, or it may be a formal written acknowledgment. Another option is to include a "confirm to phone number" field in the purchase order, as was shown earlier in the sample purchase order template. If the company is issuing purchase orders by electronic means, the supplier's computer system may automatically send back an acknowledgment message.
   Responsible party: Purchasing staff
   Control issues: This step is probably of least use when dealing with long-term business partners, but could be of considerable importance when ordering from new suppliers where the purchasing department has no idea of supplier performance levels.

8. **Monitor subsequent activity**. Following the due date of the purchase order, remove the department's copy from the pending file and verify with the receiving department that the related goods were received. If not, contact the supplier to determine the status of the order. If complete, file the purchase order by supplier name. If the purchasing system is computerized, the receiving department will flag purchase orders on-line as having been fulfilled, which effectively eliminates this step.
   Responsible party: Purchasing staff
   Control issues: For more important items, the purchasing staff might consider contacting suppliers *in advance of* the due date to ensure that items were shipped on time.

> **Tip:** If the purchasing staff finds that small residual balances were not fulfilled on a purchase order, and the company no longer requires the residual amount, issue a notification to the supplier that the order for the remaining amount has been cancelled.

9. **File documents**. When all activity associated with a purchase order has been completed, file the purchasing documents by supplier name for the current year. This will certainly include the purchase order and purchase requisition, and may also include a cancellation notice that terminates any residual unfulfilled balances on a purchase order, as well as any purchase order acknowledgments received from suppliers.
   Responsible party: Purchasing staff

The following exhibit shows a streamlined view of the purchasing procedure, not including the optional steps to obtain additional documentation, conduct a legal review, or monitor change orders. It also does not include the bidding process, which is addressed later in the Bidding Procedure section.

Purchasing Process Flow

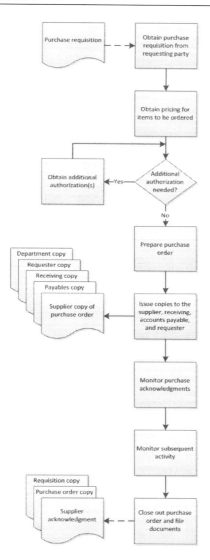

Variations on the Purchasing Procedure

A more advanced purchasing department is likely to use blanket purchase orders, where a single funding commitment is issued to cover recurring purchases for a long period of time, such as a year. Doing so eliminates the work that would otherwise be required to issue a series of purchase orders for incremental purchases. When blanket purchase orders are used, a purchase order release is issued for individual purchases, rather than a standard purchase order. This document references the governing blanket purchase order, the release number, the release date, and the details of what is being ordered. A blanket purchase order release form was shown earlier in this chapter.

Control issues: Only items included in the blanket purchase order should be ordered in a subsequent release. The internal audit staff can review this issue for compliance. Alternatively, if the purchasing system is computerized, the system can restrict purchases to authorized items, as well as track the total dollar amount of cumulative purchases under the blanket purchase order.

The Bidding Procedure

If a purchase is for a very expensive item, it may be prudent to obtain bids from multiple suppliers. If so, the purchasing department typically compiles a request for proposals (RFP) document and issues it to an approved list of suppliers. It then holds a bidder conference to clarify any uncertainties in the RFP, and then evaluates supplier bids to determine which vendor is offering the best mix of price, product, delivery, and so forth. The bidding procedure is outlined below:

1. **Prepare bidding documents.** The purchasing staff prepares a request for proposals document, which contains the required specifications for the item(s) to be purchased.
   Responsible party: Purchasing staff

   > **Tip:** Use a template to construct bidding documents, thereby improving the efficiency of the process.

2. **Issue bidding documents.** Determine the appropriate list of recipients, and issue the bidding packet to them.
   Responsible party: Purchasing staff
   Control issues: It may be useful to have a list of approved suppliers with whom the company does business; this is useful for eliminating from consideration any suppliers with whom the company has had problems in the past. At a minimum, there should be a list of banned suppliers that are not to receive bidding documents.

3. **Host a bidder conference** (optional). If a prospective purchase involves an extremely large expenditure, it may be necessary to host a bidder conference in which bidders can obtain clarification of such issues as the company's expectations, timeline, and budget.
   Responsible party: Purchasing staff

Control issues: Someone should take notes at the bidder conference and distribute the results to all bidders, including those who could not attend the conference. Doing so ensures that everyone bids based on the same information.

4. **Evaluate bids.** All bids received shall be evaluated based on the following criteria (samples are shown; actual criteria may vary):
   - Total cost to acquire (including price, freight, site preparation, setup, and training)
   - Ongoing maintenance and warranty fees
   - Disposal costs
   - Prior history with supplier

   Responsible party: Purchasing staff and others as assigned
   Control issues: It is useful to develop the evaluation criteria before the requests for proposal have been issued, which makes it more difficult for someone to later derive their own criteria to use as the basis for selecting a favorite supplier. It may also be useful to document the reasons why the winning bid was selected, in case questions are raised at a later date.

   > **Tip:** For larger purchases, it may make sense to form a bid evaluation committee, including members from all impacted departments. They may have a better idea than the purchasing staff of which bid will best meet the company's needs.

5. **Issue purchase order.** This step was dealt with in detail in the preceding procedure. Note that purchases sufficiently large to require a bidding process will probably also involve unique terms and conditions, which will require a review by legal counsel.

6. **Monitor supplier performance** (optional). The purchasing staff monitors deliveries under the purchase order, including delivery and quality performance, and corresponds with the supplier regarding any issues encountered.
   Responsible party: Purchasing staff
   Control issues: There should be an ongoing system in place for tracking supplier performance, which is used by the purchasing staff to determine which suppliers it will do business with in the future. Results should also be distributed to the suppliers, who can use the information to improve their performance.

The following exhibit shows a streamlined view of the bidding procedure, including both optional steps.

Bidding Process Flow

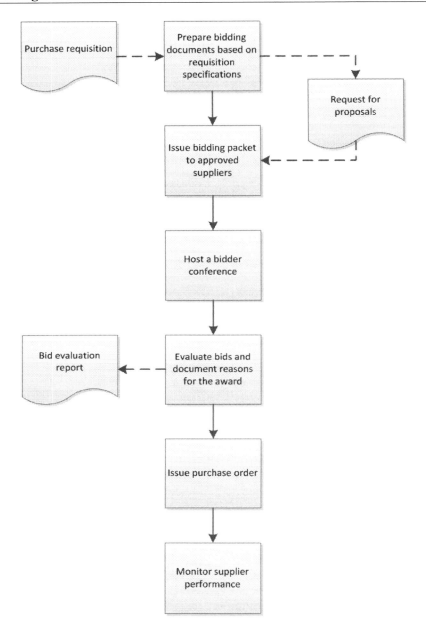

Summary

This chapter has addressed the most formal approach to purchasing, which is the process of documenting a purchase request, converting it into a bid, and using a bidding process for the more expensive purchases. While this is the classic approach to purchasing, it is so paper-intensive that it is not used for the large number of less-expensive and recurring purchases that a company engages in every day. For these other types of purchases, we use procurement cards, expense reports, and petty cash. The following three chapters deal with the procedures for these three other purchasing methods.

Chapter 9
Procurement Card Procedures

Introduction

Procurement cards are used to purchase lower-cost items, thereby avoiding the more complex and expensive process of issuing purchase orders. By consolidating the paperwork for purchases into a small number of procurement card statements, the work load of the accounts payable department can be greatly reduced.

In this chapter, we provide examples of the forms used in the procurement card processes and then move on to the various procurement card procedures. We provide separate procedures for:

- Procurement card reconciliation
- Lost procurement cards

As usual, procedural improvement tips are provided throughout the text, as well as flowcharts showing a streamlined view of each procedure.

Forms: Reconciliation Checklist

It is useful to issue monthly procurement card statements to card users with a checklist of the various reconciliation steps that they must complete before returning the statements to the accounts payable department. The following checklist shows the key reconciliation steps, which users can check off as they complete each item. The checklist is simply a reminder for card users – it does not have to be returned to the accounts payable staff.

Sample Reconciliation Checklist

Procurement Card Reconciliation Checklist

This checklist shows the steps required to reconcile your procurement card statement. The steps are:

☐ Match receipts to card statement

☐ Obtain missing receipts

☐ Complete the missing receipts form

☐ Complete the disputed expenditure form

☐ Assign account numbers to statement line items

☐ Sign approval block on the statement

☐ Make a copy of all documents and retain it for __ years

☐ Forward original documents to accounts payable department

Note: All documents must be completed and returned within three business days!

Forms: Missing Receipts Form

When a procurement card user cannot locate a receipt for an expenditure listed on the monthly card statement, he or she completes a missing receipts form. The intent of this form is to document all expenditures for which there are missing receipts, and certify that they are valid business expenses. A sample form is shown next.

Sample Missing Receipts Form

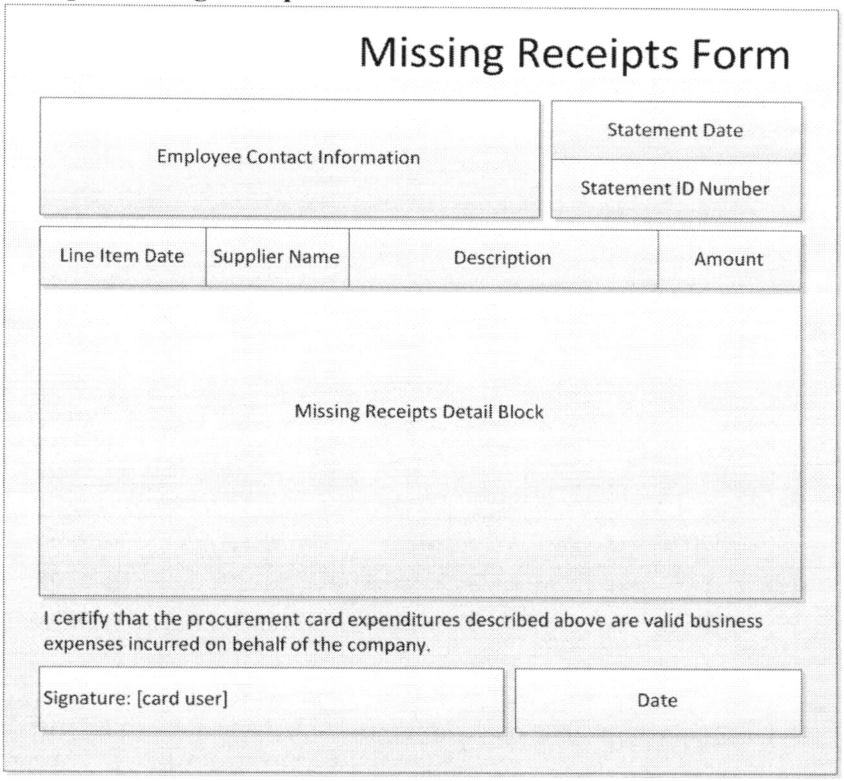

Forms: Disputed Expenditure Form

A card user completes a disputed expenditure form when he or she wants to obtain a credit for an expenditure listed on a monthly procurement card statement. There are a number of possible reasons to request a credit, so the following form format includes a number of options, as well as space at the bottom to more fully explain the situation. This form is submitted to the accounts payable department along with the monthly packet of card reconciliation information. Only one dispute is documented on each of these forms; doing so makes it easier for the accounts payable staff to track each dispute.

Sample Disputed Expenditure Form

Disputed Expenditure Form

| Employee Contact Information | | Statement Date |
| | | Statement ID Number |

Line Item Date	Supplier Name	Description	Amount

Check the box that best states the reason for the disputed expenditure:

☐ Already billed on prior statement
☐ Amount is incorrect
☐ Did not authorize the purchase
☐ Did not receive goods or services
☐ Other (see comments below)

Additional explanatory comments block

| Signature: [card user] | Date |

Return this form to the accounts payable department as part of the monthly card statement

Forms: Lost Card Notification Form

When card users learn that the procurement cards for which they are responsible are missing, they should complete a lost card notification form at once and forward it to the procurement card administrator. In many cases, the card provider already has a form for this; if not, consider using the following sample form as a template.

Sample Lost Card Notification Form

Lost Card Notification

| Employee Contact Information | Date |
| | Procurement Card Number |

Check the box that best states the reason for the card being lost:

☐ Lost (describe circumstances): _____

☐ Stolen (describe circumstances): _____

☐ Other (describe circumstances): _____

| Signature: [card user] | Date |

| Name and address of person contacted at card provider | Date Contacted |
| | Time Contacted |

☐ Send replacement by regular mail

☐ Send replacement by overnight mail (the company will be billed for this service)

| Signature: [card administrator] | Date |

Forward this form to the procurement card administrator at once

In the form, the card user completes the information above the solid line. He or she then signs the signature block in the top half of the form and forwards the form to the procurement card administrator. The administrator completes the bottom half of the form and then sends the form to the card provider.

The Card Reconciliation Procedure

The bank supplying procurement cards to a company issues a statement of card activity once a month. The company passes this information along to those employees using procurement cards, who are expected to reconcile the statement to their purchasing records. There may also be a reconciliation checklist that accompanies each card statement, which is a useful tool for reminding card users of the various reconciliation steps. The procedure for reconciling a procurement card statement is outlined below:

1. **Match receipts to statement.** Upon receipt of the monthly card statement and a reconciliation checklist from the accounting staff, match all stored receipts to the line items on the statement.
   Responsible party: Card user

   > **Tip:** To speed up the reconciliation process, consider having the accounting staff first review all card statements and accept those with small balances for which the account coding is obvious. The card user still receives a copy of the statement, but does not have to complete a reconciliation.

   > **Tip:** A high-volume card user might consider logging all purchases made with a procurement card into a transaction log. Otherwise, it may be difficult to sort through what may potentially be several hundred receipts.

2. **Obtain missing receipts.** If the receipts associated with some line items are missing, contact the supplier to see if a replacement receipt can be obtained. If a receipt cannot be obtained (which is likely), fill out a missing receipts form. This form itemizes any statement line item for which there is no receipt and states the purpose of the expense. The card user signs the form to certify that the expenses on the form are valid business expenses. A sample missing receipts form was shown earlier in this chapter.
   Responsible party: Card user
   Control issues: Track the volume of missing receipts over time by card user. There may be some users who habitually lose receipts for suspicious expenditures, which may require the revocation of their card privileges.

   > **Tip:** Adopt a cutoff level for the missing receipts form, below which no entries are required. Otherwise, employees may spend an inordinate amount of time documenting insignificant expenditures.

3. **Note disputed charges.** If line item amounts appear to be incorrect or charged in error, circle them on the account statement and note that they are in dispute. Also, complete the disputed expenditure form, which is used by the accounts payable staff to follow up with the card provider. A sample disputed expenditure form was shown earlier in this chapter.
   Responsible party: Card user

   > **Tip:** Card users are not good at resolving disputed charges, so have them provide the details for each dispute, and then have the person in charge of the procurement card program or the accounts payable staff follow up on the charges.

4. **Assign account numbers.** Write the account number to be charged next to each line item on the statement. A variation is to assign a default account number to

each card user, so that they only have to enter an account number if it varies from the default account number.
Responsible party: Card user

> **Tip:** Card users may not know which accounts are available for their use, so send each user a list of acceptable account numbers, and issue an updated version whenever there is a change to the chart of accounts.

5. **Sign approval block.** Before forwarding card statements, the accounts payable staff should have stamped an approval block on each statement, in which the card user and the department manager should sign if they approve the expenditures listed in the statement.
Responsible party: Card user and supervisor
Control issues: Someone must review and sign off on all card statements. Otherwise, there is no one in the company who will spot purchasing irregularities by card users. The check signer should not be relied upon as a statement reviewer, since that person may not be directly responsible for the expenses being incurred, and so will not review statements in detail.

6. **Forward documents.** Assemble the card statement, missing receipts form, disputed expenditure form, and receipts into a packet. Make a copy of the packet and retain it. Forward the original version of the packet to the accounts payable department.
Responsible party: Card user

The following exhibit shows a streamlined view of the card reconciliation procedure.

Card Reconciliation Process Flow

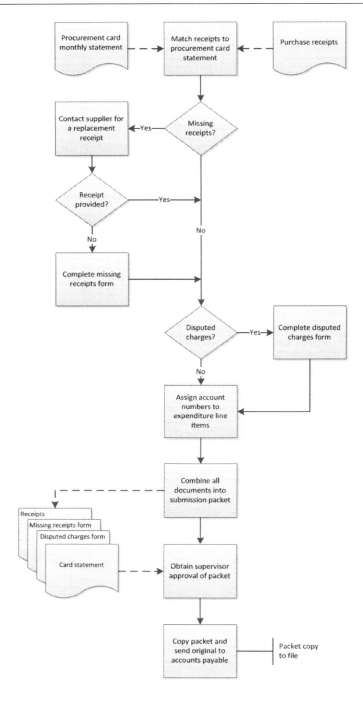

The Lost Card Procedure

There is a significant liability associated with a lost or stolen procurement card, so a company should have a system in place for rapidly notifying its card provider whenever employees become aware that a card is missing. The procedure for lost cards is outlined below.

1. **Complete lost card notification form.** Complete the lost card notification form for the employee name, date, card number, and reason fields. Then forward the form as expeditiously as possible to the procurement card administrator. A sample lost card notification form was shown earlier in this chapter.
   Responsible party: Card user
   Control issues: The importance of a prompt lost card notification should be drilled into card users, as well as where they can find the lost card notification form.

> **Tip:** If there is a procurement card user manual, include the lost card notification form in the manual, so that it is easily accessible by card users.

2. **Contact card provider.** Contact the company's contact person at the card provider about the missing card. Note on the form the name of the person contacted, as well as the date and time of notification. This information can be of some importance when determining the respective liabilities of the company and its card provider for any fraudulent charges made after the card was lost or stolen.
   Responsible party: Procurement card administrator

3. **Complete form.** Complete the bottom part of the lost card notification form, requesting the speed with which a replacement card should be forwarded by the card provider. Then sign the form and e-mail it to the provider. Retain a copy of the form, in case there are questions later about whether a notification was properly made.
   Responsible party: Procurement card administrator
   Control issues: The lost card notification form may be used as evidence in case there is a dispute with the card provider, so store it in a three-ring binder to reduce the risk of losing it.

4. **Match to received cards.** As replacement cards arrive from the card provider, match them to the related lost card notification forms. Follow up with the provider if any cards were not received by the expected dates.
   Responsible party: Procurement card administrator
   Control issues: A slightly more formal approach to matching lost card notification forms to replacement cards is to create a "card received" stamp; use it to stamp the relevant forms and fill in the date of receipt.

The following exhibit shows a streamlined view of the lost card procedure.

Lost Procurement Card Process Flow

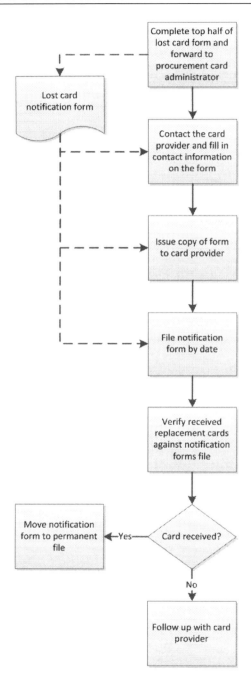

Summary

The purchasing manager usually wants to shift as much purchasing activity as possible to procurement cards, thereby reducing the purchasing workload of his or her department. This emphasis on procurement cards can mean that quite a large proportion of all expenditures are made with the cards. If so, it is critical to install a card reconciliation procedure that incorporates an approval process. Otherwise, it will be much too easy for employees to make a significant number of purchases that are not in the best interests of the company.

Chapter 10
Expense Report Procedures

Introduction

Expense reports are submitted by employees in order to be reimbursed for expenses they incurred on behalf of their company. Expense reports are quite different from normal expenditures that run through the purchasing department, since there is no authorizing purchase order or receiving report to document an expense. Given these differences, an entirely different set of procedures are needed to process expense reports.

In this chapter, we provide examples of the forms used in the expense reporting process, and then move on to the various expense report procedures. We provide separate procedures for:

- Expense report submission (manual system)
- Expense report submission (automated system)
- Expense report review

As usual, procedural improvement tips are provided throughout the text, as well as flowcharts showing a streamlined view of each procedure.

Forms: Expense Report Form

The expense report form comes in many varieties, of which there are two main types. The first is shown in the following sample format, where a common set of expense categories are listed across the top row, leaving space for many entries down the left side of the form. The alternative is to switch these placements, so that columns for each of the seven days of the week are listed across the top, with the most common expense categories listed down the left side. The format shown here has the advantage of being usable for longer periods than one week.

Sample Expense Report Form

Employee Name	Expense Report Date							Expense Report	

Date	Expenditure Description	Airline	Rental Car	Meals	Tips	Supplies	Other	Totals	
								+ Mileage Expense	
								- Advances	
								= Net Payable	

Explanation of "Other" Items			Detail of Meals Expense			Detail of Mileage Expense			
Date	Description	Amount	Date	Description	Amount	Date	Description	Miles	$

Authorized By: [signature]	Date

Both expense report formats contain additional blocks at the bottom of the report, in which employees can enter additional detailed information about certain expense categories.

The Expense Report Submission Procedure (Manual System)

When employees want to be reimbursed for expenditures, they fill out an expense report. This can be on a preprinted form, on an electronic spreadsheet, or in an on-line form. This procedure assumes the use of either a preprinted form or an electronic spreadsheet. The next procedure deals with an on-line form. This procedure includes steps for a number of expenditures commonly found on expense reports, including mileage reimbursements, per diem meals, and deductions for advances. The procedure for completing an expense report is outlined below:

1. **Enter expense items.** Enter all items to be reimbursed on the expense report, placing each one in the expense category to which it most closely relates. Attach *original* receipts for all expenses that exceed the minimum corporate receipt policy. Otherwise, if employees were to attach copies of receipts, they could then submit the originals in other expense reports and be reimbursed twice. *Responsible party:* Person submitting report

Control issues: Employees may have a hard time retaining receipts for inclusion in their expense reports, and the accounts payable staff may justifiably not want to pay for items where there is no receipt. A reasonable alternative is to have the company directly pay for as many expenses as possible, such as all airfares and hotels. Doing so greatly reduces the expenses listed on an expense report, and mitigates the control risk associated with it.

> **Tip:** Employees may not be aware of the company's travel policy, so consider summarizing its key points on the face or back of the expense report. This may keep some questionable expenses from being claimed.

> **Tip:** If employees paid in a foreign currency, the easiest way to reimburse them is at the exchange rate stated on the person's credit card statement for those expenditures, plus any foreign currency exchange fee (also listed on the credit card statement).

2. **Enter mileage.** State on the expense report the beginning and ending locations of travel on each date, as well as the miles driven between those locations. Multiply the miles driven by the mileage reimbursement rate to arrive at the total mileage amount for which to be reimbursed.
   Responsible party: Person submitting report
   Control issues: Many employees use an old expense report form from the preceding year, which does not contain the current mileage reimbursement rate. Consequently, anyone reviewing expense reports should verify that the correct rate was used. Also, the internal audit staff can compare miles claimed to the mileage calculated using any Internet-based mileage calculation tool.

3. **Enter per diem meals** (optional). If the company pays its employees a fixed amount per meal, rather than reimbursing actual meal expenses, itemize the travel dates to which per diem meals apply, and enter the per diem amounts as per the company travel policy.
   Responsible party: Person submitting report
   Control issues: The accounts payable or internal audit staff should review expense reports to verify that employees are entitled to per diem payments, and that they were traveling on the indicated dates.

4. **Enter entertainment expenses** (optional). It is customary for a business to allow its employees to spend much greater amounts for meals than normal if they are entertaining business customers. It is difficult to impose any restrictions on these expenses, but employees should at least be required to state who attended and the business purpose of the meal or meeting.
   Responsible party: Person submitting report

Control issues: It may be possible to match the names listed on the expense report to those people the employee was scheduled to meet. However, this is a weak control that does little to keep entertainment costs in check.

5. **Enter advances.** If a company pays an employee an advance to cover expenses during a trip, list the entire amount of the advance on the expense report as a deduction from the total expenses claimed.
   Responsible party: Person submitting report
   Control issues: The accounts payable staff can reference the current list of advances paid to employees when reviewing expense reports, to see if advances have been properly deducted.

6. **Explain non-corporate travel payments** (optional). The company may have a policy of having all airline and hotel payments be made by a central reservations group. If so, paying for airline or hotel arrangements with a personal credit card breaches company policy, and should be explained in an attachment to the expense report.
   Responsible party: Person submitting report
   Control issues: An alternative to this control is to have the internal audit staff look for such payments during its occasional audits of expense reports, and report their findings to senior management.

7. **Obtain approval.** All expense reports must be approved by the person whose budget will be impacted by the expense. This is usually the department manager. For higher-level positions, reports may be approved by the chief operating officer or vice president of human resources.
   Responsible party: Supervisor
   Control issues: The expense reports of the chief executive officer (CEO) could be approved by the chair of the compensation committee of the board of directors. Anyone else in the organization reports to the CEO, and so would feel pressure to approve whatever is listed in the CEO's expense report.

8. **Retain copy.** Make a copy of the expense report and retain the copy.
   Responsible party: Person submitting the expense report
   Control issues: When employees are eventually reimbursed, they can compare the payment amount to the expense report, and may protest any differences between the two.

9. **Forward to accounts payable.** Forward the expense report, with attached receipts, to the accounts payable staff for payment processing.
   Responsible party: Either the person submitting the expense report or the approving supervisor

10. **Review expense report.** The accounts payable staff examines the expense report for a variety of issues, as described later in the Expense Report Review Procedure section.
Responsible party: Accounts payable staff

11. **Generate invoice number.** Assign an invoice number to the expense report and record the expense report as an invoice in the accounts payable system for the amount payable, net of advances. Assigning an invoice number is not a minor issue, because there needs to be a way to differentiate employee expense reports in the accounting system. Since employees tend to submit multiple expense reports at the same time, it is not possible to base the invoice number on the submission date or the approval date. Instead, consider using an invoice number that is derived from the date of the first or last expense stated in the expense report (which is more likely to be unique).
Responsible party: Accounts payable staff
Control issues: The methodology for generating invoice numbers should be rigidly enforced, so there is no variability in the length or content of invoice numbers. Doing so ensures that, if the same expense report were to be submitted twice, the accounting system would reject the second submission as being already in the system.

The following exhibit shows a streamlined view of the expense report submission procedure, with some optional tasks included.

The On-Line Expense Report Submission Procedure

Some companies require their employees to use an on-line form to submit their expense reports. This is an efficient way to record and review expenses, since the form typically incorporates the company's travel policy, which automatically rejects any submissions that are not in compliance with the policy. The procedure for completing an on-line expense report form is outlined below:

1. **Enter information in system.** The on-line form will prompt the employee to enter the dates and amounts of expenditures, as well as classify them into different expense categories. The system will review these submissions based on the corporate travel policy and automatically reject those items prohibited by the policy.
Responsible party: Employee submitting report
Control issues: The accounting department should test the system whenever the corporate travel policy is changed, to see if it is dealing with employee submissions correctly.

Expense Report Submission Process Flow

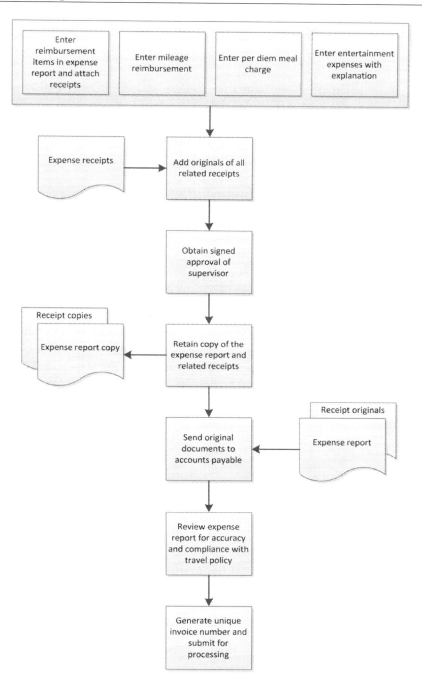

2. **Enter receipts.** The system will review the expenses submitted and decide which receipts should accompany them. Employees may have the option of scanning in the required receipts, or of mailing them to the accounts payable department.
Responsible party: Employee submitting report

3. **Obtain approval.** The system routes a digital image of the expense report to the person designated as the supervisor of the employee. The supervisor reviews and approves the document, after which the system routes it to the accounts payable department.
Responsible party: Supervisor
Control issues: If a supervisor is not available to approve an expense report, have a second person designated as a backup. Otherwise, a supervisor's vacation plans could halt the payment of an employee.

4. **Import expense report.** There should be an interface between the expense reporting system and the accounts payable system, so that expense report submissions are automatically set up for payment. Unlike the manual system, there is no need to devise a unique invoice number for each expense report. Instead, the on-line form automatically assigns a unique number when an expense report has been submitted.
Responsible party: Accounts payable staff
Control issues: The expense reporting system is the control for expense reports, so there should not be a need for any additional review of expense reports by the accounts payable staff.

The following exhibit shows a streamlined view of the on-line expense reporting procedure.

On-line Expense Reporting Process Flow

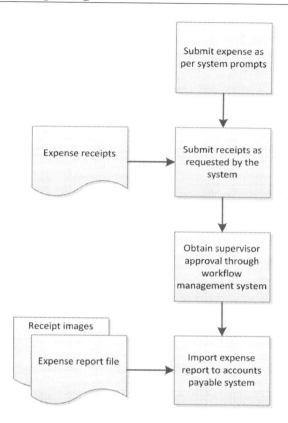

The Expense Report Review Procedure

When a company uses a manual submission process for expense reports, there is an enhanced risk of errors in the reports. This procedure gives direction to the reviewers who examine expense reports prior to issuing payments to the submitting employees. We assume that this entire procedure is conducted within the accounts payable department. However, many or all of the investigative aspects of the procedure can be shifted to the internal audit department, if the company prefers to use occasional audits of expense reports. The expense report review procedure is outlined below:

1. **Review for non-reimbursement items.** Review the expense report to see if it contains any of the items noted in the following table. If so, they are to be disallowed and subtracted from the expense report. Send an e-mail to the employee, detailing all disallowed expenses, and copy the message to the employee's supervisor.

Sample List of Non-Reimbursement Items

Adult entertainment	Expenses > 90 days old	Personal reading material
Car washes and cleaning	Finance charges on credit cards	Theft/loss of personal property
Contributions	Health club / spa fees	Toiletries
Child care	Laundry fees on short-duration trips	Traffic fines
Clothing	Lost luggage	Travel insurance
Commuting costs	Movies	Undocumented expenses

Responsible party: Accounts payable staff

Control issues: The repeated presence of non-reimbursement items on expense reports is an indicator that an employee is more likely to continue to make fraudulent reimbursement claims through his or her expense report. The accounting staff should flag the expense reports submitted by these persons for more detailed reviews than it normally conducts.

2. **Match to receipts.** Compare the expenses claimed on the expense report to the accompanying receipts, and request additional information if some receipts are missing.

Responsible party: Accounts payable staff

Control issues: If any receipts appear to have been modified, bring them to the attention of the accounts payable supervisor.

> **Tip:** It is painfully time-consuming to review every receipt associated with an expense report. An alternative is to examine 100% of the receipts for the largest expenses, and some lesser percentage of the receipts for smaller expenses.

3. **Review per diem meals.** Verify from the travel records in the expense report the dates on which travel was conducted, and verify that per diem charges were only applied for during those dates. Also verify that the per diem rates are correct, and that no actual meal expenditures are included in the expense report in addition to per diem charges.

Responsible party: Accounts payable staff

Control issues: Another issue to be aware of is when employees charge their meals on a company credit card and also charge per diem rates on their expense reports. To detect this issue, compare credit card statements to expense reports.

4. **Review mileage claims.** Review the amount of mileage reimbursement claims for reasonableness. This might include running a mileage calculation on an on-line travel site. If the miles claimed figure is within a certain percentage of the calculated amount, accept it.

Responsible party: Accounts payable staff

Control issues: If some routes are heavily traveled by employees, it might make sense to create a standard table of mileage allowed between higher-volume locations.

5. **Verify clerical accuracy.** Re-summarize the totals in the expense report for both rows and columns. If the expense report is based on an electronic spreadsheet, it is particularly likely that someone might have added rows or columns that are not reflected in the grand totals on the report.
Responsible party: Accounts payable staff
Control issues: If the accounting staff spots a formula error on an employee's expense report spreadsheet, send the employee the latest version of the spreadsheet, which (presumably) does not contain the error.

6. **Match to advances list.** Compare the expense report to the current list of employees to whom travel advances have been issued. If an advance is not deducted from the expense report, refer the matter to the accounts payable supervisor, who verifies which travel plans are associated with the advance. If the advance should have been deducted from this expense report, do so and issue an e-mail notice to the employee and the employee's supervisor regarding this change in reimbursement.
Responsible party: Accounts payable staff and accounts payable supervisor
Control issues: The accounts payable staff should have read-only access to the employee advances account in the general ledger, so that it has real-time access to the most recent information about travel advances issued.

7. **Update trend analysis** (optional). It may be useful to periodically update a trend analysis of the types of expenses being claimed by those employees who appear to be at higher risk of abusing the company's travel policy. This analysis can extend to a review of receipt copies being used across multiple expense reports, as well as a review of sequential receipt numbers across multiple expense reports (which indicates that an employee purchased a block of receipts and is using them to fraudulently claim fake expenses).
Responsible party: Accounts payable staff

The following exhibit shows a streamlined view of the expense report review procedure, not including the optional trend analysis.

Expense Report Review Process Flow

```
┌─────────────────────────────────────────────────────────────────┐
│  Review for non-      Review for missing    Review per diem       Verify clerical  │
│  reimbursement        receipts              and mileage claims    accuracy         │
│  items                                                                             │
└─────────────────────────────────────────────────────────────────┘
```

Modify expense report and notify employee and supervisor ←Yes— Adjustments?

No

Compare to advances outstanding

Contact supervisor and adjust as necessary ←Yes— Deduction needed?

No

Enter into accounts payable system

Summary

The completion and subsequent processing of expense reports is quite time-consuming, and is not even remotely cost-effective when the effort is compared to the modest sums involved. Because of this issue, consider having the company directly pay for more expenses, such as air travel and hotels. By doing so, the remaining amount of expense report reimbursements may drop to such a low level that they are less of a concern from a control perspective, and so will require less review time.

Chapter 11
Petty Cash Procedures

Introduction

A petty cash fund is typically set up for any department where there is a history of small, short-term cash requirements for operational expenditures. These funds are initially set up with a sufficient amount of cash to fund all reasonable cash requests for a short period of time, such as a few weeks to a month. The cash is stored in a drawer or cash box. When the cash level in a petty cash fund declines to a certain point, it is refreshed with more cash. Several procedures are needed to fund and pay out petty cash, as well as a number of controls to mitigate the risk that the cash in these funds is not used inappropriately.

In this chapter, we provide examples of the forms resulting from or used in the petty cash process, and then move on to the various petty cash procedures. We provide separate procedures for:

- Petty cash funding
- Petty cash disbursement
- Petty cash review

As usual, procedural improvement tips are provided throughout the text, as well as flowcharts showing a streamlined view of each procedure.

Forms: Petty Cash Transfer Form

The petty cash transfer form is used to document the transfer of cash from the cashier to the petty cash custodian. Both the cashier and custodian should retain a copy of the form as evidence of who has taken responsibility for the cash. A sample form follows.

Note that the form requires the amount transferred to be written in words, not just in numbers. This makes it more difficult for someone to fraudulently alter the numerical amount listed to a larger number, and pocket the difference paid.

Forms: Petty Cash Voucher

When someone is paid from a petty cash fund, they must complete a petty cash voucher. The voucher provides evidence that the person was actually paid, since someone must sign for the payment received. It also provides detail regarding the type of expense being reimbursed, since it provides space for both an expense description and the account number to which the expense is to be charged. The following sample voucher contains two additional features to combat fraud. First, it includes a voucher number, so that auditors can investigate missing vouchers.

Second, the form requires that the petty cash custodian not only enter the total amount paid, but also to state the amount in words; by doing so, it is much more difficult for someone to fraudulently increase the amount stated on the voucher and remove a corresponding amount from petty cash.

Sample Petty Cash Transfer Form

Petty Cash Transfer Form

Petty Cash Fund Number	Date

The Sum Of	Total Paid

For funds received:	Petty Cash Custodian: [signature]
For funds disbursed:	Cashier: [signature]

Sample Petty Cash Voucher

Petty Cash Voucher

Date	Voucher Number

Paid To	

Item Description	Account No.	Amount
Petty Cash Voucher Detail Block		
The Sum Of		Total Paid
Payment Received By: [signature]	Issued By: [initials]	

Forms: Petty Cash Book

The petty cash book is, in most cases, an actual ledger book, rather than a computer record, in which are recorded petty cash expenditures. There are two primary types of entries in the book, which are a debit to record cash received by the petty cash custodian (usually in a single block of cash at infrequent intervals), and a large number of credits to reflect cash withdrawals from the petty cash fund. These credits can be for such transactions as payments for meals, flowers, office supplies, stamps, and so forth.

An alternative format is to record all debits and credits in a single column, with a running cash balance in the column furthest to the right, as shown in the following example. This format is an excellent way to monitor the current amount of petty cash remaining on hand.

Sample Petty Cash Book (Running Balance)

Date	Purchase/Receipt	Amount	Balance
4/01/xx	Opening balance	$250.00	$250.00
4/05/xx	Kitchen supplies	-52.80	197.20
4/08/xx	Birthday cake	-24.15	173.05
4/11/xx	Pizza lunch	-81.62	91.43
4/14/xx	Taxi fare	-25.00	66.43
4/23/xx	Kitchen supplies	-42.00	24.43

Another variation on the petty cash book is to maintain it as a spreadsheet, where each item is recorded in a specific column that is designated for a particular type of receipt or expense. This format makes it easier to record petty cash activity in the general ledger. An example of this format, using the same information as the preceding example, is as follows:

Sample Petty Cash Book (Columnar)

Date	Description	Meals	Supplies	Travel
4/05/xx	Kitchen supplies		$52.80	
4/08/xx	Birthday cake	$24.15		
4/11/xx	Pizza lunch	81.62		
4/14/xx	Taxi fare			$25.00
4/23/xx	Kitchen supplies		42.00	
	Totals	$105.77	$94.80	$25.00

The petty cash book is a useful control over petty cash expenditures, since it forces the petty cash clerk to formally record all cash inflows and outflows. To ensure that this is an effective control, the petty cash book should be reviewed periodically by an internal auditor or accountant to see if the net total amount of cash available as per the book matches the actual amount of cash on hand in the petty cash fund. If not, the petty cash clerk may require additional training.

Forms: Petty Cash Reconciliation

When a person conducts a petty cash reconciliation, it can be a relatively informal compilation of the cash and vouchers in a petty cash fund. Alternatively, it can be documented more formally on a petty cash reconciliation form, of which a sample follows. The reconciliation form contains space for a summarization of the cash on hand, the total dollar amount issued based on vouchers, and an explanation of any overage or underage in the cash balance.

Sample Petty Cash Reconciliation

Petty Cash Reconciliation

Department		Date

Cash on Hand

Bills on hand	$ _____
Coins on hand	$ _____
Subtotal – bills and coins on hand	$ _____

Vouchers

Account Number	Description	Amount
_____	_____	$ _____
_____	_____	$ _____
_____	_____	$ _____
_____	_____	$ _____
_____	_____	$ _____
Subtotal – vouchers		$ _____

Overage / Shortage

Account Number	Explanation	Amount
_____	_____	$ _____
_____	_____	$ _____
Subtotal – overage / shortage		$ _____

Total

Cash on hand	–	Vouchers	+/-	Overage/Shortage	=	Total Fund
$ _____	-	$ _____	+/-	$ _____	=	$ _____

Petty cash custodian: [signature]	Date

Verified by: [signature]	Date

The petty cash reconciliation form can take the place of the petty cash book, since the form itemizes all vouchers issued. However, the form does not provide a running ending cash balance, as a petty cash book does, and so is an inferior form of documentation.

The Petty Cash Funding Procedure

When cash is added to a petty cash fund, the basic concept is to replace the amount of any cash that had previously been disbursed from the fund. This involves summarizing all disbursements made and issuing cash back to the fund for that amount. The procedure for petty cash funding is outlined below:

1. **Complete reconciliation form.** Complete a petty cash reconciliation form, in which the petty cash custodian lists the remaining cash on hand, vouchers issued, and any overage or underage. The voucher information may come from the petty cash book. An accounting staff person reviews and approves the form and sends a copy to the accounts payable staff, along with all vouchers referenced on the form. The petty cash custodian retains a copy. A sample reconciliation form was shown earlier in the Forms: Petty Cash Reconciliation section.
   Responsible party: Petty cash custodian and accounting staff
   Control issues: There should be a policy that the petty cash fund be replenished at least quarterly, since this triggers the recordation of all vouchers stored in the fund. Otherwise, the related expenses may not be recognized for a long time.

2. **Obtain cash.** The accounts payable staff creates a check made out to the cashier in the amount needed to fund petty cash to its stated limit. The cashier deposits the check and converts the funds into cash. The accounts payable staff forwards the petty cash reconciliation form to the general ledger accountant.
   Responsible party: Accounts payable staff and cashier
   Control issues: There is some risk that the cashier could abscond with the funds, but the amount represents a negligible potential loss.

> **Tip:** If it appears that the petty cash fund is being replenished too frequently, have the controller or treasurer decide if it is worthwhile to mandate a larger petty cash fund. Doing so presents a greater risk of theft, but also reduces the amount of replenishment work.

3. **Add cash to petty cash fund.** The cashier gives the cash to the petty cash custodian, who includes it in the petty cash fund. If there is a petty cash book, the custodian enters the amount of the cash received in the book, and updates the running total of cash on hand.
   Responsible party: Cashier and petty cash custodian
   Control issues: A petty cash book is useful for tracking the exact date and amount of cash added to the fund. The cashier might also use a petty cash

transfer form, as evidence that the petty cash custodian has accepted the cash. A sample form was shown earlier in the Forms: Petty Cash Transfer Form section.

4. **Record vouchers in general ledger.** The general ledger accountant records the voucher amounts listed in the petty cash reconciliation form as expense in the general ledger, and then files the form and attached vouchers.
   Responsible party: General ledger accountant
   Control issues: Since the reconciliation form passes through several people before reaching the general ledger accountant, there is a risk that it may be lost or delayed in transit. This issue can be mitigated by initially preparing the form in triplicate and sending a copy straight from the petty cash custodian to the general ledger accountant.

> **Tip:** Consider setting up a standard petty cash journal entry template in the accounting software, since the accounts charged are likely to be the same from month to month.

The following exhibit shows a streamlined view of the petty cash funding procedure.

The Petty Cash Disbursement Procedure

The disbursement procedure for petty cash is designed to provide sufficient documentation of each expenditure, as well as proof that funds were actually disbursed. The petty cash disbursement procedure is outlined below:

1. **Screen disbursement requests.** Disburse funds only for minor business expenses. The following reimbursements are specifically prohibited (the list may vary by business):
   - Compensation
   - Dues and subscriptions
   - Employee advances
   - Fixed assets
   - Personal expenses
   - Traffic citations

   Responsible party: Petty cash custodian
   Control issues: When auditing the petty cash fund, review the items reimbursed to see if they are on the prohibited list of reimbursements.

Petty Cash Funding Process Flow

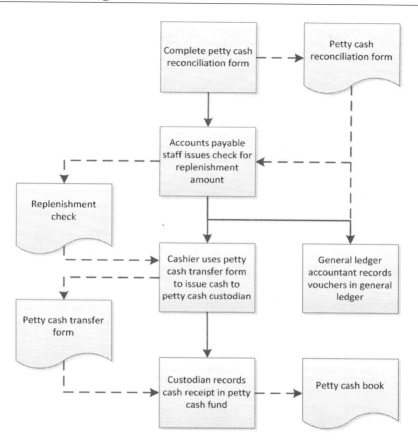

2. **Unlock petty cash.** If a disbursement request falls within the petty cash disbursement guidelines, unlock the container in which petty cash is stored. For security reasons, the petty cash fund should be locked at all times when it is not in use.
   Responsible party: Petty cash custodian
   Control issues: If petty cash is stored in a petty cash box, there is a risk that the entire box will be stolen. Accordingly, either bolt it into a drawer or simply use a locked desk drawer.

3. **Complete voucher.** The person being reimbursed completes a reimbursement voucher. This voucher states the amount disbursed, the type of expense, the date, and the person to whom the petty cash was paid. If there is a receipt for which the person is being reimbursed, staple it to the voucher. This step is needed to track the types of expenditures being made, which can then be charged to various expense accounts.
   Responsible party: Petty cash custodian

Control issues: Some petty cash custodians routinely forget to fill out vouchers for disbursements. If they continue to do so after repeated reminders, this is cause for shifting responsibility for petty cash to another person.

4. **Disburse cash.** Count the cash being disbursed, and have the recipient count it as well, to verify the amount being paid. The recipient of cash should then sign the voucher; this provides proof that the custodian did not fill out the voucher and simply pocket the corresponding amount of cash. Store all completed vouchers in the petty cash box.
Responsible party: Petty cash custodian
Control issues: Have all parties fill out and sign vouchers in ink, which makes them more difficult to fraudulently modify.

5. **Update petty cash book** (optional). Whenever a voucher is completed, the custodian should immediately update the petty cash book by adding the amount, type, and date of the expenditure and updating the running cash balance. This information can also be maintained on an electronic spreadsheet.
Responsible party: Petty cash custodian
Control issues: As was the case with filling out vouchers, some custodians do not remember to update the petty cash book. If so, consider shifting responsibility for petty cash to another person.

> **Tip:** If the petty cash fund is a small one with few monthly transactions, it may not be necessary to maintain a petty cash book at all.

> **Tip:** It may be useful for an accounting person to periodically match the petty cash book to the petty cash vouchers and initial the entries to validate that they are correct. Though this will result in an accurate petty cash book, it may also be too time-consuming.

The following exhibit shows a streamlined view of the petty cash disbursement procedure, including the optional step of updating the petty cash book.

Petty Cash Disbursement Process Flow

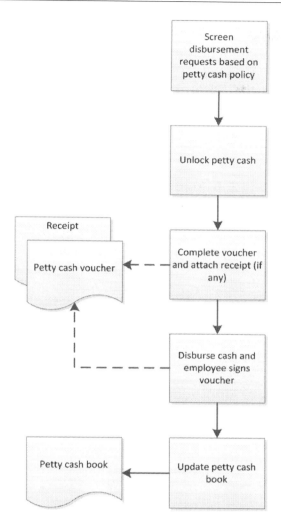

The Petty Cash Review Procedure

There tend to be a large number of problems with undocumented disbursements from petty cash funds – some due to fraud and others from improper documentation of expenditures. The petty cash review procedure is designed to look for and document these issues. The review can be treated as an audit, which means not warning the petty cash custodian of your arrival. This lack of warning is useful for detecting any personal withdrawals from the petty cash fund by the custodian. The petty cash review procedure follows:

1. **Ascertain stated balance.** Review the company's petty cash policy and determine the stated petty cash balance for the fund to be reviewed. Petty cash

funds can have different stated balances, since some experience higher transaction volumes than others.
Responsible party: Accounting or internal audit staff

2. **Calculate withdrawn cash.** Count the cash remaining in the petty cash fund and subtract it from the stated balance for the fund. The result is the amount of cash withdrawn from the fund.
Responsible party: Accounting or internal audit staff

3. **Summarize vouchers.** Add up the total expenditure listed on each petty cash voucher in the petty cash fund (the information can also come from the petty cash book). Subtract this amount from the calculated amount of cash withdrawn. The result should be zero. If there is a residual balance, there is a cash overage in the fund. If there is a negative balance, there is a cash shortage in the fund.
Responsible party: Accounting or internal audit staff

4. **Investigate variances.** Investigate any differences between the stated amount of the petty cash fund and the actual total of cash and vouchers. If the difference is unexplained, complete a voucher stating the unexplained amount, and charging it to a predetermined departmental account in the general ledger.
Responsible party: Petty cash custodian and accounting or internal audit staff
Control issues: It is useful to charge unexplained differences to an expense account set aside for that purpose. By doing so, it is much easier to track the cumulative amount of undocumented losses over time. Also, consider having a policy that requires the internal audit staff to be notified if the amount of an unexplained shortage in a petty cash fund exceeds a certain amount.

The following exhibit shows a streamlined view of the petty cash review procedure.

Summary

There are quite a few procedural steps and integrated controls for petty cash. Given the small amounts of cash involved, this means that a business is devoting an inordinate amount of its resources to guarding an exceedingly small asset, which is not cost-effective. A better approach than maintaining several petty cash funds is to have no petty cash at all. Instead, use procurement cards for most purchases, or encourage employees to pay for incidental items themselves and be reimbursed by the company. These two replacement approaches are addressed in the Procurement Card Procedures chapter and Expense Report Procedures chapter, respectively.

Petty Cash Review Process Flow

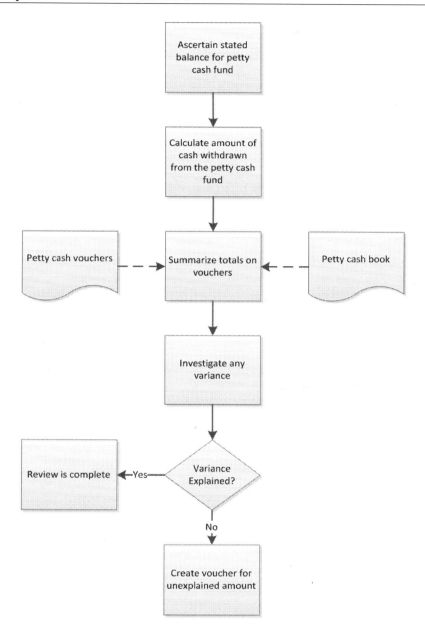

Chapter 12
Receiving Procedures

Introduction

The receiving department is typically on the receiving end of a large quantity of relatively unorganized deliveries from suppliers, which it must sort through, classify, and record in a company's information systems. The receiving staff needs a small number of carefully organized procedures to ensure that it completes these tasks accurately.

In this chapter, we provide examples of the forms used in the receiving process, and then move on to the various receiving procedures. We provide separate procedures for:

- Receiving (manual system)
- Receiving (computerized system)
- Receiving returned goods

As usual, procedural improvement tips are provided throughout the text, as well as flowcharts showing a streamlined view of each procedure.

Forms: Receiving Report

The receiving report is used by the receiving staff to specify the amount and condition of goods contained within each supplier delivery. The format shown in the following example uses standard exception codes to state the condition of goods received. An alternative format is to provide space for free-form commentary about the condition of goods received. It may also be necessary to provide space in the form for the approval of a quality assurance person, if the goods being received require examination by a specially-trained person.

Sample Receiving Report

Receiving Report

Receiving Report Number		Purchase Order Number

Supplier Name		Receiving Date

Item #	Item Description	Quantity Received	Exception Code

Receiving Report Detail Block

Attach bill of lading

Received By: [signature]	Date	Exception Codes

Forms: Return Merchandise Authorization

The return merchandise authorization (RMA) form is the authorization document needed by the receiving department to accept back goods originally shipped to a customer. It should state the RMA date, as well as a notice that the RMA is only valid for a certain number of days from that date. Setting a date limitation curtails the liability of the company. There is no need to include the price of the goods being returned, since that information will be compiled later by the billing clerk who creates a credit memo for the customer. A sample RMA follows.

Sample Return Merchandise Authorization

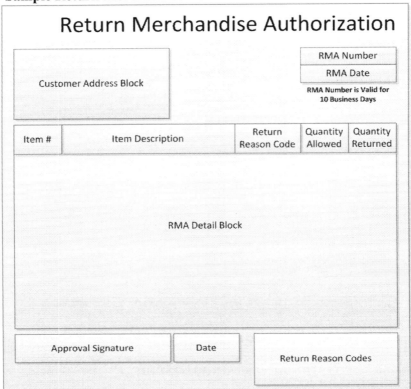

Forms: RMA Receipt Notification

It can be laborious for the receiving staff to copy RMA information onto a separate RMA receipt notification form, so an easier approach is to make a copy of the RMA, stamp it with the stamp shown in the following example, complete the information within the stamp, and enter the actual quantity returned in the "Quantity Returned" field (as noted by the arrow in the example).

Sample RMA Receipt Notification

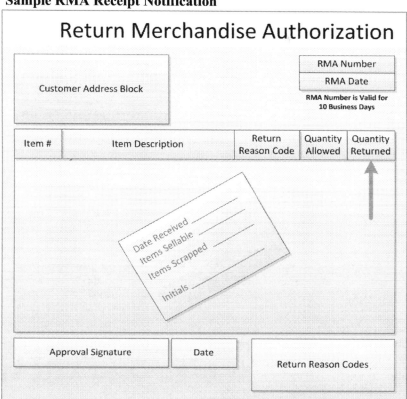

The Receiving Procedure (Manual System)

The receiving department is the gateway for the inflow of goods into a business, and so must be careful to only accept approved items, as well as to properly classify and record them. The procedure for receiving goods in an environment where there are no computer linkages between the receiving and other departments is outlined below:

1. **Match to purchase order.** When goods arrive at the receiving dock, the receiving staff compares them to its file of outstanding purchase orders to see if the receipt has been authorized. If so, the delivery is accepted, subject to inspection. If not, the receiving manager contacts the purchasing manager for authorization to reject the order.
   Responsible party: Receiving staff
   Control issues: Rejecting deliveries is a difficult control, since a critical item may be inadvertently sent back to a supplier. A less unpalatable option is to segregate items that do not have an authorizing purchase order, and allow a day to investigate them before shipping them back.

2. **Inspect goods.** Using an inspection checklist, review the delivered goods for such issues as quantity, quality, damage, and time of delivery in comparison to the requested delivery time. If there appears to be a problem, the receiving manager calls in the person most knowledgeable to examine the delivered goods. This leads to a joint decision to accept or reject some or all of the delivered goods.
    Responsible party: Receiving staff
    Control issues: In practice, the receiving department rarely rejects goods under its own authority, since the receiving staff usually does not have the knowledge required to determine if a delivery is unacceptable.

3. **Test count received items** (optional). On a random basis, open all packaging and conduct a complete count of a delivery. This step is time-consuming, but may occasionally find quantity or quality problems for which the purchasing department should be notified for further action.
    Responsible party: Receiving staff
    Control issues: This step should not be confined to high-value deliveries. A delivery of low-cost items might have a considerable impact on the production of goods if it is a key component, and has been short-shipped.

4. **Reject excess material** (optional). If the amount delivered exceeds the authorized quantity, reject the difference. It is particularly important to do so when the company has short production runs, and so is unlikely to need the additional units.
    Responsible party: Receiving staff
    Control issues: It is customary to allow a small excess amount in a delivery, since it is difficult for a supplier to obtain an exact count for some smaller items that are shipped in bulk.

5. **Pay for cash on delivery items** (optional). If a delivery requires an immediate cash payment, notify the accounting department, which handles the payment. If the supplier will not accept a check, this may take additional time for a certified check or cash payment to be prepared.
    Responsible party: Receiving staff and accounts payable staff

6. **Accept bill of lading.** If the carrier requires that the company sign for the delivery, the receiving manager signs the bill of lading, and accepts a copy of the document from the carrier. Even if no signature is required, the receiving staff should always receive a copy of the bill of lading. The original of this document is retained on file within the department. The accounts payable staff may request a copy along with the receiving report, which is used as further evidence of receipt.
    Responsible party: Receiving staff

7. **Flag customer-owned goods** (optional). If a customer delivers goods that it owns, and which the company is to modify, the receiving staff flags these items as being customer-owned. Otherwise, they will be recorded in the company's inventory records and assigned a cost, which will overstate its ending inventory valuation.
Responsible party: Receiving staff
Control issues: It is useful to physically segregate these items, as well as flagging them as being customer-owned.

8. **Tag received items.** Mark on an identification tag the part number, description, unit of measure, and quantity for each received item. This step is needed to standardize the tracking information used by the warehouse staff to store and monitor inventory.
Responsible party: Receiving staff
Control issues: Initial tagging is usually applied at the pallet level, which is sufficient to shift a coherent group of inventory items to a bin location. The warehouse staff may want to tag goods at the individual unit level once they have been stored in a bin.

Tip: It is more efficient to require suppliers to add inventory tags prior to shipping them to the company, though suppliers will rarely agree to this unless the company buys from them in considerable volume.

---

9. **Complete receiving report and log.** The receiving staff completes a receiving report for the delivery. It sends a copy to the accounts payable staff, which uses it as proof of delivery when deciding whether to pay a supplier invoice. Another copy goes to the purchasing department, which pairs it with the authorizing purchase order. The department retains a copy for its own files. The receiving manager also maintains a receiving log, which summarizes each delivery received by the department.
Responsible party: Receiving staff
Control issues: These documents are needed not only to verify receipt as part of the accounts payable process, but are also examined by the outside auditors at year-end as part of their audit testing, to see if received items have been recorded within the correct accounting period. Also, it may be useful to prenumber receiving reports, which can be tracked by the accounting or receiving staffs to spot missing documents.

10. **Forward goods.** The receiving staff shifts the goods to the warehouse entrance, where the warehouse staff takes responsibility for them and logs them into the inventory database. In many organizations, the receiving department is integrated into the warehouse, so the receiving staff logs deliveries directly into the inventory records, with the inventory location designated as the receiving area. Once the warehouse staff moves items to specific storage bins, they replace the receiving location with the bin location in the inventory record.

Responsible party: Receiving staff

The following exhibit shows a streamlined view of the manual receiving procedure, excluding the optional items.

Manual Receiving Process Flow

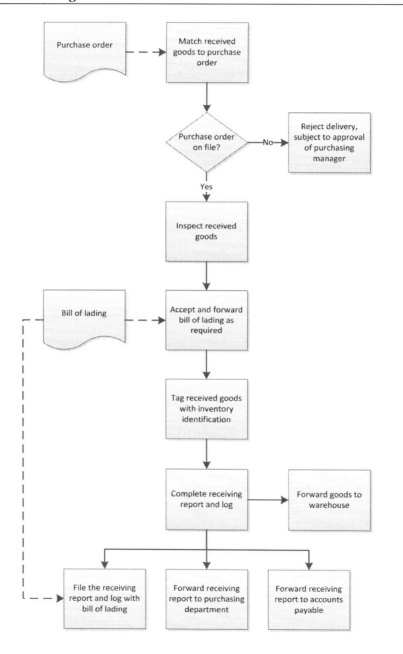

The Receiving Procedure (Computerized System)

The receiving process is greatly accelerated when the receiving staff can enter receiving information into a company-wide computer system. The following procedure shows that there is no longer a need to maintain a manual receiving report, nor is it necessary to issue reports to the accounts payable staff. The procedure steps are:

1. **Enter purchase order number.** When goods arrive at the receiving dock, the receiving staff locates the authorizing purchase order number that should be stamped on the delivery, and enters it into the on-line receiving system. The system locates the purchase order record, and (as part of the next step) the receiving staff enters the quantity received.
   Responsible party: Receiving staff
   Control issues: This system works best when all deliveries are authorized with purchase orders. When there is no authorization in the system, the manual receiving procedure must be used instead.

2. **Inspect goods.** An automated receiving system may have an on-line receiving checklist. If so, enter all issues found into the on-line form, which is then routed to the purchasing and materials management departments for additional action. If there appears to be a problem that requires immediate resolution, the receiving manager calls in the person most knowledgeable to examine the delivered goods. This leads to a joint decision to accept or reject some or all of the delivered goods. Once quantities have been confirmed, enter them in the computer system. Doing so automatically subtracts the received amount from the authorized amount in the purchase order, notifies the accounts payable staff of the receipt, and logs the goods into the inventory database.
   Responsible party: Receiving staff

3. **Test count received items** (optional). This step is identical to the step described for the manual receiving process.

4. **Reject excess material** (optional). This step is identical to the step described for the manual receiving process.

5. **Pay for cash on delivery items** (optional). This step is identical to the step described for the manual receiving process.

6. **Accept bill of lading**. This step is similar to the step described for the manual receiving process, but the receiving staff may scan the bill of lading into the system and make the image available to the accounts payable staff for supplier payment purposes.

7. **Flag customer-owned goods** (optional). This step is similar to the step described for the manual receiving process, but may also involve flagging the goods in the computer system as being customer-owned.

8. **Tag received items.** Once the receiving staff locates the purchase order in the computer system that relates to a delivery and updates quantities based on its inspection, the system should provide a bar coded label to attach to the pallet or box.
   Responsible party: Receiving staff
   Control issues: Initial tagging is usually applied at the pallet level, which is sufficient to shift a coherent group of inventory items to a bin location. The warehouse staff may want to tag at the individual unit level once goods have been stored in a bin.

Tip: It is less important to require suppliers to pre-tag inventory items (as suggested in the last procedure) when a company can automatically generate its own inventory tags.

---

9. **Forward receiving report.** Once the inspection and tagging of a delivery has been completed, flag the delivery as completed in the computer system. This generates a receiving report that is made available to the accounts payable staff for payment processing purposes. The system also automatically generates a receiving log.
   Responsible party: Receiving staff
   Control issues: As long as there is a good backup system in place, there is no need to print and store receiving reports or the receiving log, since they can be printed on demand as needed.

10. **Forward goods.** The receiving staff shifts the goods to the warehouse entrance, where the warehouse staff takes responsibility for them. The goods should already be logged into the computer system as being in the receiving location, so the warehouse staff moves items to specific storage bins and then replaces the receiving location with the bin location in the inventory record.
    Responsible party: Receiving staff

The following exhibit shows a streamlined view of the computerized receiving procedure, excluding the optional items.

Computerized Receiving Process Flow

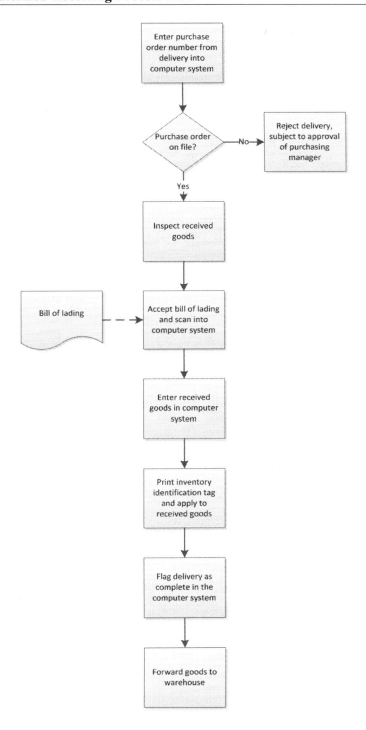

The Receiving Returned Goods Procedure

When a customer wants to return goods, the order entry staff reviews its request and grants a return merchandise authorization (RMA) if the request is valid. The RMA number associated with the authorization is required by the receiving staff to accept the return of goods. The procedure for returning goods is outlined below:

1. **Issue RMA number.** When a customer wants to return goods that it purchased from the company, it contacts the company's order entry staff. The order entry staff determines the reason for the return; if valid, it issues a return merchandise authorization number to the customer. The customer is instructed to write the RMA number on the outside of the package to be returned. The use of RMA numbers is quite important in some industries, where retailers and wholesalers would otherwise return all unsold goods to a company.
   Responsible party: Order entry staff
   Control issues: Any RMA number should be valid only for a certain period of time. Otherwise, the company may be forced to accrue an expense for goods that may never be returned.

2. **Forward copy to receiving.** The order entry staff maintains a master log of all RMA numbers issued, and also sends a notification to the receiving department for each new issuance, detailing exactly which items are allowed in each return shipment.
   Responsible party: Order entry staff and receiving staff

3. **Match against RMA.** When a delivery of returned goods arrives at the receiving dock, the receiving staff matches the RMA number posted on the delivery to their file of outstanding return merchandise authorizations. If there is no corresponding RMA number in their file, they reject the delivery.
   Responsible party: Receiving staff
   Control issues: In practice, the receiving staff is unlikely to reject a delivery without first contacting the order entry department to see if there is an RMA on file that never reached the receiving department.

4. **Review received items.** When customers return goods, the merchandise is not necessarily in as organized or pristine a condition as when it left the company. Accordingly, review the state of the packaging and products in a delivery, and note any issues on the RMA receipt notification described in the next step. This review may result in a reduced credit memo, as well as a routing to the repair department to fix damaged goods.
   Responsible party: Receiving staff

5. **Notify of receipt.** The receiving staff creates three copies of an RMA receipt notification. One copy goes to the order entry staff, which uses the notification to flag an RMA number in its master log as having been fulfilled. Another copy

goes to the billing department, which uses it as the basis for generating a credit memo to the customer. The receiving department retains the original and staples it to the RMA (if the RMA is a separate document). If the full amount of the RMA has not yet been received, the documents are returned to the file of open authorizations. If the full amount *has* been received, the documents are stored in a file of completed return merchandise authorizations.

Responsible party: Receiving staff

Control issues: This step has a built-in control, which is that customers will complain to the accounting department if they do not receive a credit memo for returned goods.

Tip: The entire process of notifying various parties of the presence or fulfillment of return merchandise authorizations is much easier if the information is stored in a central database. In such a computerized system, the order entry staff creates the initial RMA record, the receiving staff updates it with the quantity of received goods, and the system notifies the billing department to issue a credit memo.

The following exhibit shows a streamlined view of the procedure for receiving returned goods.

Summary

The receiving department is governed by extremely regimented receiving procedures from which it rarely deviates. Thus, the driving force behind improving the efficiency of this department is to enhance the underlying procedures. It is particularly cost-effective to install a computer linkage between the purchasing, receiving, and accounting departments and to modify the receiving procedures to take advantage of this linkage. By doing so, the receiving staff will find it much easier to log in received items, evaluate them, and forward information to other parts of the company.

Receiving Returned Goods Process Flow

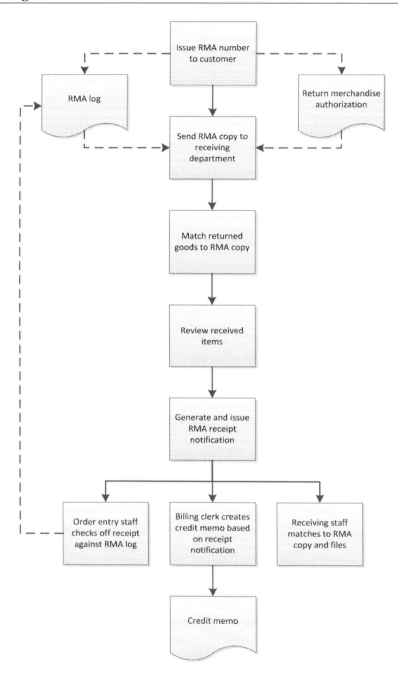

Chapter 13
Accounts Payable Procedures

Introduction

The accounts payable process involves the examination and scheduling of supplier invoices and other payment requests, which can be accomplished through manual, computerized, and evaluated receipts systems. It is also necessary to have procedures in place to issue checks, process supplier credits, and void checks. These are mostly high-volume applications, and therefore require detailed procedures that are rigidly followed to ensure that payments are properly authorized and paid.

In this chapter, we provide examples of the forms resulting from or used in the accounts payable process, and then move on to the various accounts payable procedures. We provide separate procedures for:

- Supplier invoice processing (manual system)
- Supplier invoice processing (integrated system)
- Accounts payable credits processing
- Evaluated receipts processing
- Check payment issuance
- Void checks

As usual, procedural improvement tips are provided throughout the text, as well as flowcharts showing a streamlined view of each procedure.

Forms: Check Request Form

When someone wants to request a payment from within the company, they should complete a check request form. This form states the name and mailing address of the entity to be paid, as well as the vendor identification number under which the entity's information is stored in the accounting system (if any). The form also includes the tax identification number for the entity, since it may be necessary to issue a Form 1099 tax report to them at the end of the calendar year. The account to be charged for the expense can be stated on the form, though many employees may not use it, since their knowledge of account codes may be limited. Finally, there should be a check request approvals block, on which are noted the varying levels of authorization needed, based on the amount requested. A sample form follows.

Sample Check Request Form

Check Request Form

Payee Name		Payee Vendor Number
Payee Mailing Address		Tax ID Number
		Amount to Pay
Check Mailing Instructions		Account to Charge

Reason for Check Request

Check Request Approvals Block

Forms: Adjustment Letter

If the accounts payable staff decides to pay less than the full amount stated on a supplier invoice, it should notify the supplier of the reason for the short payment with an adjustment letter. This letter should state the amount of the short payment and the reason(s) for it. There should also be contact information listed, in case the supplier wants to discuss the issue with the accounts payable staff. A sample adjustment letter format follows.

The Supplier Invoice Processing Procedure (Manual System)

Though most companies operate with a computer-based accounting system, it is considerably less likely that they coordinate the information between the accounting, purchasing, and receiving databases. When there is no inter-linking of this information, use the following procedure to process supplier invoices:

1. **Store purchase order.** When the purchasing department creates a purchase order to authorize the purchase of goods or services, they send a copy of the purchase order to the accounts payable staff. Upon receipt, the accounts payable staff stores the copy in an unmatched purchase orders file, sorted by supplier name.
   Responsible party: Accounts payable staff

Sample Adjustment Letter

Adjustment Notification

Supplier Address Block	Company Logo	Company Address Block

To whom it may concern:

[Company name] has short-paid your invoice number _____ by the amount of $_____, for the following reasons:

☐ Damaged goods

☐ Incorrect items delivered

☐ Incorrect quantity delivered

☐ Items delivered after requested due date

☐ Price on invoice does not match purchase order

☐ Quality test failed

> Additional Comments Block

If you would like to discuss these issues with us, please contact the accounts payable department at [phone number].

2. **Store receiving report.** When a supplier delivers goods to the receiving dock, the receiving staff completes a receiving report that references the supplier name, purchase order number, and number of units received, and sends a copy (sometimes including a copy of the bill of lading) to the accounts payable staff. Upon receipt, the accounts payable staff stores the copy in an unmatched receiving reports file, sorted by supplier name.
   Responsible party: Accounts payable staff

3. **Review supplier invoice.** When a supplier invoice is received, examine it to ensure that it contains the following information:
   - Supplier pay-to address
   - Payment terms
   - Purchase order reference number (optional)
   - List of services provided (for service contracts)
   - List of hours worked (for service contracts)

If the required information is not listed, obtain it from the supplier and add it to the invoice.
Responsible party: Accounts payable staff

> **Tip:** A payment can also be initiated by a check request form, which must be signed by the person whose budget will be impacted by the resulting expense. The form should contain payment information, the reason for the expenditure, and the appropriate approvals for the expenditure level required. A sample form was presented earlier in this chapter.

4. **Conduct three-way match.** Match the invoice with the receiving report issued by the receiving department and the purchase order issued by the purchasing department. If there is no receiving report or purchase order, contact the issuing department to see if there is a missing document. If the price stated on the supplier invoice does not match the price stated on the purchase order, contact the purchasing department for further instructions. If the quantity stated on the supplier invoice does not match the amount stated on the receiving report, contact the receiving department for further instructions.
Responsible party: Accounts payable staff
Control issues: The three-way matching process will probably uncover a number of small variances between the various documents. To keep three-way matching from being an excessively onerous control, consider allowing invoice payment without further review, as long as the variances are within predetermined limits.

> **Tip:** If some suppliers persistently submit incorrect billing information, the accounting staff may need to discuss the issue with them. This takes time, but is more efficient over the long-term if payment problems can be eliminated. Thus, there may need to be an additional step following the matching process, to contact suppliers about problems found.

> **Tip:** Three-way matching can be a very good control, but it is also very inefficient. A more cost-effective alternative is to only require it for supplier invoices that exceed a certain dollar amount. It is also not needed for such ongoing payments as taxes, utilities, insurance, legal and accounting fees, and royalties.

5. **Obtain approval** (optional). If there is no purchase order for a supplier invoice, or if the invoice is an expense report from an employee, or if the invoice is for services (for which there is no receiving report), send the invoice to the person whose budget will be impacted by it and ask for an approval signature. It is customary to first make a copy of the invoice before sending the document to the approver, to ensure that the invoice will not be lost. It may also be useful to maintain a log of all invoices that have been sent out for approval, and cross

them off the list as they are returned. The accounts payable staff can use the log to follow up on any unapproved invoices.

Responsible party: Accounts payable staff

Control issues: This is a difficult control to follow, since many supervisors consider invoice authorizations to be an annoyance, and therefore delay returning approved documents to the payables department. One option is to use *negative approvals*, where supervisors are notified that invoices will be paid unless they say otherwise. This means that the payables staff can immediately enter invoices into the accounting system, rather than waiting for approval.

Tip: Approvers may not know why they were sent an invoice, or may not know where to write their approval on the document. To mitigate these issues, create an approval stamp that contains an approval line, and use this stamp on all invoices before sending them out for approval.

---

6. **Create vendor master file record** (optional). If the company has not done business with a supplier before, create a vendor master file record for it in the accounting system. This record contains such information as the supplier's payment address, tax identification number, contact information, and payment terms.

   Responsible party: Accounts payable staff

7. **Obtain Form W-9** (optional). Check the Form W-9 file to see if there is a completed form for the supplier. Alternatively, check the vendor master file to see if a tax identification number has been listed for the supplier. If not, contact the supplier and request that a form be sent. Upon receipt, file the form in the Form W-9 file.

   Responsible party: Accounts payable staff

Tip: The Form W-9 is the source document for the tax identification number used in the Form 1099 that is sent to qualifying suppliers at year-end. The company is in the best position to obtain this document when it can withhold payments from suppliers, so be sure to tell suppliers that no payment will be forthcoming until a completed form is received.

---

8. **Enter invoice.** Enter the invoice into the accounting system for payment. Set the invoice date in the system at the invoice date noted on the invoice, rather than the current date (otherwise it will be paid late). Also, set the system to take advantage of any early payment discounts allowed by the supplier.

   Responsible party: Accounts payable staff

   Control issues: It may be advisable to enter invoices into the accounting system before any of them are sent out for approvals (see the preceding step concerning invoice approvals). Doing so eliminates the risk that an invoice is not entered into the system in time to be paid by its due date.

> **Tip:** When invoices contain no unique invoice number, there is a significant risk of paying them twice, since the accounting software cannot uniquely identify them. To avoid this issue, enforce a policy for creating invoice numbers. Such a policy typically converts the invoice date into an invoice number.

9. **Issue adjustment letter** (optional). If the amount to be paid differs from the amount stated on the supplier invoice, consider sending an adjustment letter to the supplier, stating the amount of and reason for the difference. This can keep the supplier from charging late payment fees and pestering the accounts payable staff with questions about the unpaid difference.
Responsible party: Accounts payable staff

The following exhibit shows a streamlined view of the supplier invoice processing procedure in a manual environment. It only includes those optional steps most likely to occur on an ongoing basis.

Supplier Invoice Process Flow

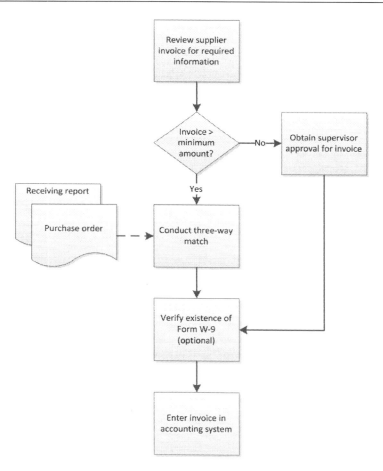

The Supplier Invoice Processing Procedure (Integrated System)

If a company has a computer system that comprehensively integrates the information stored in all of its departments, there is an opportunity to streamline the accounts payable process by shifting a portion of the three-way matching process (described in the last procedure) to the receiving department. The following procedure shows how this more advanced approach to invoice processing can be used.

1. **Conduct match at receiving dock**. When the purchasing staff creates a purchase order to authorize a purchase, they create a purchase order record in the computer system. This record is made available to the receiving department in the computer terminals at the receiving dock. They take the purchase order number from the shipping information provided by the supplier and enter it into the computer, which presents them with the purchase order record. The receiving staff then enters the quantity received into the purchase order record.
   Responsible party: Receiving staff

2. **Review supplier invoice.** This is the same step described earlier in the manual invoice processing procedure.

3. **Conduct two-way match.** Upon receipt of an invoice from the supplier, match the invoice with the purchase order in the computer system, against which receipts have already been logged. If there is a difference between the quantity received and the quantity stated on the invoice, the company should pay the quantity recorded by the receiving staff. If the price stated on the supplier invoice does not match the price stated on the purchase order, contact the purchasing department for further instructions.
   Responsible party: Accounts payable staff
   Control issues: The two-way match is less time-consuming than the three-way match detailed in the last section, but is still inefficient enough to limit its use to larger invoices.

4. **Obtain approval** (optional). This is the same step described earlier in the manual invoice processing procedure.

5. **Obtain Form W-9** (optional). This is the same step described earlier in the manual invoice processing procedure.

6. **Enter invoice.** This is the same step described earlier for the manual invoice processing procedure. A variation is for the accounts payable staff to enter each line item in the invoice into the computer system, which then automatically conducts the three-way match described for the preceding procedure. However, it can be time-consuming to enter longer invoices in this manner.

> **Tip:** It is also possible to scan supplier invoices into the computer system. The scanning software is preconfigured to know where key information is located on each supplier's invoice, which the software then extracts and stores. This method is time-consuming to set up, and is likely to reject the invoices of suppliers whose invoice characteristics have not been entered into the system.

7. **Issue adjustment letter** (optional). This is the same step described earlier in the manual invoice processing procedure.

Note the absence of a step to create a vendor master file record, since the purchasing staff should have already created this record when they issued the initiating purchase order.

The following exhibit shows a streamlined view of the supplier invoice processing procedure in an integrated system.

Accounts Payable Credits Processing Procedure

It will sometimes be necessary to apply to a supplier for a credit against an invoice, and to appropriately record this credit in the accounting system. The procedure for accounts payable credits processing is outlined below:

1. **Notify accounts payable.** When an employee wants to request the reduction of a supplier invoice by obtaining a credit, he or she notifies the accounts payable staff, which records the following information regarding the proposed credit:
   - Supplier contact information
   - Related supplier invoice number
   - Related company purchase order number
   - Reason for the proposed credit
   - Status of any returned goods

   Responsible party: Accounts payable staff

   Control issues: The documentation of a proposed credit can easily be lost, so consider either recording the information on consecutively-numbered documents, recording it in a log, or assigning all credits to a single accounts payable person. Any of these alternatives make it less likely that a proposed credit will *not* be pursued.

Supplier Invoice Process Flow (Integrated System)

```
                    ┌──────────────────┐
                    │  Review supplier │
                    │ invoice for required │
                    │    information   │
                    └──────────────────┘
                             │
                             ▼
                        ◇ Invoice >
                          minimum          ──No──▶  ┌──────────────────┐
                          amount?                   │ Obtain supervisor │
                                                    │ approval for invoice │
                                                    └──────────────────┘
                   ┌──Yes──┐    └──Yes──┐                    │
                   ▼                    ▼                     │
         ┌──────────────┐      ┌──────────────┐              │
         │ Conduct two-way │   │ Conduct purchase │          │
         │  match with    │    │ order match at  │           │
         │ purchase order and │ │ receiving dock │           │
         │    invoice     │    └──────────────┘              │
         └──────────────┘              │                     │
                   └────────┬──────────┘                     │
                            ▼                                 │
                   ┌──────────────┐                          │
                   │ Verify existence of │  ◀──────────────────┘
                   │    Form W-9   │
                   │   (optional)  │
                   └──────────────┘
                            │
                            ▼
                   ┌──────────────┐
                   │ Enter invoice in │
                   │ accounting system │
                   └──────────────┘
```

2. **Issue credit request** (optional). Complete a form letter, requesting a credit and stating the reason for the request. Retain a copy for monitoring purposes, and send the original to the supplier.
   Responsible party: Accounts payable staff
   Control issues: Periodically review the file of credit request copies to see which ones have not received a reply, and follow up with the supplier.

> **Tip:** Wherever possible, have either the purchasing department or the accounts payable staff handle all product returns and credits. If individual employees handle this task, they are likely to not follow through on supplier submission requirements, resulting in no credits being issued.

3. **Obtain return merchandise authorization (RMA) and ship** (optional). Contact the supplier's order entry or customer service staff and request an RMA. If granted, have the shipping department return the relevant goods to the supplier, identified by the RMA number.
    Responsible party: Accounts payable staff
    Control issues: Keep a log of all granted RMA numbers and match them against received credits. Follow up on any RMA numbers for which no credit has yet been received.

4. **Enter supplier credit.** Upon receipt of a credit from a supplier, enter it into the accounts payable system.
    Responsible party: Accounts payable staff
    Control issues: It is also useful to examine vendor statements of account to see if there are any credits listed on the statements that are not listed in the company's accounts payable system. It is quite possible that these credits were lost in transit to the accounts payable department, and were therefore never entered into the accounting system.

> **Tip:** It is possible that there are multiple vendor master file records for a single supplier, so first verify which record is being used to store invoices, and then enter the credit against that same record. Otherwise, the credit may be applied to the wrong record and so will not be applied against a payment.

The following exhibit shows a streamlined view of the accounts payable credits processing procedure.

Accounts Payable Credits Process Flow

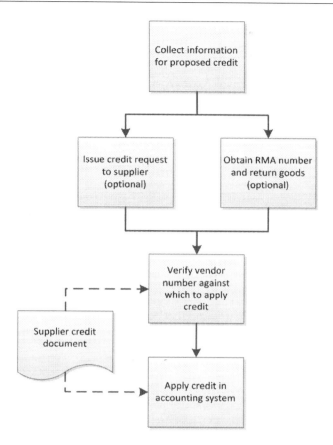

The Evaluated Receipts Processing Procedure

The evaluated receipts system involves sourcing all cost of goods sold items through a small number of suppliers, who are then authorized to deliver their raw materials on a just-in-time basis directly to the company's production lines. Once manufacturing has been completed, the company uses its bills of material to determine what must have been delivered to the company, and pays based on this information and the price listed in its authorizing purchase order. The supplier does not have to send an invoice, and may even be discouraged from doing so. Though this approach is extremely efficient, it also requires a very well-organized manufacturing and purchasing system. The procedure for evaluated receipts processing is outlined below:

1. **Issue master purchase order.** The purchasing department issues a master purchase order to a supplier, authorizing a general quantity of goods to be acquired over the purchasing period, at a specific price.
   Responsible party: Purchasing department

2. **Issue purchase order release.** The purchasing department issues a release against the purchase order, detailing exactly how many units are to be delivered, and the date and time of delivery. This may be an automated release from the materials management system.
Responsible party: Purchasing department
Control issues: Even if the system automatically issues purchase order releases, it may be reasonable to have the purchasing staff manually review the larger releases to ensure that they are accurate.

3. **Calculate production totals.** Once production has been completed, compile the grand total of all units produced. An automated counting system, such as a fixed bar code scanner on a conveyor belt, may be sufficient for conducting this count.
Responsible party: Production department
Control issues: Production totals *must* be accurate, since they are the basis for paying suppliers, as noted in the next step.

> **Tip:** There should also be a system in place for tracking materials that were scrapped during the production process, since the company must add this information to the production totals to arrive at the supplier payment information described in the next step.

4. **Calculate delivered amount.** The accounting system multiplies the number of units produced by the unit quantities stated in the bill of materials for each unit to arrive at the amount of materials delivered by the supplier. The system then multiplies the amount of materials delivered by the unit cost specified in the master purchase order to arrive at the payment due to the supplier, and automatically authorizes payment to the supplier.
Responsible party: Accounts payable staff

> **Tip:** There is no need for a supplier invoice in the evaluated receipts system. In fact, an invoice increases the amount of paperwork that the accounts payable staff must sort through, and so should be discouraged.

The following exhibit shows a streamlined view of the evaluated receipts processing procedure.

Evaluated Receipts Process Flow

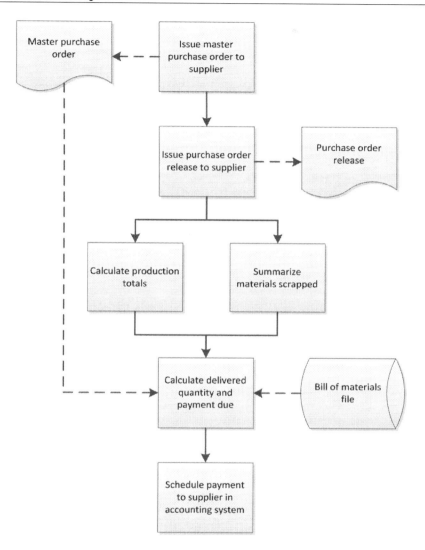

The Check Payment Issuance Procedure

The predominant mode of payment to suppliers is to print a check, though the use of direct deposit and wire transfers is also common. The check payment issuance procedure is outlined below, while the procedural variations for direct deposits and wire transfers are noted in the next section.

1. **Print payment due dates report.** Any accounting software package includes a standard report that itemizes the invoices that are now due for payment. The accounts payable staff should print this report prior to the next scheduled date on

which it makes payments. This report only works if the accounting staff has previously entered the standard payment terms for each supplier in the vendor master file in the accounting software. The system should automatically present invoices that are available for early payment discounts.

Responsible party: Accounts payable staff

Control issues: It is important not to miss due dates, so running the due dates report should be on the daily schedule of activities in the accounting department.

> **Tip:** If you are operating a manual accounts payable system, store supplier invoices in folders that are organized by due date.

2. **Approve payments.** The accounts payable manager or controller review the report to see if any prospective payments should be delayed. If so, they cross out these items.

   Responsible party: Accounts payable manager or controller

   Control issues: To ensure that only the approved items are paid, consider crossing out line items in ink, initialing the crossed-out items, and later matching printed checks to the report.

3. **Select payments.** Access the payments module in the accounting software and select all approved invoices listed on the payment due dates report. Print a preliminary check register and match it against the approved payment due dates report to ensure that only approved invoices are being paid.

   Responsible party: Accounts payable staff

   Control issues: The matching process noted here is quite important; otherwise, the software may automatically pay *all* invoices that are currently due for payment.

4. **Obtain check stock.** Go to the locked cabinet where check stock is stored, and extract a sufficient number of checks for the check run. Re-lock the cabinet.

   Responsible party: Accounts payable staff

   Control issues: It is critical to keep unused check stock locked up at all times. We will return to this issue later, when we log out the range of check numbers used. Also, if there is a check stamp or plate, store it in a different locked location, which makes it more difficult for someone to fraudulently create a check payment.

5. **Print checks.** Enter the beginning check number for the unused checks into the accounting software. Print the checks. Verify that the checks were properly aligned and that all checks were printed. If not, re-print the batch of checks. Otherwise, accept the check run in the software and print a final check register.

   Responsible party: Accounts payable staff

   Control issues: It is useful to match the final check register to the approved payment due dates report, to ensure that the accounts payable staff has only paid authorized invoices.

> **Tip:** It is customary to retain a copy of the final check register, but there is no particular reason to do so, since the accounting system stores this information and can usually print a replacement report on demand.

6. **Return unused checks.** Return all unused checks to the locked cabinet. Note in a check usage log the check number range that was used. This step is needed to uncover cases where checks may have been fraudulently removed from the stock of unused checks.
   Responsible party: Accounts payable staff
   Control issues: The check usage log should be stored in a locked location, so that no one can steal unused checks and modify the log to hide the theft.

7. **Sign checks.** Attach all supporting documentation to each check. Then schedule a check signing meeting with an authorized check signer. Be available during the meeting to answer any questions posed by the check signer. The check signer examines the supporting materials for any check where there is a concern about the payment. If a check is for an unusually large amount, consider requiring an additional signature on the check, thereby providing another level of authorization.
   Responsible party: Accounts payable staff and authorized check signer
   Control issues: Check signing is a control, but may not be necessary in cases where the purchasing department has authorized a payment in advance with a signed purchase order. If so, a signature stamp or plate can be used instead of a check signer.

8. **Issue checks.** Attach any required remittance advices to checks, and mail them to recipients. Then attach the company's copy of remittance advices to supporting documents, and file them by supplier name.
   Responsible party: Accounts payable staff
   Control issues: In a purely manual payables environment, there is a risk of paying an invoice more than once, so a reasonable control is to stamp each paid invoice, or even perforate it, with a "paid" stamp. This control is not needed in a computerized environment, where the accounting system tracks the payment status of all invoices.

9. **Issue positive pay file** (optional). If the company uses a positive pay system, compile information about the newly-printed checks into a file and send it to the bank. The bank then matches submitted checks against this file and rejects those not listed in the file.
   Responsible party: Accounts payable staff
   Control issues: The positive pay notification must encompass manual checks. Otherwise, a special check may be written outside of the normal check printing process, and then be rejected by the bank because no positive pay file was submitted for it.

The following exhibit shows a streamlined view of the check payment issuance procedure, not including the optional use of positive pay.

Check Payment Issuance Process Flow

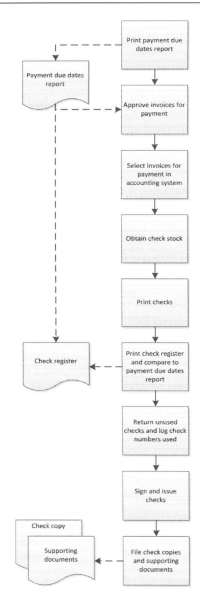

Payment Alternatives

The preceding procedure was designed for the issuance of payments by check. However, payments can also be made by direct deposit or wire transfer. These two alternatives are:

- *Direct deposit.* This involves payments using the Automated Clearing House (ACH) system, which is a digital payment that is usually completed in one or two business days. The direct deposit procedure is the same as the one used for check payments, through the point where payments are approved. After that point, the accounts payable staff either prepares a direct deposit file for transmission to the company's bank, or accesses the bank's secure direct deposit site and manually sets up each payment. The bank then sends a confirmation to the company, stating the amounts and payees associated with each direct deposit transaction. The accounts payable staff notes in the accounting system that the related invoices were paid by direct deposit.
  Responsible party: Treasury and accounts payable staff
  Control issues: There is no check signer involved in direct deposit, so consider requiring a second person to review and approve direct deposit transactions prior to their issuance.

- *Wire transfer.* This involves an electronic payment from the company's bank to the supplier's bank. It is typically completed within one day, though some international wire transfers can require a longer clearing period. The procedure is identical to the one used for direct deposit, except that the approval of an authorized person is usually required. Wire transfers are not recommended, since the associated fees are much higher than for other payment methods.
  Responsible party: Treasury and accounts payable staff
  Control issues: There is a significant risk of someone using wire transfers to fraudulently send large amounts of company funds to unauthorized accounts. Consequently, the wiring procedure should be armored with multiple layers of approvals.

> **Tip:** Electronic payments are frequently made outside of the normal flow of accounts payable transactions, which means that someone has to manually record these payments in the accounts payable system. If they forget to do so, there is a risk that duplicate payments will be made. To mitigate this risk, set up a default payment type for each supplier in the vendor master file, and consider any variation from that payment type to be a policy violation that requires extra approvals.

The Void Checks Procedure

There will be times when a check is created but is either replaced internally or lost in transit to the recipient. These checks should be voided in the accounting system in order to avoid having a checks-in-transit figure on the bank reconciliation that is higher than the actual amount in transit. The void checks procedure is outlined below:

1. **Deface check.** If the check is still on-hand internally, deface the check with a "Void" perforation or stamp.
    Responsible party: Accounts payable staff
    Control issues: A check that is not defaced can still be cashed, so this step is of some importance.

    > **Tip:** For informational purposes, it may be useful to write the reason for the void on the back of the check.

2. **Issue a stop payment** (optional). If the check was lost in transit to the recipient, there is still a chance that it may eventually be received and cashed. In these situations, it is best to contact the bank and issue a stop payment flag on the check, which means that the bank will not accept the check if someone ever tries to cash it. The bank will charge a fee for this service.
    Responsible party: Accounts payable staff
    Control issues: This step is only needed if the company does not have control of the check.

    > **Tip:** Depending on the circumstances, it may be possible to charge the check recipient for the bank's stop payment fee.

3. **Designate as void.** Access the accounts payable module in the accounting system and flag the check as being void. This will remove the check from the "checks in transit" portion of the bank reconciliation, as well as re-designate the supplier invoice being paid by the check as unpaid.
    Responsible party: Accounts payable staff
    Control issues: It may be useful to call up the aged accounts payable report to see if the invoice(s) being paid by the check now appear on the report as unpaid. If not, the check was probably not voided correctly.

4. **File voided check.** File the voided check in a separate voided checks folder. It is possible that the voided checks will be reviewed by the auditors as part of their year-end audit, so keep these checks segregated for their use.
    Responsible party: Accounts payable staff

The following exhibit shows a streamlined view of the void checks procedure.

Void Checks Process Flow

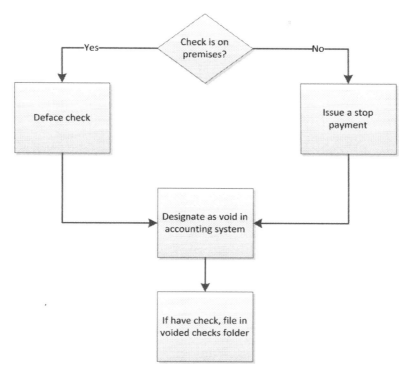

Summary

The typical accounts payable department processes thousands of payments each year. Given the high transaction volume, it is wise to have detailed procedures in place for all possible variations on the processing of invoices and related payments. If procedures are absent, not sufficiently detailed, or weakly enforced, there is a strong likelihood that incorrect payments will be made, which will require a substantial effort to investigate and correct.

It is useful to obtain the services of the internal audit department for periodic testing of the accounts payable system. Doing so may spot potential control weaknesses and lead to the enhancement of some procedures. By engaging in testing on a regular basis, it should be possible to operate an industrial-grade accounts payable function with minimal errors.

Chapter 14
Inventory Procedures

Introduction

The inventory area is a key one for any retail, manufacturing or distribution business, since inventory forms a large part of its asset base and also drives its sales. Of particular concern is the accuracy of the inventory records that a company maintains, since this is crucial for fulfilling customer orders and ensuring that items are manufactured in accordance with the production plan.

In this chapter, we provide examples of the forms used in the handling of inventory, and then move on to the various inventory procedures. We provide separate procedures for:

- Physical inventory count
- Cycle counting
- Obsolete inventory investigation
- Inventory valuation

The inventory picking procedure is described in the Shipping Procedures chapter.

As usual, procedural improvement tips are provided throughout the text, as well as flowcharts showing a streamlined view of each procedure.

Forms: Inventory Count Tag

The inventory count tag is used to document the amount and type of inventory in a storage location. The following sample is for a tag with a punch hole in the top center, which can be used to tie the count tag to an inventory item. A count team fills out the information on the form and signs it at the bottom. There is also space for a reviewer to signify that the count has been verified. This tag is usually printed as a two-part form, so that the second page is given to an inventory clerk for compilation, and the front part is affixed to the inventory item that was counted.

The Physical Inventory Count Procedure

In a business that does not have accurate inventory records, it is necessary to periodically conduct a complete count of the inventory. This is usually done at the end of a month, quarter, or year, to coincide with the end of a reporting period. As the following procedure will show, it takes a great deal of effort to complete an accurate physical inventory count, so companies tend to limit the number of counts completed per year.

Sample Inventory Count Tag

1. **Order count tags.** Order a sufficient number of two-part count tags for the amount of inventory expected to be counted. These tags should be sequentially numbered, so that they can be individually tracked as part of the counting process. A sample form was shown earlier in this chapter.
   Responsible party: Warehouse manager

2. **Preview inventory.** Review the inventory several days in advance of the scheduled inventory count. If there are missing part numbers, or if items appear to be in a condition that would be difficult to count (such as not being bagged or boxed), notify the warehouse staff to make the necessary corrections.
   Responsible party: Warehouse manager
   Control issues: It is useful to mark each designated item with brightly-colored tape or tags, to make them easier to identify for remediation purposes.

3. **Pre-count inventory.** Go through the inventory several days in advance and count any items that can be placed in sealed containers. Seal them in the containers and mark the quantity on the sealing tape. This makes the counting

task much easier during the actual count. If a seal is broken, a counting team will know that they need to re-count the contents of a container.
Responsible party: Warehouse staff

4. **Complete data entry.** If there are any remaining data entry transactions to be completed, do so before the physical inventory count begins. This includes transactions for issuances from the warehouse, returns to the warehouse, and transfers between bin locations within the warehouse.
Responsible party: Warehouse staff

> **Tip:** This issue is much less of a concern when the warehouse staff uses portable data entry terminals to scan inventory transactions, since the transactions are completed at once.

5. **Notify outside storage locations.** If the company has any outside storage facilities or third-party locations that hold company inventory on consignment, notify them that they should count their inventory on hand as of the official count date and forward this information to the warehouse manager.
Responsible party: Warehouse manager
Control issues: This step is frequently forgotten, so maintain a list of all locations where inventory is held, and include this information in the checklist of physical count activities.

6. **Freeze warehouse activities.** Stop all deliveries from the warehouse, and also segregate all newly-received goods where they will not be counted. Otherwise, the inventory records will be in a state of flux during the inventory count, and so will not be entirely reliable.
Responsible party: Warehouse manager

7. **Instruct count teams.** Assemble two-person teams to count the inventory, and instruct them in their counting duties. These duties involve having one person count inventory while the other person marks down the information on a count tag. One copy of the tag is affixed to the inventory, while the team retains the other copy.
Responsible party: Warehouse manager

> **Tip:** Prepare these instructions in advance in a guidebook that the count teams can reference as they complete their counting tasks.

8. **Issue tags.** An inventory clerk issues blocks of count tags to the count teams. Each team is responsible for returning a specific numeric range of count tags, whether or not the tags are used. Maintaining control over all count tags ensures that lost tags will be investigated promptly.
Responsible party: Inventory clerk

Control issues: The inventory clerk stores the delivered count tags in their exact numerical order, or else the numeric ranges of tags issued to count teams will be scrambled.

9. **Assign count areas.** Assign a specific range of bins to each count team. Note these locations with a highlighter on a map of the warehouse. The inventory clerk maintains a master list of which areas of the warehouse have been counted, and which teams have been assigned to each area.
   Responsible party: Warehouse manager

10. **Count inventory.** One person on each team counts a specific item within a bin location, and then the other person marks the bin location, item description, part number, quantity, and unit of measure on a count tag. The team affixes the original copy of the tag to the inventory item, and retains the copy.
    Responsible party: Count teams
    Control issues: The internal or external auditors may accompany the count teams to review their counting methods, as well as to conduct their own test counts of the inventory.

11. **Verify tags.** Upon completion of a count area, each count team returns to the inventory clerk, who verifies that all tags were returned. If there are more warehouse areas to be counted, assign a new area to the count teams and issue them new blocks of count tags as necessary.
    Responsible party: Inventory clerk and warehouse manager

Tip: If a count tag is missing, go to the part of the warehouse where the next closest inventory tag numbers were affixed to inventory items. Both parts of the two-part tag were probably affixed to an inventory item nearby.

---

12. **Enter tag information.** Enter the information on the count tags into an online data entry form. Once data entry is completed, print a report showing all tag numbers entered, sorted by tag number, and look for any gaps in the numbers. Investigate any numbering gaps found. This will ensure that all count tags issued were included in the file.
    Responsible party: Inventory clerk
    Control issues: It may make sense to have a second person re-enter the information on all tags, and have the system note any differences between the two sets of entered information. This is a time-consuming way to spot data entry errors.

13. **Investigate unusual results.** Re-sort the inventory report several ways to look for unusual information, and investigate the tag entry associated with each one. For example:
    - Sort the report by dollar total, and review the highest and lowest extended totals to see if they are reasonable.

- Sort the report by unit of measure to see if any unusual units of measure appear.
- Run a comparison of the report to the most recent inventory report prior to the physical count, to see which unit totals have changed significantly.

Responsible party: Warehouse manager

Control issues: Someone other than the original count team should investigate each variance item, since a third party is more likely to spot an anomaly that was overlooked by the original team.

The following exhibit shows a streamlined view of the physical inventory count procedure. In the flowchart, all activities occurring prior to the counting day can be completed at the same time, and so are listed as a group.

The Cycle Counting Procedure

Cycle counting is used to continually count small portions of an inventory and update the accounting records when any variances are found. Cycle counting works best if the warehouse area is already very well organized and all items are properly boxed and labeled; otherwise, the cycle counters spend too much time on housecleaning and not enough on counting. The procedure for cycle counting is outlined below:

1. **Assign count area.** Assign a section of the warehouse to each cycle counter. This is typically a small area of the warehouse, since the intent of cycle counting is to engage in a small amount of counting every day. The count area may also be scattered throughout the warehouse, in case the focus is less on blocks of bin locations and more on counting higher-value or higher-usage items.
   Responsible party: Warehouse manager
   Control issues: To ensure that cycle counts eventually cover the entire warehouse area, the warehouse manager should keep track of the areas counted over a reasonably long period of time (such as a year).

   > **Tip:** It may be more efficient to assign each cycle counter to a certain part of the warehouse on a long-term basis; doing so allows them to become more familiar with the inventory items in their areas of responsibility, which makes their cycle counts more efficient and accurate.

2. **Print cycle counting report.** Print a separate cycle counting report for each cycle counter for just the designated count area. This report includes the bin location, item number, item description, unit of measure, quantity on hand, and an empty field in which to enter the amount counted.
   Responsible party: Warehouse manager

Physical Inventory Count Process Flow

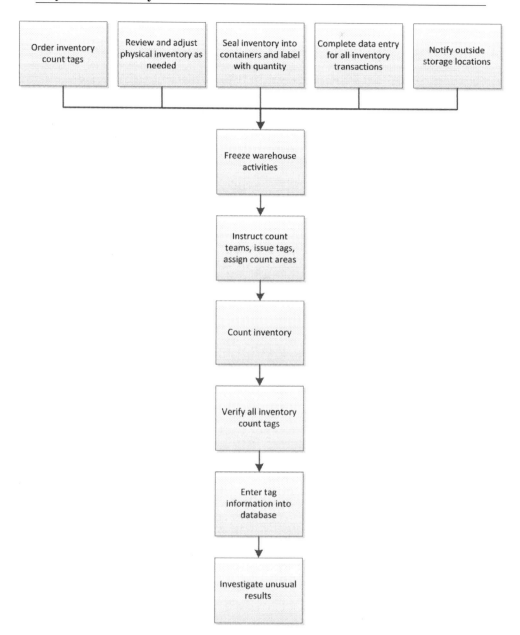

3. **Count inventory.** Each cycle counter traces all items listed on the report to their physical locations, counts the amount on hand, and enters it in the blank space on the report.
   Responsible party: Cycle counters

Control issues: The cycle counters also trace items in the designated bins back to the cycle counting report, to see if any items are in stock that are not recorded in the inventory records.

4. **Investigate variances.** If there is a difference between the amount printed on the cycle counting report and the count total written on it by the cycle counter, investigate the reason for the difference. If warranted, adjust the inventory record to reflect the new count. This is the key step in the cycle counting process, for the investigation and correction of the reasons for inventory errors will gradually improve the accuracy of all inventory items.
   Responsible party: Cycle counters and warehouse manager

> **Tip:** In many cases, the reason for a variance is that the data entry for an inventory transaction has not yet been completed, which causes the inventory record to be incorrect. It may be necessary to wait a day to see if such an entry appears, before making an adjustment to an inventory record.

The following exhibit shows a streamlined view of the cycle counting procedure.

The Obsolete Inventory Investigation Procedure

At the end of their fiscal years, many companies conduct a thorough review of their on-hand inventory and find that a significant proportion of their ending inventory is obsolete, and so must be written off. To avoid being surprised by a large inventory write-off, use the following procedure to periodically examine the inventory for obsolete items and record the expected write-off in a reserve account.

1. **Run "where used" report.** If the company uses a material requirements planning system, run a "where used" report to determine whether any inventory items are not being used in products currently being produced by the company. If such items exist, determine the quantity of each one currently in stock. This is the primary method for locating obsolete inventory, since it focuses on those inventory items for which there is no expectation of usage.
   Responsible party: Cost accountant
   Control issues: This step only works if the company's inventory records and bills of materials are very accurate. If not, the business may find itself disposing of inventory that it will need in the near future.

Cycle Counting Process Flow

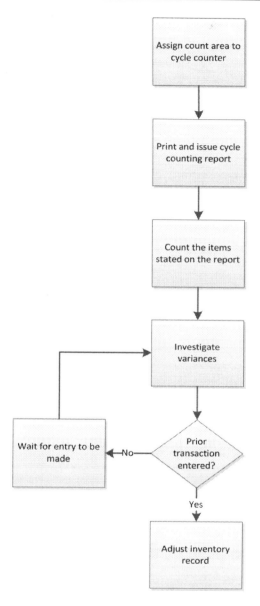

2. **Use ancillary techniques.** There are a number of additional methods available for locating obsolete inventory. For example:
    - *Change orders.* The engineering staff sometimes issues engineering change orders, where they swap out one part for another in the fabrication of a product. Review these change orders to see which items were eliminated and if there are any quantities still remaining in stock.

- *Inventory tags*. After a physical inventory count, leave the count tags on all inventory items. Then wait a few months to see how many inventory tags are still visible. These tags may indicate the presence of unnecessary inventory. This approach works well when a business does not have accurate inventory record keeping systems.
- *Last day used*. The inventory system may track the last date on which an inventory item was used. If so, run a report listing the last day used for all inventory items, and examine those for which a considerable time period has passed since the last usage date.
- *Preceding obsolete report*. Review the last report issued for obsolete inventory items, and see if any of the targeted items are still in stock.
- *Usage volume analysis*. Compare the amount of inventory on hand to the amount of annual usage. This approach may reveal situations where there is too much inventory on hand.

Responsible party: Cost accountant
Control issues: These activities are less effective than the "where used" report, since they ignore the possible usage of inventory items in the future. Consequently, be sure to have someone from the engineering and production departments verify that any items selected are indeed obsolete.

3. **Manually review targeted items** (optional). If inventory record keeping is poor, take the preliminary list of obsolete inventory items into the warehouse and verify that the items exist, and in the quantities indicated on the report.
   Responsible party: Cost accountant

4. **Investigate disposition alternatives.** Work with the purchasing staff to determine the most cost-effective ways to dispose of the items indicated as obsolete. Possible methods are:
   - Return to supplier (possibly net of a restocking fee)
   - Sell to a third party reseller
   - Scrap (which may net a small amount of scrap revenue from a scrap dealer)
   - Donate to a not-for-profit (which may generate a tax credit)
   - Incorporate into the design of a product (which can require a substantial period of time before the parts are used)

Generally, the disposition method selected is the one generating the smallest net loss to the company.
Responsible party: Cost accountant and purchasing staff

5. **Authorize dispositions.** Call a meeting of the warehouse manager, purchasing manager, engineering manager, production manager, and controller, and present to them the proposed list of inventory dispositions, along with the total loss

expected from the disposition. This group should formally vote for the action, which is then documented in formal meeting minutes.

Responsible party: Cost accountant, warehouse manager, purchasing manager, engineering manager, production manager, and controller

Control issues: This is a key step, for it must be clear that inventory items are absolutely not needed before any disposition activities begin. Otherwise, a business may find that items were disposed of that are needed for future production requirements.

6. **Update reserve account.** Summarize the total amount of expected losses for all inventory items that have been tagged as obsolete but not yet disposed of, and forward this information to the general ledger accountant. The expected loss is the recorded cost of an inventory item, minus any expected proceeds from its disposition. The general ledger accountant uses the information to adjust the reserve for obsolete inventory, which is a contra account that offsets the inventory account in the general ledger.

   Responsible party: Cost accountant and general ledger accountant

   Control issues: Put this task on the closing activities checklist, so that the accounting staff will not forget to engage in it as part of each period-end close.

The following exhibit shows a streamlined view of the obsolete inventory investigation procedure.

The Inventory Valuation Procedure

At the end of each reporting period, the cost accountant compiles the value of the ending inventory, which appears in the balance sheet. There are a number of ways to compile this information, depending upon the cost layering assumptions used by a company, such as the weighted-average method or first-in first-out method. In the following procedure, we assume that a company uses the standard costing method, where a predetermined standard cost is assigned to each inventory item. We also assume that actual overhead costs for a period are allocated to the various inventory accounts, rather than using a standard overhead charge per period. You should modify this procedure to match the costing system used by your business.

1. **Review change log.** Review the change log for the bills of material in the computer system to see if there were any unusual changes during the accounting period. Verify unusual items with the engineering manager. If any changes prove to be incorrect, have the engineering staff correct the files.

   Responsible party: Cost accountant

   Control issues: Review the change log after the engineering staff has made its corrections, to ensure that the proper file alterations were made.

Obsolete Inventory Process Flow

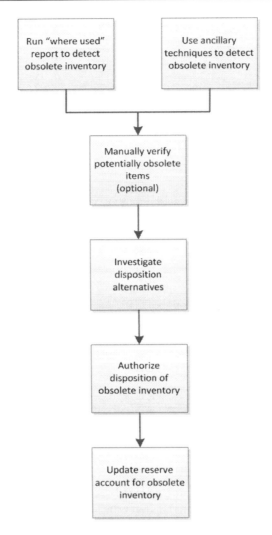

2. **Verify high-valuation items.** Print a report listing the extended inventory valuation for each inventory item, sorted in declining order by dollar amount. Go to the warehouse and verify that the quantities on hand are correct for the top items on the list comprising most of the inventory value. If items are incorrect, bring the matter to the attention of the warehouse manager, who should correct the on-hand balance if there is an error.

    Responsible party: Cost accountant

    Control issues: Verify that there are no inventory transactions in process that have not yet been recorded in the system. Otherwise, the comparison may yield incorrect results.

3. **Verify low-valuation items.** Run the same extended inventory valuation report from the last step, but sorted in increasing order by dollar amount. Review the lowest-valued items for reasonableness. This is an area in which valuation errors are likely to appear, since an expensive item may have originally been entered incorrectly into the inventory database, resulting in a low stated valuation on the report.
   Responsible party: Cost accountant

4. **Charge variance to expense.** Compile the actual cost of direct materials and direct labor for the reporting period and add it to the beginning balances of these cost items (as stated in the general ledger). Compare the result to the extended amount of these standard costs generated by the accounting system. Charge any variance between the two balances to expense, so that the amount of cost recorded on the books matches the actual cost incurred.
   Responsible party: Cost accountant
   Control issues: This is a step frequently skipped during a monthly close. However, waiting until year-end to make the adjustment could generate an unexpectedly large variance. Thus, it is better to include this step (as a reminder) in the standard period-end closing checklist.

5. **Review cost pool contents.** Examine the items in the overhead cost pool that are to be allocated to overhead. Verify that they only include items from expense categories that are allowed in the cost pool. If not, shift them back to their original expense classifications so that they can be charged to expense in the current period.
   Responsible party: Cost accountant
   Control issues: There should be a formal list of expense types that are allowed in a cost pool. Changes to this list should not be made without the approval of the controller. Otherwise, the amount of overhead allocated each month may vary considerably over time.

6. **Review allocation methodology.** Verify that the method used to allocate overhead costs in the cost pool have not varied from the method used in prior periods.
   Responsible party: Cost accountant
   Control issues: Any changes in the overhead allocation methodology should be approved by the controller. Otherwise, random changes may impact how costs are recognized by the company, leading to irregular alterations in the reported level of profitability.

7. **Allocate overhead.** Allocate inventory based on the costs summarized into the cost pool and the allocation methodology. Document the amount of allocation being made to each inventory classification, and forward this information to the general ledger accountant for entry into the general ledger.
   Responsible party: Cost accountant

Control issues: This allocation should be thoroughly documented and attached to the journal entry. It may be reviewed by the company's auditors.

8. **Test inventory totals.** Compare the inventory totals for each inventory classification to those for the past few periods, as well as for the same date in the preceding year. Also compare the inventory level to the amount of revenue generated in the most recent period, and examine this proportion for reasonableness for the past few periods. If any of these relationships appear to have changed to a material extent in the current period, review the detailed inventory records, standard costs, and overhead allocation for errors.
Responsible party: Cost accountant
Control issues: This step matches the reasonableness tests that will be performed by the outside auditors as part of their year-end audit procedures.

Again, this procedure is designed for a business that uses standard costing for its direct materials and direct labor costs, and then allocates actual overhead costs, rather than using standard overhead costs. This approach is not used by all businesses, so you may need to modify this procedure to meet the needs of your company.

The following exhibit shows a streamlined view of the inventory valuation procedure.

Summary

From both a financial and operational perspective, the key goal in inventory management is to ensure that inventory records are *accurate*. This calls for an unending series of cycle counts to locate and correct errors in inventory records, and perhaps an occasional physical inventory count for those inventory systems that have not yet attained a high level of record accuracy. Tracking obsolete inventory is a less necessary clean-up task that may eventually eliminate some items from stock, but which has no particular impact on the underlying accuracy of the inventory records.

Inventory Valuation Process Flow

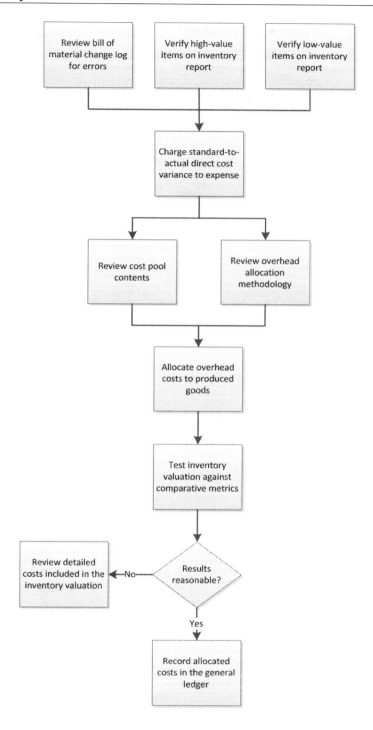

Chapter 15
Payroll Procedures

Introduction

One of the most fundamental and critical accounting areas is payroll. It is one of the more complex areas in which to process transactions, and has a highly critical audience – employees. If the payroll staff makes a mistake, not only does word of the error spread quickly, but it also requires an inordinate amount of time to locate the problem, correct it, and issue a revised payment. For these reasons, payroll procedures are unusually detailed and must be followed rigorously.

In this chapter, we provide examples of the forms resulting from or used in the payroll process, and then move on to the various payroll procedures. There are several types of payroll situations, so we provide separate procedures for:

- Adding an employee
- Timecard data collection
- Commission calculations
- Payroll processing
- Issuing payments to employees

As usual, procedural improvement tips are provided throughout the text, as well as flowcharts showing a streamlined view of each procedure.

Forms: For the New Hire

The Form I-9 is a standard form issued by U.S. Citizen and Immigration Services (uscis.gov). It requires that a prospective employee prove his or her identification and right to work in the United States. This is a two-page form, of which the first page is shown the below. The second page itemizes the types of acceptable evidence.

Sample Form I-9

U.S. Department of Justice		OMB No. 1115-0136
Immigration and Naturalization Service		**Employment Eligibility Verification**

Please read instructions carefully before completing this form. The instructions must be available during completion of this form. ANTI-DISCRIMINATION NOTICE: It is illegal to discriminate against work eligible individuals. Employers CANNOT specify which document(s) they will accept from an employee. The refusal to hire an individual because of a future expiration date may also constitute illegal discrimination.

Section 1. Employee Information and Verification. To be completed and signed by employee at the time employment begins.

Print Name: Last	First	Middle Initial	Maiden Name
Estevez	Jill	M	Smith

Address (Street Name and Number)	Apt. #	Date of Birth (month/day/year)
123 Main Street		10/01/1985

City	State	Zip Code	Social Security #
Anywhere	CO	80111	422-54-6913

I am aware that federal law provides for imprisonment and/or fines for false statements or use of false documents in connection with the completion of this form.

I attest, under penalty of perjury, that I am (check one of the following):
☑ A citizen or national of the United States
☐ A Lawful Permanent Resident (Alien # A_____
☐ An alien authorized to work until ___/___/___
(Alien # or Admission #) _____

Employee's Signature	Date (month/day/year)

Preparer and/or Translator Certification. (To be completed and signed if Section 1 is prepared by a person other than the employee.) I attest, under penalty of perjury, that I have assisted in the completion of this form and that to the best of my knowledge the information is true and correct.

Preparer's/Translator's Signature	Print Name

Address (Street Name and Number, City, State, Zip Code)	Date (month/day/year)

Section 2. Employer Review and Verification. To be completed and signed by employer. Examine one document from List A OR examine one document from List B and one from List C, as listed on the reverse of this form, and record the title, number and expiration date, if any, of the document(s).

	List A	OR	List B	AND	List C
Document title:	Passport				
Issuing authority:	Natl Passport				
Document #:	0123456789				
Expiration Date (if any):	10/1/15		___/___/___		___/___/___
Document #:					
Expiration Date (if any):	___/___/___				

CERTIFICATION - I attest, under penalty of perjury, that I have examined the document(s) presented by the above-named employee, that the above-listed document(s) appear to be genuine and to relate to the employee named, that the employee began employment on (month/day/year) 7/1/11 and that to the best of my knowledge the employee is eligible to work in the United States. (State employment agencies may omit the date the employee began employment.)

Signature of Employer or Authorized Representative	Print Name	Title
	Joe Emilio	HR Director

Business or Organization Name	Address (Street Name and Number, City, State, Zip Code)	Date (month/day/year)
Orion Designs	42 Center, Arvada, CO 80007	07/-1/2011

Section 3. Updating and Reverification. To be completed and signed by employer.

A. New Name (if applicable)	B. Date of rehire (month/day/year) (if applicable)

C. If employee's previous grant of work authorization has expired, provide the information below for the document that establishes current employment eligibility.

Document Title:_____	Document #:_____	Expiration Date (if any): ___/___/___

I attest, under penalty of perjury, that to the best of my knowledge, this employee is eligible to work in the United States, and if the employee presented document(s), the document(s) I have examined appear to be genuine and to relate to the individual.

Signature of Employer or Authorized Representative	Date (month/day/year)

Form I-9 (Rev. 11-21-91)N Page 2

The Form W-4 is a standard form issued by the Internal Revenue Service (irs.gov), in which employees designate the number of withholding allowances that they want to claim. It is the basis for the amount of income taxes withheld from their pay. A sample form follows.

Sample Form W-4

Form **W-4**	**Employee's Withholding Allowance Certificate**	OMB No. 1545-0074
Department of the Treasury Internal Revenue Service	► Whether you are entitled to claim a certain number of allowances or exemption from withholding is subject to review by the IRS. Your employer may be required to send a copy of this form to the IRS.	2013

1 Your first name and middle initial	Last name	2 Your social security number
John D.	Smith	012-34-5678

Home address (number and street or rural route)	3 ☐ Single ☑ Married ☐ Married, but withhold at higher Single rate.
213 Main Street	Note. If married, but legally separated, or spouse is a nonresident alien, check the "Single" box.
City or town, state, and ZIP code	4 If your last name differs from that shown on your social security card, check here. You must call 1-800-772-1213 for a replacement card. ► ☐

5	Total number of allowances you are claiming (from line **H** above **or** from the applicable worksheet on page 2)	5	2
6	Additional amount, if any, you want withheld from each paycheck	6 $	50
7	I claim exemption from withholding for 2013, and I certify that I meet **both** of the following conditions for exemption.		
	• Last year I had a right to a refund of **all** federal income tax withheld because I had **no** tax liability, **and**		
	• This year I expect a refund of **all** federal income tax withheld because I expect to have **no** tax liability.		
	If you meet both conditions, write "Exempt" here . . . . ►	7	

Under penalties of perjury, I declare that I have examined this certificate and, to the best of my knowledge and belief, it is true, correct, and complete.

Employee's signature
(This form is not valid unless you sign it.) ►   **Date** ►

8	Employer's name and address (Employer: Complete lines 8 and 10 only if sending to the IRS.)	9 Office code (optional)	10 Employer identification number (EIN)
Big Widget Company			84-1234567

For Privacy Act and Paperwork Reduction Act Notice, see page 2.	Cat. No. 10220Q	Form **W-4** (2013)

Forms: The Timecard

A timecard is usually printed on heavier-weight paper and is stored in a central timecard rack. Employees can fill it out by hand, or they can insert it into a punch clock, which stamps the time on it. There are separate columns for the beginning and ending times when regular hours and overtime hours are worked. There is also a small block next to each day of regular and overtime hours, in which the payroll staff enters the total time worked for that day. They then accumulate these daily totals into overtime and regular time totals at the bottom of the timecard. Both the employee and his or her supervisor should sign the card. A sample timecard appears in the next exhibit.

Sample Timecard

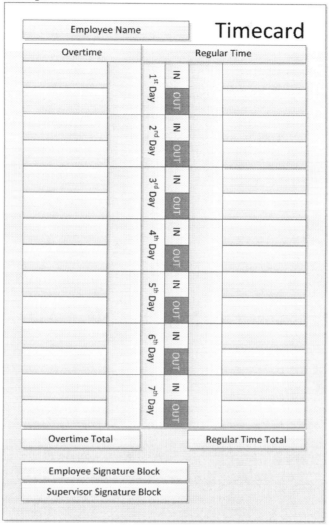

The timesheet differs from the timecard in that there is no provision for a time stamp by a punch clock. Instead, employees are expected to fill out the timesheet by hand. This is a relatively simple document, as illustrated in the following sample. Employees state the time period worked and the number and types of hours worked. There is also space for supervisory approval of the document. The name of the supervisor is stated near the top of the form, in case the payroll staff wants to contact that person with a question about information on the timesheet.

Sample Weekly Timesheet

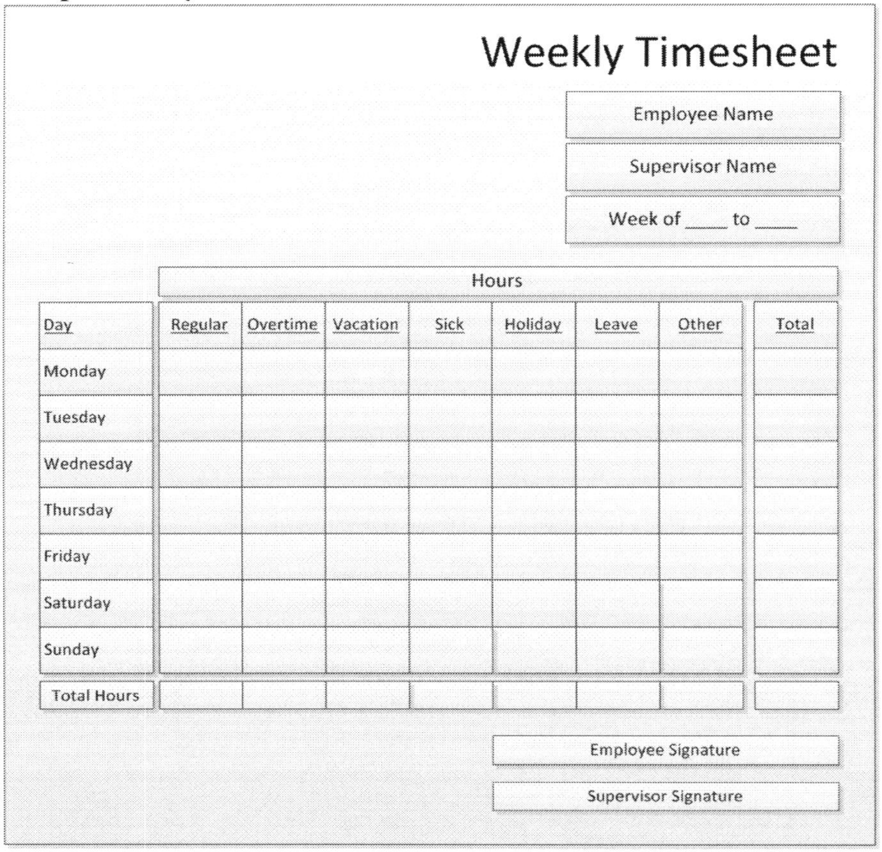

Weekly Timesheet

| Employee Name |
| Supervisor Name |
| Week of _____ to _____ |

Day	Hours							
	Regular	Overtime	Vacation	Sick	Holiday	Leave	Other	Total
Monday								
Tuesday								
Wednesday								
Thursday								
Friday								
Saturday								
Sunday								
Total Hours								

| Employee Signature |
| Supervisor Signature |

In some organizations, time tracking is only intended for hours that can be billed to customers. In this situation, the timesheet is structured so that the employee can enter the name of the client, the project, and the task. This information is not used for paying employees (unless they are only paid for billed hours) but rather for creating customer invoices. A sample billing timesheet is shown below.

Sample Billing Timesheet

Billing Timesheet

| Employee Name |
| Supervisor Name |
| Week of _____ to _____ |

Billing Information			Hours							
Client	Project	Task	Mon	Tue	Wed	Thu	Fri	Sat	Sun	Total
		Total Hours								

| Employee Signature |
| Supervisor Signature |

Forms: The Paycheck and Remittance Advice

If a company pays its employees with checks, it should issue not only the paycheck, but also a remittance advice that details the calculation of the payment. A sample paycheck and remittance advice is shown below. The presented format can be altered to include additional information, such as the remaining amount of earned vacation time.

Sample Paycheck and Remittance Advice

			Check Number
Employer Name Employer Address			Check Date

Pay to the order of: [text of amount paid]	$____.__

Employee Name Employee Address	Signature Block

Employee Number	Employee Name	Pay Period	**Deductions**		
			Deduction Type	Deduction this Period	Deduction YTD
Earnings					
Hours Worked	Pay Rate	Pay this Period	Pay YTD		
				Total Deductions	
	Gross Pay			Net Pay	

The paycheck and remittance advice shown here can also be adapted to direct deposit payments. The paycheck part of the document is stated as being non-negotiable, and that the payment was made by direct deposit. In all other respects, the document is the same.

The Adding an Employee Procedure

The task of adding an employee should fall upon the human resources department, rather than the payroll staff. However, smaller organizations may have no human resources department, so the work is shifted to the payroll staff. The procedure for adding an employee is outlined below, to be used by either department:

1. **Complete Form I-9.** Verify the employee's authorization to work in the United States, and complete the Form I-9, Employment Eligibility Verification. This is a major issue that can prevent someone from working for a business, so be sure to complete the Form I-9 before an employee begins work. Otherwise, the company puts itself at risk of paying someone whom it is not legally allowed to employ.
   Responsible party: Payroll clerk or human resources clerk
   Control issues: Timing is the control point. This form must be completed *at once*. If an employee presents an excuse for not being able to complete the form prior to his or her start date, delay the start date until the form has been completed and verified.

2. **Complete Form W-4.** Have the employee fill out a Form W-4, Employee's Withholding Allowance Certificate. This document does not have to be completed on the first work day of the employee, but must be completed by the time the next payroll processing begins. Otherwise, there will be no way to determine the correct amount of income taxes to deduct from the employee's gross pay.
Responsible party: Payroll clerk or human resources clerk
Control issues: Because there is not an absolute requirement to have the Form W-4 completed at the point of hiring, there is a tendency for it to be ignored until the payroll staff is calculating payroll, at which point it can prolong the completion of payroll. Consequently, the best approach is to require that it be completed at the same time as the Form I-9.

Tip: The human resources or payroll staffs should contact all employees once a year about updating the information on their W-4 forms. See the author's most recent annual edition of *Payroll Management* for more information.

---

3. **Verify approval** (optional). The payroll clerk verifies the authorization signature on the employee offer sheet. This is not entirely necessary, since the person who authorizes the employee hire is probably the same person who forwards the new employee information to the payroll clerk.
Responsible party: Payroll clerk or human resources clerk
Control issues: This step is designed to keep a false (or "ghost" employee) from being created, to which payments can then be directed. An enhanced control is to require a senior manager to approve all employee offer sheets.

4. **Create employee record.** Create a record for the employee in the payroll system and enter the information noted below. The exact types of information required will be mandated by the payroll system. A more comprehensive set of information may be required if the record is kept in a human resources system, from which a subset of information is extracted for processing payroll. The minimum set of information to include is:
   - Employee name
   - Employee address
   - Employee social security number
   - Employee marriage status
   - Number of withholding allowances claimed
   - Start date
   - Department code
   - Base wage or salary
   - Shift worked
   - Shift differential
   - Banking information (for direct deposit)

Responsible party: Payroll clerk or human resources clerk

Control issues: Access to employee records in the system should be severely restricted. Otherwise, it would be quite easy to alter payment information or create ghost employees to which payments can be directed.

5. **Create employee folder.** Create an employee folder, insert all related documents in it, and store it in a locked storage area.
   Responsible party: Payroll clerk or human resources clerk
   Control issues: It is of considerable importance to lock up these files, especially if they contain bank account information or social security numbers that could be fraudulently used.

> **Tip:** Consider buying fastener folders and a two-hole punch, so that you can securely store employee-related documents in chronological order within each folder.

The following exhibit shows a streamlined view of the adding an employee procedure, including the optional step.

Adding an Employee Process Flow

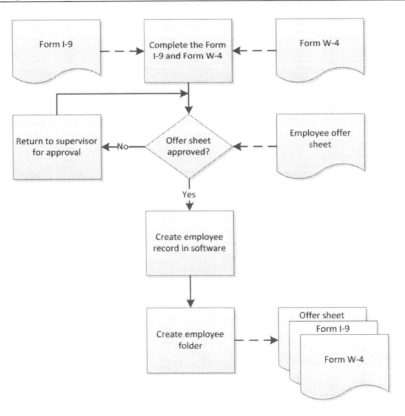

The Timecard Data Collection Procedure

There are quite a few steps involved in the collection of timecard information, for the payroll staff wants to have 100% assurance that it has obtained the correct time information from all employees. Otherwise, it may need to engage in the manual adjustment of pay, which is even more time-consuming than the steps noted here. The detailed procedure, including responsibilities and basic controls, follows:

1. **Issue reminder.** Issue a reminder to employees a few days in advance of the payroll to make sure their timecards are up-to-date. This is especially important for those employees who have a history of being late in making timecard submissions.
   Responsible party: Payroll clerk

   > **Tip:** A useful side effect of issuing reminders in advance is that, if done by e-mail, some employees away from the office will have configured their e-mails to issue out-of-office notices. The payroll staff then knows which employees will not be submitting timecards.

2. **Print employee list.** Print a list of all employees who are supposed to submit timecards. This should be the official list of employees maintained by the human resources department (if there is such a department) as of the payroll date.
   Responsible party: Payroll clerk
   Control issues: Do not use an old copy of the employee list, since it may vary from the actual group of employees as of the payroll date, which may in turn result in some employees not submitting timecards without the payroll staff knowing about it.

   > **Tip:** It may be useful to highlight the names on this list of those employees who are most likely to not submit their timecards in a timely manner, so that the payroll staff can focus on collecting those timecards.

3. **Sort timecards.** Sort all timecards received by employee last name. This makes it easier to match timecards received to the employee list for verification purposes.
   Responsible party: Payroll clerk

4. **Determine missing submissions.** Compare the timecards to the employee list, and note which employees have not yet submitted their timecards.
   Responsible party: Payroll clerk
   Control issues: This step is a very important one from a control perspective, since it is the best way to determine which employees have not submitted timecards.

5. **Determine missing employees.** Compare the employee list to the schedule of employees who are on vacation, and cross off the names of those employees who did not submit timecards and who are on vacation. As noted earlier, sending e-mail reminders makes this task easier, since out-of-office messages may be returned to the payroll clerk.
Responsible party: Payroll clerk

6. **Notify management.** Notify management of the remaining employees who have not submitted timecards. This is needed to obtain timecards from the most recalcitrant employees. Otherwise, the payroll staff is placed in the difficult position of issuing reminders to employees who may be substantially senior to them in the organization.
Responsible party: Payroll clerk

7. **Review for errors.** Review all timecards for errors, such as missing beginning and ending times, and vacation used that has not been earned, and return them to employees for correction. An alternative is to return the timecards to supervisors, on the grounds that they can more efficiently track down employees to correct any timecard problems.
Responsible party: Payroll clerk

> **Tip:** Though employees should usually make all alterations to their own timecards, it may be possible to adopt a set of rules for filling in missing information on a timecard, and having the payroll clerk initial these items to indicate who made them. This approach can improve the speed with which timecard processing is completed.

8. **Approve overtime.** Forward all timecards containing overtime hours to management for approval. It may be necessary to retain copies of these timecards, in case there is a history of timecards being lost by supervisors. Another approach is to walk the timecards through the organization to obtain immediate reviews and approvals; though it uses payroll staff time, it ensures that timecards will be reviewed at once.
Responsible party: Supervisors
Control issues: This step is of considerable concern in those businesses where a large amount of overtime is used, since the overtime premium is so expensive. Alternatively, it may be a minor item that can simply be audited from time to time in an environment where overtime is rarely used.

9. **Verify timecard returns** (optional). Verify that all timecards returned for correction or approval have been returned to the payroll department.
Responsible party: Payroll clerk

> **Tip:** An easy way to verify timecard returns is to make a copy of the employee list, highlight the names of those employees whose timecards are out for correction or approval, and check them off as the timecards are returned.

10. **Summarize hours worked.** Add up the time worked on each timecard and note the total hours worked on the card. If the timecard is designed to include subtotals by day (see the sample timecard in the Forms: The Timecard section), fill in the subtotals and then enter the grand total for the entire timecard.
    Responsible party: Payroll clerk (possibly more than one – see the control issue)
    Control issues: It is very easy to make mistakes in this step, so consider having a second person verify the timecard totals.

11. **Forward for processing.** Forward the approved and summarized timecards to the payroll clerk for entry into the payroll processing system.
    Responsible party: Payroll clerk

The following exhibit shows a streamlined view of the timecard data collection procedure:

The Commission Calculation Procedure

The commission calculation procedure is viewed with trepidation by many payroll departments, especially if the assignment of invoices to salespeople is disorganized or the commission plan is complex. Both issues must be addressed before a functional commission procedure can be implemented. The detailed procedure, including responsibilities and basic controls, follows:

1. **Obtain invoice list.** Obtain a summary of invoices issued during the calculation period, sorted by salesperson. It may be necessary to compile this information from individual invoices, if the company uses a manual billing system or the computer system does not assign each invoice to a salesperson.
   Responsible party: Payroll clerk
   Control issues: There can be arguments over who "earned" an invoice for commission purposes, which can lead to side deals to split commissions, and which generally muddies the calculation of commissions. It is best to keep this issue from arising by enforcing a streamlined commission system that only allows an invoice to be credited to a single salesperson.

2. **Enter information on spreadsheet.** Transfer report totals by salesperson to a spreadsheet.
   Responsible party: Payroll clerk (possibly more than one – see the control issue)
   Control issues: It is possible that the responsible clerk will transfer information into the spreadsheet incorrectly. If there is evidence of this problem, have a second person verify the information.

Timecard Data Collection Process Flow

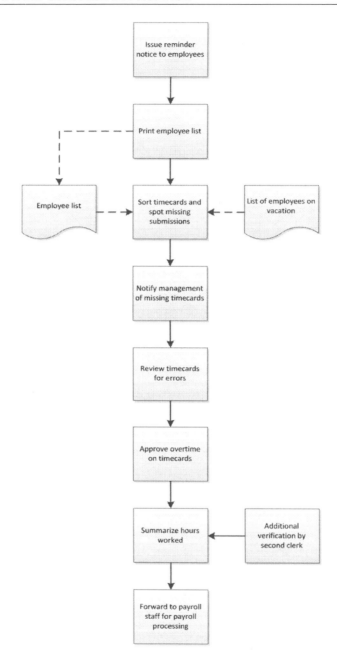

> **Tip:** The step outlined here is a labor-intensive one, especially if there are many salespeople. If possible, consider constructing a report in the accounting software that states totals by salesperson, and export it to an electronic spreadsheet for further modification.

3. **Adjust spreadsheet.** Adjust the spreadsheet for:
   - Commission splits
   - Additional bonuses issued during the period
   - Commission increases caused by target levels being met
   - Subtractions for unpaid customer invoices more than ___ days old
   - Different commissions for specific products or services sold

   Responsible party: Payroll clerk

   Control issues: The main control problem here is the use of too many commission adjustments. A complex commission plan introduces so many variables into the compensation calculation that it is difficult to ever be correct. Thus, a simple commission plan results in reduced computational errors.

4. **Forward spreadsheets for approval.** Send the completed spreadsheets to the sales manager for review. The sales manager will examine which invoices were assigned to each sales person, subtractions for unpaid invoices, commission rates, bonuses, splits, and so forth. This may call for the adjustment of the spreadsheets to incorporate changes made by the sales manager.

   Responsible party: Sales manager

   Control issues: Have the sales manager initial each commission spreadsheet to indicate his or her approval.

> **Tip:** Since commissions must be included in the next scheduled payroll, the review of commissions is a time-sensitive task. Accordingly, schedule a review session with the sales manager to go over the commission calculations, to ensure that the review is completed in a timely manner.

5. **Forward for data entry.** Forward the approved commission spreadsheets to the payroll clerk for entry into the payroll processing system.

   Responsible party: Payroll clerk

   Control issues: Match the list of forwarded commission spreadsheets to a list of current salespeople employed by the company. This will detect whether any spreadsheets have been lost. Otherwise, the payroll staff may have to create a manual commission check for an irate salesperson who was not paid.

The following exhibit shows a streamlined view of the commission calculation procedure.

Commission Calculation Process Flow

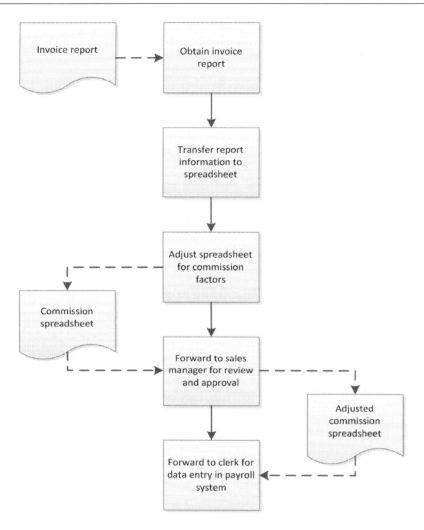

The Payroll Processing Procedure

The payroll processing procedure, like the timecard data collection procedure, can produce errors in several places, which calls for a detailed process flow that incorporates several controls. The actual process flow may vary somewhat from the steps noted below, since there may be differences related to the use of manual, computerized, or outsourced payroll processing solutions. The most likely version of the procedure, including responsibilities and basic controls, follows:

1. **Update employee master file.** The payroll clerk will probably receive notification of a number of changes to employee information that impact the

processing of payroll. If so, update the employee master file in the payroll software with the following changes:

- Change of employee name
- Change of employee address
- Change of employee pay rate
- Change of employee marriage status and/or withholding allowance
- Change of employee payment method
- Change of shift worked
- Change of employee status to inactive

Responsible party: Payroll clerk

Control issues: The notifications containing these changes may contain confidential information, so the payroll clerk should keep them in a locked location.

Tip: Notifications can arrive at any time, so the payroll clerk might consider entering them in the employee master file at once, rather than waiting for the designated payroll processing day. Doing so reduces the amount of work to be done during regular payroll processing.

---

2. **Set pay period.** Verify that the payroll module is set for the correct pay period. Outsourced payroll systems usually do this automatically, or at least make it quite clear what the current payroll period is. A commercial off-the-shelf software package may not be so clear about this.

   Responsible party: Payroll clerk

   Control issues: It is *very* important to set the correct payroll period; otherwise, the entire payroll must be cancelled and re-run. Thus, enforce the use of a checklist to process payroll, and include verification of the pay period on that list.

3. **Enter time worked.** Enter the amount of regular and overtime hours worked by each employee in the payroll system. If the company manually calculates payroll, this step and the next step are not needed. If the company uses computerized time clocks to assemble its timekeeping information, the information may be ported directly into the payroll software.

   Responsible party: Payroll clerk (possibly more than one – see the control issue)

   Control issues: There is a risk that the information entered will be done so incorrectly, so it may be necessary to have a second person verify the information in the payroll system. Also, compare the hours entered to the employee list to ensure that all data has been entered.

4. **Enter manual payments.** Enter the amounts of any manual paychecks that have not yet been recorded in the payroll system. These may be pay adjustments from previous periods, or payments related to the initial hiring or the termination of employees.

   Responsible party: Payroll clerk

Control issues: Manual payments may be difficult to locate, since they are sometimes issued through the accounts payable system, which is usually operated by other accounting staff. It may be necessary to review the accounts payable check register to see if any of these manual payments were made.

5. **Calculate termination pay.** Manually calculate the amount payable to any employee who has left the company, including their unused vacation time and severance pay. This usually only involves those employees who have left the company voluntarily, since forcible terminations require near-immediate payments that usually fall outside of the normal payroll processing period.
Responsible party: Payroll clerk
Control issues: Have a supervisor approve the calculation of termination pay.

6. **Alter deductions.** Enter any changes to the standard deductions from employee pay, including the following:
   - Cafeteria plan
   - Charitable contributions
   - Dental insurance
   - Disability insurance
   - Garnishments
   - Life insurance
   - Medical insurance
   - Pension plans
Responsible party: Payroll clerk
Control issues: These changes should be stated on a standard form that the employee signs. Otherwise, there is a risk of a change being made that the employee subsequently disavows.

7. **Calculate pay.** Have the software process all pay calculations for the period. If the company manually calculates pay, use the tax tables provided by the federal and state governments to determine the proper amount of tax withholdings.
Responsible party: Payroll clerk (possibly more than one – see the control issue)
Control issues: If payroll is calculated manually, it is possible (if not likely) that there will be pay calculation errors. To mitigate these errors, consider having an experienced clerk verify the calculations.

8. **Review reports.** If payroll calculations are either outsourced or use payroll software, print the following reports and review the underlying transactions for errors. Process payroll again until these issues have been corrected.
   - Negative deductions report (can indicate a data entry error or fraud)
   - Negative taxes report (can indicate a data entry error or fraud)
   - Preliminary payroll register (the key document used to locate errors)
   - Sorted list of wages paid (focus on excessively high or low wage amounts to spot potentially inaccurate hours worked or wage rates)

- Trend line of payroll expense by department (can indicate wages being charged to the wrong department)

Responsible party: Payroll clerk

Control issues: Several of these reports can indicate fraud, and so should be printed and reviewed by someone other than the payroll clerk, such as the controller or payroll supervisor.

9. **Issue payments.** Once the analysis of reports indicate no further errors, process payments to employees. This is dealt with in the next procedure.

Responsible party: Payroll clerk

Control issues: As indicated in the next procedure.

10. **Issue management reports** (optional). Issue payroll reports to management that are related to the payroll just completed. Examples of such reports are a trend line of overtime by employee and a trend line of compensation expenses by department. This information might be used to adjust management practices within the business.

Responsible party: Payroll clerk

11. **Back up data.** Once the payroll has been completed, back up the data related to it. If payroll processing is outsourced, this is handled by the supplier. If in-house software is being used, archive the data. If a manual system is used, put the payroll register in locked storage.

Responsible party: Payroll clerk or IT person

Control issues: This is an item that should be on a checklist of required activities for each payroll.

12. **Lock down the period.** Lock down the payroll period in the payroll module for the period just completed, to prevent unauthorized changes. This is essentially the same as Step 2; by locking down the payroll period, we are essentially shifting forward to the next payroll period.

Responsible party: Payroll clerk

13. **Deposit taxes.** Deposit payroll taxes and verify their transmission to the government. If the company has outsourced its payroll processing, this step is handled by the supplier.

Responsible party: Payroll clerk or treasury clerk

Control issues: Responsibility might be assigned to the treasury clerk, who is more accustomed to making payments outside of the company. However, doing so means that payment information must be successfully shifted from the payroll department to the treasury department every time, which can introduce the possibility of a payment failure.

> **Tip:** The single best reason for outsourcing is to shift the tax filing burden to a supplier. If a company has a history of failed or incorrect filings, outsourcing may be a cost-effective option.

14. **Store timecards.** File the timecards near the payroll department. It is quite possible that employees will question their pay, in which case the most recent timecards should be easily accessible for review. After a month or two, the timecards can be shifted to longer-term storage.
    Responsible party: Payroll clerk

15. **Investigate errors.** If there are payroll processing problems, be assured that employees will find them! Investigate all transaction errors encountered, and initiate changes to mitigate their continued occurrence. This may involve the alteration of procedures or the imposition of new controls.
    Responsible party: Payroll manager or controller
    Control issues: Keep track of the types of errors encountered over time, which gives management a good idea of which issues must be addressed, and which appear to be outlier events that can be safely ignored.

The following exhibit shows a streamlined view of the payroll processing procedure. The last five tasks are not necessarily sequential, and so are presented as occurring at the same time.

The Employee Payment Procedure

This procedure is an expansion of the Issue Payments step noted in the preceding payroll processing procedure. It duplicates a few steps from the last procedure, which is intended to better present the entire flow of the payment process. The detailed procedure, including responsibilities and basic controls, follows:

1. **Review payroll register.** Print the preliminary payroll register and review it for errors. Adjust transactions as necessary to correct errors, and re-process payroll as needed. This is the primary report used to spot payroll errors. The other reports noted in the preceding procedure are targeted at specific types of problems.
   Responsible party: Payroll clerk

2. **Approve register.** Have a supervisor review and initial the final version of the payroll register.
   Responsible party: Payroll manager or controller
   Control issues: This is an important control step, since it may be the only time in the payroll process that someone verifies the amounts to be paid to employees.

Payroll Processing Flow

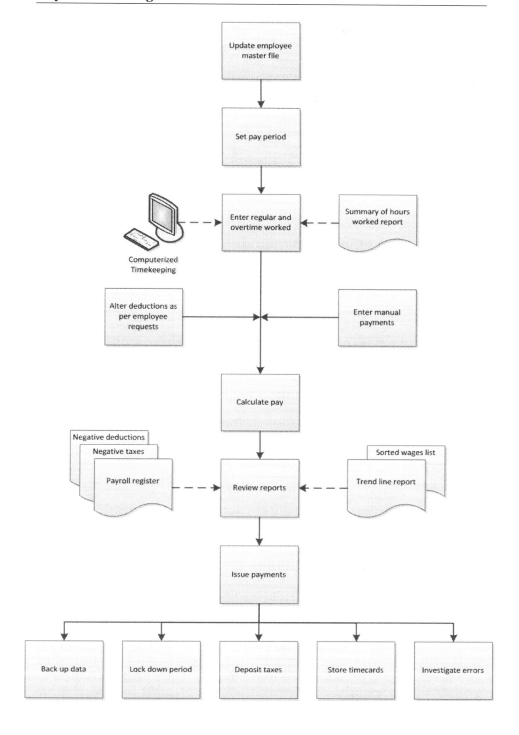

3. **Obtain check stock.** Remove check stock from the locked storage cabinet. If payroll processing is outsourced, the supplier stores and prints checks on behalf of the company.
   Responsible party: Payroll clerk
   Control issues: If a signature plate or stamp is used to sign checks, store it in a separate locked location, so that someone wanting to commit fraud must access two separate locked locations.

4. **Print and review checks.** Print paychecks for those employees receiving paychecks. Review and reprint them if necessary. This step is not needed if payroll is outsourced.
   Responsible party: Payroll clerk
   Control issues: It may be useful to periodically have the internal audit staff compare the bank's records of checks cleared to the amounts listed on the approved payroll register, to ensure that no additional checks were fraudulently issued or payment amounts altered.

5. **Accept batch.** Accept the printed batch in the payroll software, which records the payments in the accounting records. This step is not needed if payroll is outsourced.
   Responsible party: Payroll clerk

6. **Return unused check stock.** Return any remaining unused checks to the locked storage area, and log the range of check numbers that were used.
   Responsible party: Payroll clerk
   Control issues: Store the log separately from the check stock. Otherwise, someone could steal check stock and modify the log to make it appear that the checks were legitimately used.

7. **Print and store final register** (optional). The payroll software may require that a final payroll register be printed. If so, print and store it in the payroll archives area.
   Responsible party: Payroll clerk
   Control issues: If this step is used, the internal audit team can compare it to the approved payroll register to see if the listed payments are the same.

8. **Export direct deposit file.** Export the direct deposit payments file to the direct deposit processor, and verify receipt of the file by the processor. Correct any direct deposit failures that arise. The company may print direct deposit remittance advices in-house, or the direct deposit processor may do so.
   Responsible party: Payroll clerk and direct deposit processor
   Control issues: It may be necessary to have a supervisor review the payments file before it is delivered to the direct deposit processor. This review should involve a comparison to the payroll register to ensure that the correct amounts will be paid.

9. **Sign checks.** Have an authorized check signer sign all paychecks.
   Responsible party: Authorized check signer
   Control issues: If the company uses a signature plate or stamp instead of a check signer, it is more important than ever to have a supervisor formally review and approve the final payroll register, as well as to subsequently compare paid amounts to that register. These controls are needed to replace the missing check signer control.

10. **Stuff checks.** Stuff the checks and direct deposit remittance advices into envelopes for delivery to employees. If payroll is outsourced or direct deposit remittances are printed by a direct deposit processor, the supplier may handle this task.
    Responsible party: Payroll clerk or supplier

11. **Deliver checks.** Deliver the paychecks and remittance advices to supervisors for delivery to employees. For off-site locations, send paychecks and remittance advices by overnight delivery service.
    Responsible party: Payroll clerk
    Control issues: It is better to deliver paychecks and remittance advices to supervisors than mailing them directly to employees, since this ensures that someone is verifying the existence of all employees. Otherwise, a payment might be fraudulently issued to a ghost employee.

Tip: It is usually more efficient to send payments directly to employees. If so, a reasonable detective control is to have the internal audit staff track down employees for a random selection of payments to ensure that they exist.

The following exhibit shows a streamlined view of the employee payment procedure.

Summary

The processing of payroll involves several procedures, of which most contain many steps. Also, there are verifications at various points to ensure that all of the payroll information has been accounted for, and is correct. Given the complexity of these tasks, it makes considerable sense to create a checklist for each procedure, and force the payroll staff to follow it and initial each step. Only through this level of rigorous enforcement can a payroll manager hope to consistently process payroll with minimal errors.

Employee Payment Process Flow

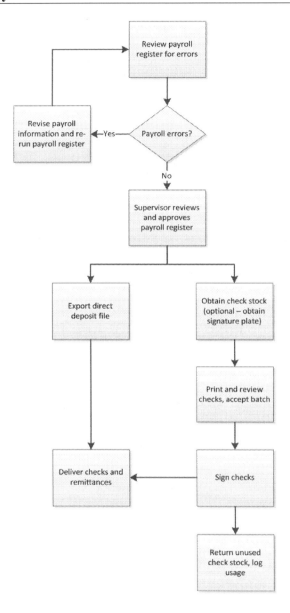

Chapter 16
Fixed Asset Procedures

Introduction

There are a number of possible transactions that can potentially be generated over the useful life of a fixed asset, ranging from the initial budgeting for it to its eventual disposal. Given the significant cost of fixed assets, you should adhere to a carefully-defined set of procedures for these transactions so that only necessary assets are acquired, they are accounted for correctly, and eliminated only when it makes economic sense to do so. Without the procedures listed in this chapter, you will have a heightened risk of investing in assets that are not needed, or of accounting for them incorrectly.

In this chapter, we provide examples of the forms resulting from or used in the fixed asset process, and then move on to the various fixed asset procedures. There are several types of fixed asset situations, so we provide separate procedures for:

- Capital request form completion
- Capital request form analysis
- Post installation review
- Asset recognition
- Interest capitalization
- Asset record creation
- Asset revaluation
- Asset exchange
- Depreciation
- Impairment analysis
- Asset retirement obligation analysis
- Intangible asset analysis
- Asset tracking
- Asset disposal

Procedural improvement tips are provided throughout the text, as well as flowcharts showing a streamlined view of each procedure.

Forms: Capital Request Form

The key form used for fixed assets is the capital request form. It is intended to provide a summary that identifies a proposed fixed asset, why it is needed, and its impact on the business. The following sample shows how the form could be structured, though it may need to be modified to meet the specific needs of a business. This form is typically treated as a cover page, with additional analyses attached that may cover a number of additional pages.

Sample Capital Request Application

Capital Request Form

Project Name	Project Number
Project Sponsor	Sponsor Contact Information

Submission Date

Project Type

- [ ] Constraint improvement
- [ ] Cost reduction
- [ ] Environmental/legal requirement
- [ ] Risk reduction
- [ ] Scheduled equipment replacement
- [ ] Other

Project Description

Description Block

Financial Summary

Year 1 Revenue	-	Year 1 Expenses	=	Year 1 Cash Flow
Year 2 Revenue	-	Year 2 Expenses	=	Year 2 Cash Flow
Year 3 Revenue	-	Year 3 Expenses	=	Year 3 Cash Flow

| Net Present Value | Internal Rate of Return | Payback Period |

Constraint Summary

| Throughput Impact |
| Operating Expenses Impact |
| ROI Impact |

Approvals

All proposals	Financial analyst signature	Attorney signature
< $25,000	Department manager signature	
$25,000+	CEO signature	

Forms: Asset Disposal Form

The asset disposal form is used to formalize the disposition of assets. Ideally, the purchasing department should be involved in disposals, since it presumably has the most experience in obtaining the best prices for goods. Consequently, a large part of the form is set aside for the use of the purchasing staff, which describes how the asset is disposed of and the amount of funds (if any) received. There is space to state billing information, in case the buyer is to be billed. There is also a separate section containing a checklist of activities that the accounting staff must complete. A sample of the form is presented below.

Sample Asset Disposal Form

Asset Disposal Form

Asset Tag Number	Asset Serial Number	Current Location

Asset Description

Reason for Disposal

☐ No longer usable   ☐ Being traded in
☐ Past recommended life span ☐ Lost or stolen*
☐ Being replaced   ☐ Other _____

* Contact building security to file a police report

Department Manager Approval Signature

For Use by Purchasing Department

Type of Disposition   If buyer is to be invoiced, state billing information:

☐ Sold ($_____)
☐ Donated
☐ Scrapped   Buyer billing information
☐ Other _____

Purchasing Manager Approval Signature	Disposal Date

For Use by Accounting Department

Accounting Actions Completed

☐ Asset removed from general ledger	Initials	Date
☐ Asset removed from fixed asset register	Initials	Date
☐ Buyer billed for sale amount	Initials	Date
☐ Cash receipt recorded	Initials	Date

The Capital Request Form Completion Procedure

Given the large amount of funding involved in some fixed asset purchases, it is of some importance to ensure that the form is completed consistently and includes all required materials. Otherwise, the people evaluating a proposal will be operating from inadequate information that may lead to the wrong decisions. The procedure for completing the capital request form is outlined below:

1. **Obtain form.** Obtain a capital request form from the financial analyst.
    Responsible party: Person requesting the purchase
    Control issues: It is of some importance for the financial analyst to maintain the entire stock of capital request forms, so that outdated versions do not float around the company. Otherwise, someone might use an old form that does not include the most recent requirements.

2. **Complete form header.** The financial analyst inserts the project number in the form header. Complete the project name and description in the header fields of the form.
    Responsible party: Financial analyst and person requesting the purchase
    Control issues: The financial analyst adds the project number in order to keep track of pending projects. The analyst can then poll project sponsors from time to time to monitor the progress of their applications.

3. **Itemize cash flows.** Itemize the revenues and expenses generated by the project in each of its first three years. This should include expenditures for the purchase of the requested asset, as well as the cash flow impact of any changes in working capital (particularly inventory), incremental changes in gross profits, and the impact of any changes in depreciation on income taxes.
    Responsible party: Person requesting the purchase

> **Tip:** It is advisable to create a guide for using the capital request form that includes examples of cash flows. Otherwise, project sponsors tend to submit proposals that do not contain complete cash flow information.

4. **Note legal and risk issues.** Fully document any legal or risk mitigation reasons for acquiring the asset, as well as the date by which the company will be out of compliance if it does not make the investment.
    Responsible party: Person requesting the purchase

5. **Note constraint issues.** Note the change in throughput at the bottleneck operation and any change in operating costs that is tied to the proposed investment.
    Responsible party: Person requesting the purchase. This may call for the assistance of an industrial engineer or the financial analyst.

Control issues: Since constraint analysis is an advanced concept, project sponsors may not understand what is being requested. Consequently, it may be necessary to require the participation of an expert in assembling this information. If so, insert an approval block in the capital request form and have the expert sign it, to show that a qualified person supplied the information.

6. **Calculate net present value.** Note the net present value (NPV) associated with the proposed investment, and attach a detailed derivation of the NPV. Contact the financial analyst for the discount rate and tax rate to use in the NPV calculation.
   Responsible party: Person requesting the purchase. This may call for the assistance of the financial analyst.

   > **Tip:** It may be useful to release a net present value calculation spreadsheet that project sponsors can use to derive NPV. The spreadsheet could also contain a formula for the internal rate of return and payback period, if the company chooses to include these metrics in the capital request form.

7. **Add supporting materials.** Attach to the proposal a detailed itemization of all cash flow estimates related to the asset, as well as assumptions regarding changes in revenues, profit margins, tax rates, and other business conditions that may alter the outcome of owning the asset. The department manager then signs the cover page and forwards the packet of information to the financial analyst.
   Responsible party: Person requesting the purchase

   > **Tip:** Consider providing a checklist of the backup materials that should be attached to the capital request form. This checklist could be attached to the main form, so that project sponsors cannot possibly avoid it.

8. **Review package.** The financial analyst examines the packet to ensure that all paperwork is included, that all assumptions appear reasonable, and that the calculations are correct. These tasks are addressed in the following procedure. The financial analyst then signs the cover page and forwards the packet to the corporate attorney for review.
   Responsible party: Financial analyst

9. **Approve package.** The corporate attorney reviews the packet for risk issues, includes commentary on any risk issues found, and then signs the cover page. If the expenditure level requires no further approvals, the attorney forwards the packet to the controller. If an additional approval is required, the packet is sent to the next-highest approver listed in the signature block of the capital request form.
   Responsible party: Corporate attorney and additional approvers

The following exhibit shows a streamlined view of the capital budgeting form completion procedure.

Capital Request Form Process Flow

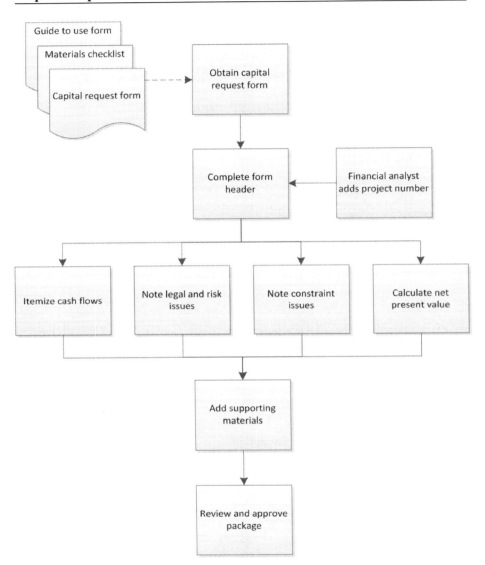

The Capital Request Form Analysis Procedure

The procedure for completing the capital budgeting analysis is outlined below:

1. **Review for completion.** Upon receipt of the capital request form from the project sponsor, review it to see if any fields have not been completed, or have

been insufficiently completed. If there are issues, contact the project sponsor and go over the information that is missing. Hold any further review until the form has been revised and re-submitted.
Responsible party: Financial analyst

> **Tip:** Consider creating a standard checklist of review items for the financial analyst to examine, including a listing of all attachments expected to be filed with the capital request form.

2. **Review calculations.** Review the calculations that accompany the application to verify that they are correct, and verify that the totals in the supporting documentation are used in the lead page of the application.
Responsible party: Financial analyst

3. **Review assumptions.** Review all assumptions noted in the supporting documentation to see how they compare to the assumptions used in other applications, both currently and in the recent past. If the assumptions vary significantly from those used elsewhere, contact the project sponsor for justification.
Responsible party: Financial analyst

4. **Review cash flows.** Review all cash flow projections with the project sponsor, as well as the purchasing, engineering, and sales departments to see if the amount and timing of the projected cash flows are reasonable.
Responsible party: Financial analyst
Control issues: The project sponsor is the person most likely to be optimistic in the discussion of cash flows, so be sure to consult with people in other departments to gain an alternative perspective.

5. **Examine previous results.** Examine the post-implementation reviews of projects that were previously submitted by the same project sponsor, and note in the application if this person has a history of projecting results that cannot be realized, as well as the extent of these variances.
Responsible party: Financial analyst

6. **Describe risk.** If the project appears to have a high level of risk, note this issue in the application, and discuss with the controller whether to apply a higher discount rate to the net present value calculation to incorporate risk more fully into the cash flows associated with the application.
Responsible party: Financial analyst and controller

7. **State recommendation.** Following the review, evaluate whether the application should be approved. State the recommendation in the application, along with reasons.
Responsible party: Financial analyst

Control issues: This step is an important one, since it provides an in-depth, independent evaluation. It also presents a problem if the request form is coming from the supervisor of the financial analyst (probably the controller or CFO). In this case, it may be necessary to obtain an independent appraisal of the proposal from someone elsewhere in the company.

8. **File copy.** Copy the application and store the copy.
   Responsible party: Financial analyst
   Control issues: It may be necessary to store the copy in a locked location. This provides evidence of what was originally submitted, in case someone later attempts to modify the application in order to fraudulently gain approval.

9. **Forward for approval.** Forward the original version of the application to the next person on the approval list, and request that it be returned following that person's review.
   Responsible party: Financial analyst

10. **Monitor approvals.** Monitor the progress of the approvals through the company, and shift the document to the next approver as needed.
    Responsible party: Financial analyst
    Control issues: At each step in the approval process, the application should always be returned to the financial analyst. This allows the analyst to track who has the application, as well as to physically present it to the next person on the approval list and emphasize the importance of returning it as soon as possible.

11. **Communicate results.** If the application is rejected, communicate this result to the project sponsor, as well as the reasons why it was rejected. If the application is approved, communicate this information to the sponsor, and notify the accounting and purchasing departments of the approval.
    Responsible party: Financial analyst
    Control issues: The notification to the accounting and purchasing departments should take the form of a copy of the capital request form, with all approval signatures included, and with an approval stamp on it.

The following exhibit shows a streamlined view of the capital request form analysis procedure. Note that many of the review steps can be conducted at the same time, so they are presented as a group, rather than separately.

Capital Request Form Analysis Process Flow

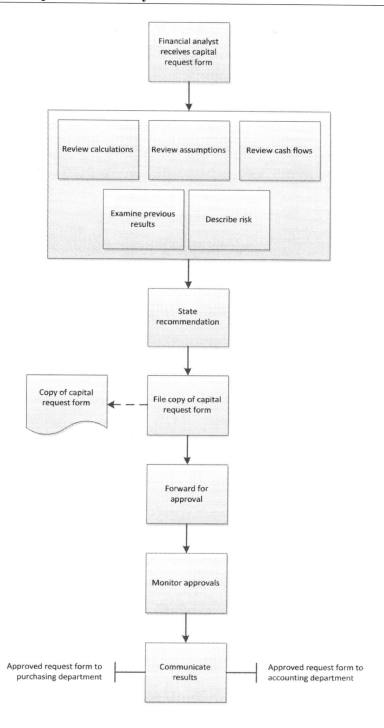

The Post Installation Review Procedure

It is highly advisable to conduct a post installation review to see if an approved project has generated the results predicted in the original capital request form. This procedure is intended for the financial analyst, and so can be quite specialized, with references to specific types of analysis to conduct. The following procedure may require significant alterations to meet the needs of a specific business:

1. **Schedule review.** Once a fixed asset has been installed for a certain period of time, schedule a post implementation review. There is a danger in conducting this review too soon, since it takes time for all of the revenues and expenditures associated with a project to become apparent.
   Responsible party: Financial analyst

2. **Examine assumptions.** Compare the business assumptions detailed in the application to actual business conditions, and quantify how these changes impacted the project results.
   Responsible party: Financial analyst

3. **Review expenditures.** Compare the forecasted expenditures in the application to actual expenditures, and investigate why any additional expenditures were needed.
   Responsible party: Financial analyst
   Control issues: It may be useful to review all expenditures related to the project, and verify that they were charged to the project, rather than to another project or to expense. This can sometimes happen when the project sponsor tries to make a project look less expensive than it really is.

4. **Review cash flows.** Compare the forecasted positive cash flows in the application to actual positive cash flows, and investigate any significant variances. This is essentially revenue projections, and is a prime area in which expectations may lag actual results.
   Responsible party: Financial analyst

5. **Review throughput.** Compare the forecasted changes in throughput with actual results, and investigate any significant variances. Throughput is revenues minus all totally variable expenses, and increasing it is the primary reason for many capital expenditures, especially in the manufacturing area.
   Responsible party: Financial analyst

6. **Investigate legal justification.** Validate with corporate counsel any legal reasons given for an asset purchase, and whether that legal basis for the decision has since changed. This step is useful for noting purchases made in anticipation of a law or regulation that is not subsequently enacted.
   Responsible party: Financial analyst and corporate counsel

7. **Investigate risk justification.** Validate with the corporate risk manager any risk-related reasons given for an asset purchase, and whether this basis for the decision has since changed. This can be an interesting area of investigation, for the risk profile of a business changes constantly, so the investigation may reveal a number of issues that require additional asset purchases.
Responsible party: Financial analyst and risk manager

8. **Notify project sponsor.** Route a preliminary copy of the post implementation review findings to the project sponsor for comments, and include the sponsor's comments in the final report.
Responsible party: Financial analyst and project sponsor
Control issues: Send the report to the project sponsor by e-mail, and include a copy of the e-mail in the review folder. This provides evidence that the sponsor was notified of the findings. An alternative is to have the project sponsor sign for his or her copy of the report. In either case, the point is to ensure that all parties are notified of the report results, and that a chance for a rebuttal is given.

9. **Forward report to management.** Forward a summary of the review findings to the management team, along with any recommendations regarding how to improve the capital budgeting process in the future. The post implementation review is detective in nature, since it does not directly prevent expenditures. However, it can indirectly prevent expenditures in the future if recommendations are made to adjust the capital budgeting process. Thus, the recommendations in this report can be of some importance.
Responsible party: Financial analyst
Control issues: A higher-level person, such as the CFO, should review the recommendations of the financial analyst from time to time to see if the capital budgeting process has been improved. This can reduce unnecessary expenditures in the future.

10. **Review again** (optional). For larger projects, it may be useful to conduct another analysis at a longer interval, such as annually, to see if the project results have changed.
Responsible party: Financial analyst

> **Tip:** A company policy could drive the use of additional post implementation reviews, such as stating that all expenditures of over $1 million shall be reviewed once a year throughout their useful lives.

The following exhibit shows a streamlined view of the post installation review procedure. Note that many of the post installation review steps can be conducted at the same time, so they are presented as a group, rather than separately.

Post Installation Review Process Flow

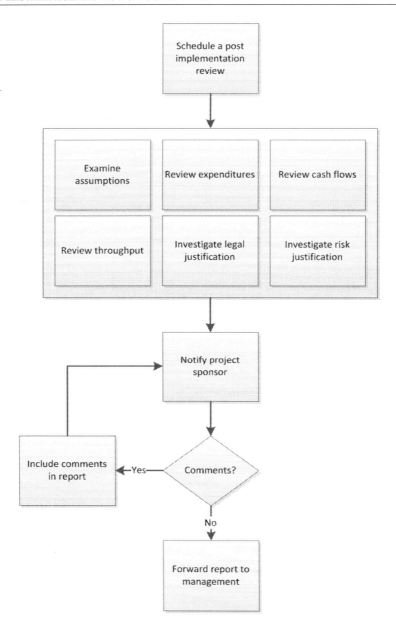

The Asset Recognition Procedure

One of the areas in which a procedure can be quite useful is for the initial recognition of a fixed asset in the accounting system. The procedure for completing the asset recognition process is outlined below:

1. **Determine base unit.** Determine the base unit for the asset. This determination is based upon a number of factors, such as whether the useful lives of various components of the asset are significantly different, at which level you prefer to physically track the asset, and the cost-effectiveness of tracking assets at various levels of detail. Reviewing the base units used for other assets may assist in this determination.
   Responsible party: Fixed asset accountant

> **Tip:** It is more efficient to aggregate expenditures into a smaller number of base units, where possible. Otherwise, the larger number of assets to be tracked requires too much accounting staff time.

2. **Compile cost.** Compile the total cost of the base unit. This is any cost incurred to acquire the base unit and bring it to the condition and location intended for its use. These activities may include the construction of the base unit and related administrative and technical activities.
   Responsible party: Fixed asset accountant
   Control issues: This step involves having a system in place for ensuring that purchases are coded to the correct fixed assets. This may involve a summary sheet given to the accounts payable staff, detailing which fixed assets are currently active, and which expenditures should be coded to them.

3. **Match to capitalization limit.** Determine whether the total cost of the base unit exceeds the corporate capitalization limit. If it does not, charge the expenditure to expense. Otherwise, continue to the next step.
   Responsible party: Fixed asset accountant

> **Tip:** This step can also be handled within the accounts payable department, where the clerks can assign expenditures to expense accounts, rather than to fixed asset accounts, if the amounts are clearly below the capitalization limit. Under this approach, the fixed asset accountant can be consulted if expenditures are very close to the limit.

4. **Assign to asset class.** Assign the base unit to the most appropriate asset class for which there is a general ledger category (such as furniture and fixtures, office equipment, or vehicles).
   Responsible party: Fixed asset accountant

> **Tip:** Again, this step can also be handled within the accounts payable department. The fixed asset accountant may be consulted regarding items where the asset class is unclear.

5. **Create journal entry.** Create a journal entry that debits the asset account for the appropriate asset class and credits the expenditure account in which the cost of

the base unit had originally been stored. If there is a general ledger accountant, this person will record the entry in the accounting system.

Responsible party: Fixed asset accountant and general ledger accountant

Control issues: Be sure to include supporting documentation in a fixed assets binder or journal entry binder, so that the outside auditors can review the information as part of their annual audit.

The following exhibit shows a streamlined view of the asset recognition procedure, and assumes that the transaction is recorded in both a journal entries binder and a fixed assets binder.

Asset Recognition Process Flow

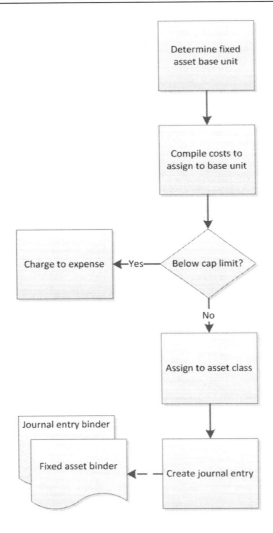

The Interest Capitalization Procedure

If you always purchase and install fixed assets quickly, there is no need for an interest capitalization procedure. However, if there are situations where you are constructing an asset over a prolonged period of time, consider adding the following procedure:

1. **Construct table.** Construct a table that includes the amounts of expenditures made during a construction period and the dates when the expenditures were made.
   Responsible party: Fixed asset accountant

   > **Tip:** Only create and update this table at the end of each month, after all accounts payable have been processed. Doing so ensures that all expenditures will be included in the table.

2. **Determine ending capitalization date.** Determine the date on which interest capitalization ends, which should be the date on which the asset has been brought to the condition and location intended for its use.
   Responsible party: Fixed asset accountant

3. **Calculate capitalization period.** Calculate the capitalization period for each expenditure, which is the number of days from the expenditure to the end of the interest capitalization period.
   Responsible party: Fixed asset accountant

4. **Calculate capitalization rate.** Calculate the capitalization rate, which is the interest rate applicable to the company's borrowings during the construction period. If you have incurred a specific borrowing to finance the asset, use the interest rate on that borrowing. This information may come from the treasurer.
   Responsible party: Fixed asset accountant
   Control issues: The capitalization rate chosen can impact short-term profit levels, so always document the reason for using that rate; the outside auditors will probably review the document.

5. **Calculate interest to capitalize.** Multiply the capitalization rate by each expenditure, and multiply the result by the fraction of a year represented by the capitalization period for each expenditure, to arrive at the interest to be capitalized for that expenditure.
   Responsible party: Fixed asset accountant
   Control issues: This step is subject to error, so it might make sense to have a second person review the calculations.

6. **Compare to actual interest expense.** If the total calculated interest capitalization is more than the total interest cost incurred by the company during

the calculation period, only capitalize the total interest cost incurred by the company during the calculation period.

Responsible party: Fixed asset accountant

7. **Record capitalized interest.** Record the interest capitalization as a debit to the project's fixed asset account and a credit to the interest expense account. If there is a general ledger accountant, this person will probably record the journal entry in the accounting system.

Responsible party: Fixed asset accountant and general ledger accountant

Control issues: Be sure to include supporting documentation in a fixed assets binder or journal entry binder, so that the outside auditors can review the information as part of their annual audit.

The following exhibit shows a streamlined view of the interest capitalization procedure. It assumes that the transaction is recorded in both a journal entries binder and a fixed assets binder, and that steps 2, 3, and 4 can be completed at approximately the same time.

Interest Capitalization Process Flow

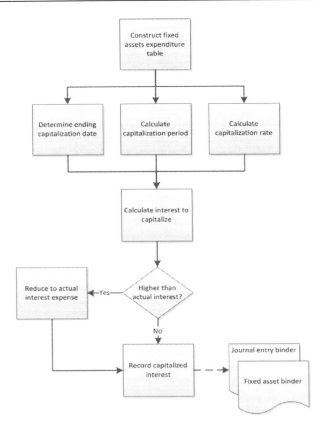

The Fixed Asset Record Creation Procedure

The exact types of information recorded for a fixed asset will vary by business, which means that the following procedure may need to be adjusted. The following sample procedure is intended for the recordation of a manufacturing asset:

1. **Create record.** Create a new record for the asset and assign the next sequential record number to it. If being recorded in a computer system, the software will assign the record number. If not, the fixed asset accountant will do so.
   Responsible party: Fixed asset accountant
   Control issues: If this is a manual system, the fixed asset accountant maintains a sequential list of record numbers to assign to each fixed asset, so that no numbers are inadvertently duplicated or missed.

2. **Write a description.** Describe the asset in one sentence. If this asset is similar to other company assets, use the same description format. Otherwise, consider using a manufacturer-provided description. For some of the more esoteric assets, it may not be clear what an item is, in which case the accountant should ask the project sponsor for a description.
   Responsible party: Fixed asset accountant

3. **Enter tag number.** List the number on the company-provided tag (if any) affixed to the equipment. If no tag was used, enter "No Tag."
   Responsible party: Fixed asset accountant
   Control issues: This step is important for keeping track of assets, but is not necessary for items that are immovable, such as multi-ton manufacturing equipment.

4. **Enter serial number.** Enter the manufacturer-provided serial number on the equipment. If you cannot find the serial number, contact the manufacturer to find out where it should be located. If there is no serial number, enter "No Serial Number."
   Responsible party: Fixed asset accountant
   Control issues: This is a good backup identification for a fixed asset, if the company-provided tag number is lost. Serial numbers tend to be affixed to assets with epoxy or bolted on, and so are not easily lost.

5. **Note asset location.** Note the location of the asset. Where possible, specify the location at least by building, and preferably by room. If it is located in the production area, specify the work center in which it is located.
   Responsible party: Fixed asset accountant

6. **Assign responsibility.** State the name or at least the position title of the person who is responsible for the asset.
   Responsible party: Fixed asset accountant

Control issues: Notify the responsible person once a fixed asset has been assigned to him or her, and verify that it is included on all asset reports for that person's area of responsibility. This means that the person is more likely to maintain a watch over the asset.

7. **Record the acquisition date.** State the month and year on which the asset was ready for its intended use, and whether it was actually used as of that date.
Responsible party: Fixed asset accountant
Control issues: The outside auditors may investigate this data item, since it establishes when depreciation should begin. Consequently, it may be useful to assemble documentation supporting why a particular date was selected.

8. **Enter cost.** Enter the total initial capitalized cost of the asset. This should match the amount recorded in the general ledger or fixed asset journal for the asset. Do not use the amount listed on the supplier invoice, since other costs may have been added. This step assumes that the fixed asset software is not having information interfaced directly to it from the general ledger or fixed asset journal.
Responsible party: Fixed asset accountant

9. **Assign to asset class.** Assign the asset to an asset class by comparing its characteristics to the standard asset classes used by the company. If in doubt, review related assets to determine the classes to which they were assigned. This is an important step, since useful lives and depreciation methods are frequently assigned automatically, based on the asset class.
Responsible party: Fixed asset accountant
Control issues: The impact of an incorrect asset class assignment can be so severe that the controller may want to sign off on these designations.

10. **Enter useful life.** If the system does not automatically assign a useful life based on the asset class, state the useful life. If the manufacturer recommends an unusual useful life, discuss the issue with the controller; it may require the creation of a new asset class for the asset.
Responsible party: Fixed asset accountant
Control issues: Document all departures from the standard useful life, since the outside auditors may investigate unusual useful lives.

Tip: Create a table that states the useful life and depreciation method for each asset class, and follow it as closely as possible for all assets. The intent is to introduce some consistency to the assignment of useful lives to assets.

---

11. **Enter warranty period** (optional). State the warranty period. This may be a standard warranty provided by the manufacturer, or an extended warranty that the company purchased. There is no warranty for many assets, so this step is optional.

Responsible party: Fixed asset accountant
Control issues: Consider creating a warranties report to go along with this field, so that management can see which warranties are about to expire on the company's fixed assets.

12. **Record contact information.** Enter the manufacturer's contact information. This may include the e-mail, telephone, and address for the supplier's field servicing, customer service, warranty, and sales departments.
    Responsible party: Fixed asset accountant

> **Tip:** The maintenance staff may also need this information for repair and servicing issues, so give them read-only access to the fixed asset records.

13. **Approve record.** Have the controller or assistant controller review and approve the file. Correct any issues noted by the reviewer.
    Responsible party: Fixed asset accountant and controller

14. **Store the record.** If the information is recorded in an entirely manual system, store it by asset class and then by record number in the fixed asset record files.
    Responsible party: Fixed asset accountant
    Control issues: This is not necessary for computerized systems, as long as there is a proper backup system in place.

The following exhibit shows a streamlined view of the fixed asset recordation procedure, including the optional step involving the entry of warranty information. There is no exact sequence to the entry of most of the information, so it is stated as a group of actions.

The Asset Revaluation Procedure

Under International Financial Reporting Standards (IFRS), you are allowed to revalue fixed assets, but only for entire asset classes – you cannot selectively revalue some assets and not others within the same asset class. Within that restriction, use the following procedure for completing an asset revaluation:

1. **Schedule the revaluation.** Consult the asset class revaluation schedule to determine when the next revaluation is to be completed. This should be listed on the department calendar of activities as a recurring event.
   Responsible party: Fixed asset accountant
   Control issues: Asset revaluations are so rare that it is easy to overlook them. Thus, placing them on the schedules of the CFO or controller may be the only way to ensure that they are revisited in a timely manner.

Fixed Asset Recordation Process Flow

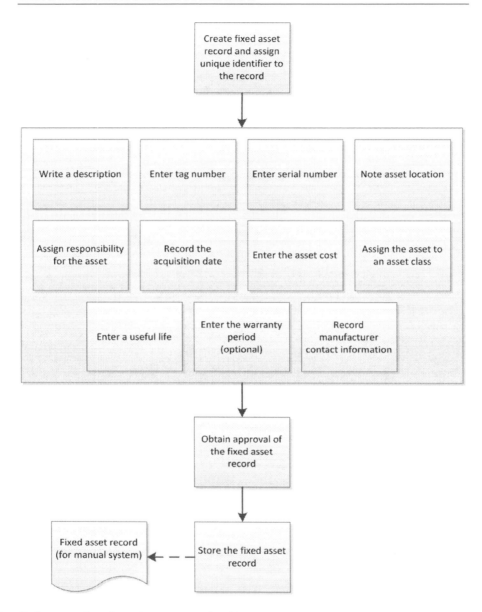

2. **Print revaluation list.** Run a detailed schedule of the fixed assets within the asset classes to be revalued.

   Responsible party: Fixed asset accountant

   Control issues: Run this report as late as possible in order to include those assets most recently acquired by the business.

3. **Hire appraiser.** Hire an independent appraiser to conduct the revaluations, and forward the detailed schedule to the appraiser.
Responsible party: Fixed asset accountant

> **Tip:** It may be more efficient and less expensive to retain the services of the same appraiser for each revaluation, since this person or business has built up an experience base with the assets owned by the company.

4. **Value based on cash flows** (optional). In cases where the appraiser is unable to derive a market valuation, use estimates of future cash flows associated with the assets in question, discounted to their present values. Use the company's incremental cost of capital as the discount rate. The treasury department can provide the cost of capital, and the financial analyst can assist with cash flow estimates.
Responsible party: Fixed assets accountant and financial analyst
Control issues: If cash flows are used as the basis for revaluations, document the reasons for specific cash flows. The outside auditors will probably want to review them as part of the annual audit.

> **Tip:** To build consistency from year to year in developing cash flow estimates, create each new estimate on the same model used for the last estimate.

5. **Account for a gain.** If there is an upward revaluation adjustment, debit the fixed asset account for the amount of the incremental increase and credit a gain in other comprehensive income. If the increase reverses a revaluation decrease for the same asset, recognize the gain in profit or loss to the extent of the previous loss, and record any remaining gain in other comprehensive income.
Responsible party: Fixed asset accountant

6. **Account for a loss.** If there is a downward revaluation adjustment, recognize the loss in profit or loss with a debit, and credit the fixed asset account. If the decrease reverses a previous revaluation increase for the same asset, recognize the loss in other comprehensive income to the extent of the previous gain, and record any remaining loss in profit or loss.
Responsible party: Fixed asset accountant

7. **Adjust accumulated depreciation.** If there is a revaluation adjustment, eliminate all existing accumulated depreciation by debiting the accumulated depreciation account and crediting the offsetting amount to the fixed asset account.
Responsible party: Fixed asset accountant

8. **Adjust other factors.** If there is a revaluation adjustment, examine the depreciation schedule being used for the asset to see if its useful life, deprecia-

tion method, or salvage value should be changed. Because of the change in the carrying amount of the asset caused by the revaluation, the amount of prospective depreciation expense recognized per period should change, even in the absence of any other changes in assumptions.

Responsible party: Fixed asset accountant

Control issues: Adjusting the depreciation expense per period is not in the normal schedule of activities, and so will probably be ignored. To remedy this, create a checklist of activities for the revaluation process that includes both this and the preceding step.

The following exhibit shows a streamlined view of the asset revaluation procedure, including the optional step.

The Asset Exchange Procedure

If you acquire a fixed asset through a non-monetary exchange, use the following procedure to arrive at the proper recorded cost for it:

1. **Record cost based on surrender value.** The cost of the asset received is the fair value of the asset surrendered to the other party. Recognize a gain or loss on the difference between the recorded cost of the asset surrendered and the asset received.
   Responsible party: Fixed asset accountant
   Control issues: This item is closely watched by the company's outside auditors, so consider having a third-party appraiser document the fair values of exchanged assets.

2. **Record cost based on receipt value.** If you cannot determine the fair value of the asset surrendered, instead use the fair value of the asset received. Recognize a gain or loss on the difference between the recorded cost of the asset surrendered and the asset received.
   Responsible party: Fixed asset accountant
   Control issues: As just noted, employ an outside appraiser to fully document the fair value of assets involved in an asset exchange.

3. **Record cost based on surrender cost.** If you cannot determine the fair value of either asset, record the cost of the asset received at the cost of the asset surrendered.
   Responsible party: Fixed asset accountant

4. **Adjust for large cash payment.** If the asset exchange involves the payment of cash that is 25 percent or more of the fair value of the exchange, recognize the transaction at its fair value, using either steps 1 or 2 in this procedure.
   Responsible party: Fixed asset accountant

Asset Revaluation Process Flow

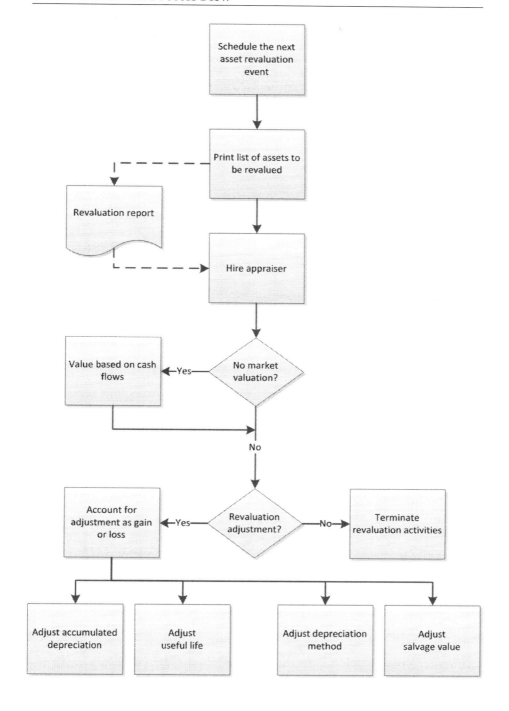

5. **Adjust for small cash payment.** If the asset exchange involves the payment of cash that is less than 25 percent of the fair value of the exchange, then (if you are the recipient of the cash) record a gain to the extent that the amount of cash received exceeds a proportionate share of the cost of the surrendered asset. If the transaction results in a loss, record the entire loss at once. If you are paying the cash, record the asset received at the sum of the cash paid plus the cost of the asset surrendered.
Responsible party: Fixed asset accountant

The following exhibit shows a streamlined view of the asset exchange procedure for the first three steps just described.

Asset Exchange Process Flow

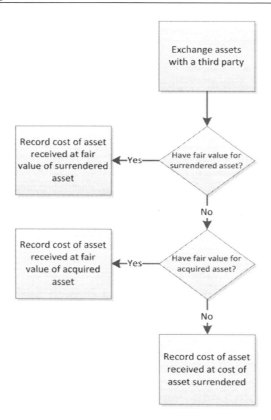

The Depreciation Procedure

There should be a detailed depreciation procedure that specifies exactly how to categorize each fixed asset and how to depreciate it based on the asset class to which it is assigned. There are several possible procedures, of which the first is listed below:

1. **Assign an asset class.** Match the fixed asset to the company's standard asset class descriptions. If you are uncertain of the correct class to use, examine the assets already assigned to the various classes, or consult with the controller.
   Responsible party: Fixed asset accountant
   Control issues: The controller could review a fixed asset register at the end of each month that only shows assets added during the month, just to see if assets have been placed in the correct asset classes.

2. **Assign depreciation factors.** Assign to the fixed asset the useful life and depreciation method that are standardized for the asset class of which it is a part. This is automatically assigned in some computerized systems, where the assignment of an asset class automatically assigns a useful life and depreciation method to an asset.
   Responsible party: Fixed asset accountant
   Control issues: Any wide variability of useful lives and especially of depreciation methods within an asset class is to be avoided, not only for efficiency reasons, but also because the outside auditors may request documentation of the reason for each departure from the standard depreciation factors.

3. **Determine salvage value.** Consult with the purchasing or industrial engineering staffs to determine whether the asset is expected to have a salvage value at the end of its useful life. If this salvage value exceeds the company's policy for minimum salvage values, make note of it in the depreciation calculation.
   Responsible party: Fixed asset accountant

   > **Tip:** If the company has an entirely manual system for tracking depreciation (such as an electronic spreadsheet), the error rate for calculations is higher when salvage values are included. To mitigate this issue, only include salvage values when they are quite large.

4. **Create depreciation calculation.** Create the depreciation calculation based on the useful life and depreciation mandated for the asset class using the asset cost less any salvage value. This is done automatically for assets entered into a fixed asset software package, but must otherwise be generated manually.
   Responsible party: Fixed asset accountant (plus a reviewer – see the control issue)
   Control issues: In a manually compiled depreciation system, it is extremely likely that there will be errors in the spreadsheet. Examples are of depreciating past the useful life, not including designated salvage values in the calculation, and not adjusting subtotals and totals to include new assets. This can be mitigated by having a second person review the depreciation spreadsheet for errors.

The procedure thus far has only addressed the calculation of depreciation for a single fixed asset. Once each calculation is set up, you will not need to address it again until either the end of the useful life of the asset or when there is a change in estimate. You also need to deal with the aggregation of the depreciation for all fixed assets in a periodic journal entry, which is addressed in the following procedure:

1. **Print depreciation report.** Print the depreciation report, sorted by asset class.
   Responsible party: Fixed asset accountant
   Control issues: it may be useful to test this report periodically to ensure that its totals match those in the general ledger. This is not an issue if the company is using fixed asset software that is integrated with the general ledger, but can be a major issue when the fixed asset information is maintained separately.

2. **Create journal entry.** Create the monthly depreciation journal entry, using the standard depreciation template. The standard entry is to record a debit for the depreciation expense (in total or by department), and to record a credit to the accumulated depreciation account for each asset class. This information comes from the totals on the depreciation report.
   Responsible party: Fixed asset accountant
   Control issues: It is a very good idea to create a standard depreciation template in the accounting software, since this ensures the consistent use of the correct accounts.

3. **Enter the transaction.** Have the general ledger accountant record the journal entry in the accounting software.
   Responsible party: General ledger accountant

4. **File backup materials.** Attach the depreciation report to the journal entry form and file it in the journal entries binder.
   Responsible party: General ledger accountant
   Control issues: The fixed asset accountant might also want to keep a copy of this entry and supporting documents for reference purposes.

There are so few steps associated with the creation and recordation of depreciation transactions that we will dispense with a flowchart of the process flow.

The Impairment Analysis Procedure

Both Generally Accepted Accounting Principles (GAAP) and IFRS require that you periodically review fixed assets for impairment. This should be a formal, documented process that steps the user through the specifics of the required testing. The procedure for completing the impairment analysis procedure is outlined below:

1. **Sort fixed asset register.** Sort the fixed asset register in declining order by net carrying amount (i.e., the gross cost of an asset, less all accumulated deprecia-

tion and accumulated impairment associated with it). This is usually accomplished in computerized systems by exporting the information to a spreadsheet and then sorting it.

Responsible party: Fixed asset accountant

2. **Select items for testing.** Select for testing any fixed assets having a net carrying amount greater than $\_\_\_$. Export these items to a spreadsheet. Realistically, the items are already in the spreadsheet used for sorting purposes in the preceding step, so just eliminate all other fixed assets from the spreadsheet.

Responsible party: Fixed asset accountant

3. **Calculate undiscounted cash flows.** Determine the sum of the undiscounted cash flows expected from each asset over its remaining useful life and final disposition, and add this amount next to each asset in the spreadsheet. This step may require the participation of the financial analyst who conducts the post implementation reviews of fixed assets.

Responsible party: Fixed asset accountant

4. **Calculate impairment.** If the cash flow total is less than the net carrying amount, the difference is an impairment. Note this amount in the spreadsheet.

Responsible party: Fixed asset accountant

5. **Approve and record.** Forward the spreadsheet to the controller along with a proposed journal entry. The controller reviews and approves the impairment calculations and journal entry, and forwards the paperwork to the general ledger accountant for entry into the accounting system. The entry reduces the net carrying amount of the asset to its fair value, as represented by the remaining cash flows.

Responsible party: Fixed asset accountant, controller, and general ledger accountant

Control issues: The outside auditors will undoubtedly review any impairment transaction, so be sure to completely document all impairment entries.

6. **Allocate the impairment.** If impairment was recorded for an asset group, apportion the impairment amount among the assets in the group on a pro rata basis that is based on the carrying amounts of the assets.

Responsible party: Fixed asset accountant

Control issues: The justification for this allocation may be reviewed by the outside auditors, so fully document the allocation methodology.

7. **Adjust depreciation calculation.** Adjust the remaining depreciation on the asset to reflect its reduced carrying amount.

Responsible party: Fixed asset accountant

Control issues: This step is likely to be forgotten, since it is separate from the other impairment analysis tasks. However, a lack of depreciation adjustment can lead to the too-rapid depreciation of an asset that has already experienced an impairment reduction, so be sure to insert a depreciation review reminder in the monthly task list of the fixed asset accountant.

The following exhibit shows a streamlined view of the impairment analysis procedure.

The Asset Retirement Obligation Procedure

There is an obligation to record a liability for any asset retirement obligation, particularly under GAAP. Use the following procedure to initially account for such an obligation:

1. **Ascertain applicability.** Determine whether there is an obligation to engage in asset retirement expenditures at the end of the useful life of the asset under review. The person responsible for an asset is most likely to be aware of such obligations, though it may also have been documented in the attachments to the initial capital request form.
   Responsible party: Fixed asset accountant and person responsible for the asset

   > **Tip:** Certain types of assets tend to have asset retirement obligations, so consider clustering them into one or a few asset classes, to better track them.

2. **Estimate applicable time period.** Estimate the number of years before which the company will engage in asset retirement activities and incur related expenditures.
   Responsible party: Fixed asset accountant and person responsible for the asset

3. **Estimate cash flows.** Estimate the timing and amounts of the cash flows associated with any required asset retirement obligations. If there are a range of probabilities, incorporate them into a weighted-average estimate of cash flows. This will likely require the services of the company's financial analyst, as well as the input of the person responsible for the asset.
   Responsible party: Fixed asset accountant, financial analyst, and person responsible for the asset
   Control issues: Be sure to document these cash flows thoroughly, since they will certainly be examined by the company's outside auditors.

4. **Determine risk-free rate.** Calculate the credit-adjusted risk-free rate.
   Responsible party: Fixed asset accountant and financial analyst
   Control issues: Document how this rate is arrived at, and use the same system for deriving it in each successive accounting period, to be consistent.

Impairment Analysis Process Flow

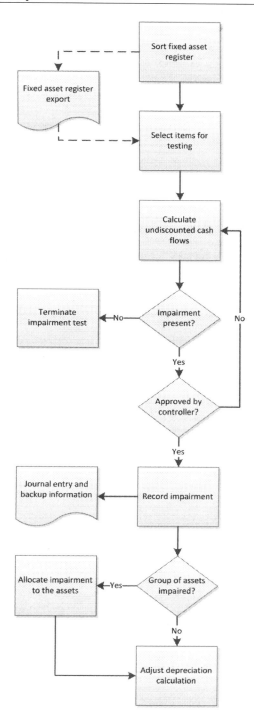

5. **Calculate discounted cash flows.** Discount the estimate of cash flows to their present value using the credit-adjusted risk-free rate. The financial analyst should have considerable experience with this task, so have that person handle it.
Responsible party: Fixed asset accountant and financial analyst

6. **Record obligation.** Record the present value of the asset retirement obligation as a credit to the asset retirement obligation liability account, and a debit to the fixed asset account to which the obligation relates. The entry may be handled by the general ledger accountant.
Responsible party: Fixed asset accountant and general ledger accountant
Control issues: The general ledger accountant should file a copy of the journal entry and supporting materials in the journal entry binder.

7. **Create tracking table.** Create a table for this initial liability layer that shows increases in the carrying amount of the liability over time, with the incremental increases attributed to accretion expense. Include in the table the straight-line depreciation of the initial carrying amount of the liability.
Responsible party: Fixed asset accountant and perhaps the financial analyst (see the control issue below)
Control issues: The tracking table is an important document for maintaining information about asset retirement obligations, so it may be useful to have a second person, such as the financial analyst, periodically review it for errors and missing information.

8. **Record accretion expense.** Using the information in the table, set up accretion expense as a debit to the accretion expense account and a credit to the asset retirement obligation liability. Also, record the depreciation expense as a debit to the depreciation expense account and a credit to the accumulated depreciation account. This entry may be handled by the general ledger accountant.
Responsible party: Fixed asset accountant and general ledger accountant
Control issues: The general ledger accountant should file a copy of the journal entry and supporting materials in the journal entry binder.

> **Tip:** Accretion expense is a recurring entry, so set up a recurring entry for it in the accounting software, which ensures that it will be generated in each successive accounting period.

The following exhibit shows a streamlined view of the asset retirement obligation procedure.

Asset Retirement Obligation Process Flow

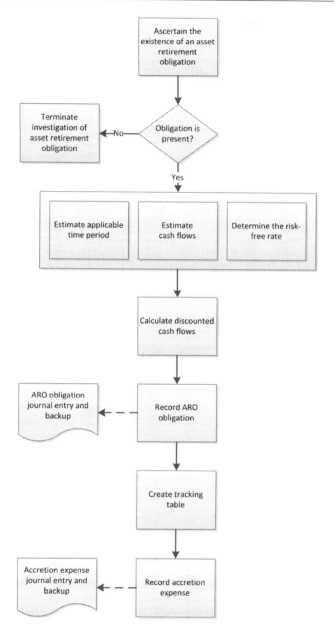

The Intangible Asset Analysis Procedure

Most procedures that apply to tangible fixed assets should also apply to intangible assets. In addition, IFRS allows you to revalue intangible fixed assets under very limited circumstances. Use the following procedure to revalue intangible assets:

1. **Schedule the revaluation.** Consult the asset class revaluation schedule to determine when the next revaluation is to be completed. This should be an annual review that is listed on the accounting department's schedule of activities.
   Responsible party: Fixed asset accountant

2. **Create revaluation schedule.** Run a detailed schedule of the intangible assets within the asset classes to be revalued. This can be a simple export into a spreadsheet if the assets are stored in a software module, or the original document may already be a spreadsheet.
   Responsible party: Fixed asset accountant

3. **Hire appraiser.** Hire an independent appraiser to conduct the revaluations, and forward the detailed schedule to the appraiser. It is easiest to rehire the appraiser from the previous review, since this person already knows about the company's assets, and so is more likely to be efficient in conducting an appraisal.
   Responsible party: Fixed asset accountant

4. **Test for an active market.** In cases where the appraiser is unable to derive a market valuation by reference to an active market, you cannot revalue the intangible asset. Stop any additional revaluation activities for these assets. The appraiser should be able to provide an opinion on this issue.
   Responsible party: Fixed asset accountant and appraiser
   Control issues: Document any determination to consider an active market to exist, since this drives all subsequent revaluation activities.

5. **Account for upward revaluation.** If there is an upward revaluation adjustment for those qualifying intangible assets, debit the fixed asset account for the amount of the incremental increase and credit a gain in other comprehensive income. If the increase reverses a revaluation decrease for the same asset, recognize the gain in profit or loss to the extent of the previous loss, and record any remaining gain in other comprehensive income. The general ledger accountant makes the entry into the accounting system.
   Responsible party: Fixed asset accountant and general ledger accountant
   Control issues: Fully document this transaction for the outside auditors, who will certainly inspect all revaluations.

6. **Account for downward revaluation.** If there is a downward revaluation adjustment for those qualifying intangible assets, recognize the loss in profit or loss with a debit, and credit the fixed asset account. If the decrease reverses a previous revaluation increase for the same asset, recognize the loss in other comprehensive income to the extent of the previous gain, and record any remaining loss in profit or loss. The general ledger accountant makes the entry into the accounting system.

Responsible party: Fixed asset accountant and general ledger accountant
Control issues: Fully document this transaction for the outside auditors, who will certainly inspect all revaluations.

7. **Adjust accumulated amortization.** If there is a revaluation adjustment, eliminate all existing accumulated amortization by debiting the accumulated amortization account and crediting the offsetting amount to the intangible fixed asset account. The general ledger accountant makes this entry.
Responsible party: Fixed asset accountant and general ledger accountant
Control issues: The controller may want to approve this entry, since it may have a significant impact on the accumulated depreciation balance.

8. **Adjust useful life.** If there is a revaluation adjustment, examine the amortization schedule being used for the intangible asset to see if its useful life should be changed. Because of the change in the carrying amount of the asset caused by the revaluation, the amount of prospective amortization expense recognized per period should change, even in the absence of any other changes in assumptions.
Responsible party: Fixed asset accountant
Control issues: All prospective changes to the useful life of an asset should be discussed with the controller, since it impacts the amount of amortization recognized per month.

The following exhibit shows a streamlined view of the intangible asset analysis.

The Asset Tracking Procedure

In a larger business with multiple locations and many fixed assets, a fixed asset audit can be a large-scale endeavor that requires the full-time commitment of several people, as well as tight coordination between them to ascertain the existence and condition of fixed assets. The following procedure assumes that a larger-scale audit is needed:

1. **Freeze asset transfers.** Notify all department managers that you are freezing asset transfers between departments for the duration of the audit. This is needed to ensure that all assets to be audited are not in the process of being transferred elsewhere.
Responsible party: Fixed asset accountant

> **Tip:** This step will freeze transfers, but not necessarily any asset purchases or disposals, so there is still a chance that some asset location information will be incorrect.

Intangible Asset Analysis Process Flow

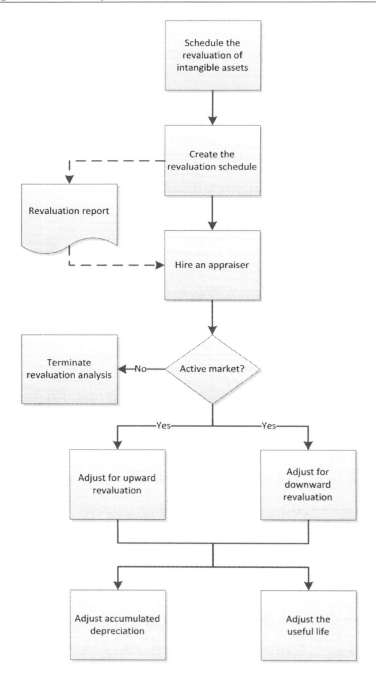

2. **Complete transfer documentation.** Verify that all asset transfer documents have been properly approved and entered into the fixed asset tracking database.
   Responsible party: Fixed asset accountant

3. **Print location report.** Print the fixed asset location report, sorted for the facility in which you plan to conduct the audit.
   Responsible party: Fixed asset accountant

4. **Match assets to report.** As you move through the facility, match the tag number and/or serial number of each asset to the report. Check off those found and note their condition. If the fixed asset database also notes the location of each tag or serial number on an asset, print out this information on the fixed asset location report.
   Responsible party: Fixed asset accountant

> **Tip:** Consider having a qualified maintenance technician assist with this audit, since the fixed asset accountant is probably not qualified to assess the condition of assets.

5. **Note exceptions.** If you find what appear to be fixed assets that are not on the report, note their identification information and locations. See if these are leased assets or assets that are supposed to be in other locations. Review these items with the person responsible for the facility in which you conducted the audit.
   Responsible party: Fixed asset accountant

> **Tip:** Any notification to a responsible party should be in the form of a memo, so there is a record of fixed asset exceptions and the dates on which notifications were sent.

6. **Report back on exceptions.** Have the responsible persons report to you regarding missing assets, and verify their assertions.
   Responsible party: Persons responsible for fixed assets
   Control issues: It may be necessary to interview other people as well as the responsible parties regarding missing assets, since the responsible parties may have fraudulently taken or sold the assets.

7. **Report remaining exceptions.** Report exceptions to the managers of the responsible persons for further action.
   Responsible party: Fixed asset accountant
   Control issues: This notification should be extended to senior management, along with commentary regarding control problems that might have led to the exceptions, as well as any trends in asset losses in certain areas. Senior management may use this information to institute procedural or staffing changes.

8. **Update fixed asset database.** Process the asset transfer documentation for any fixed assets that are proven to have been shifted to another location without any supporting documentation.
Responsible party: Fixed asset accountant
Control issues: Be sure to notify the former and current responsible parties of the formal asset transfer, and send them asset reports that contain the updated information. This officially notifies them of their areas of responsibility.

9. **Update accounting records.** Notify the accounting department of any fixed assets that have been confirmed to be permanently missing, with a request to eliminate them from the general ledger, along with the recognition of any gain or loss, as needed. The general ledger accountant will document and create the required journal entries.
Responsible party: Fixed asset accountant and general ledger accountant
Control issues: Have the controller approve any larger adjusting entries, thereby bringing significant asset custody issues to his or her attention.

10. **Notify internal audit.** Notify the internal audit staff of assets that have been confirmed to be permanently missing, as well as of any other control problems found, with a request for them to review the systems that caused these problems to arise.
Responsible party: Fixed asset accountant

11. **Issue asset condition report.** Report to the chief financial officer, maintenance manager, and financial analyst the condition of the fixed assets found, which is used to update the forecasts for future asset purchases, as well as the need for additional maintenance.
Responsible party: Fixed asset accountant

The following exhibit shows a streamlined view of the fixed asset tracking procedure.

The Asset Disposal Procedure

The disposal of an asset may require the participation of a number of employees in the accounting and purchasing departments, so a broad-based disposal procedure may require the use of several smaller procedures that are linked together to provide comprehensive coverage of the transaction. The following procedure assumes that a company is relatively small, so that only a few people are involved.

Asset Tracking Process Flow

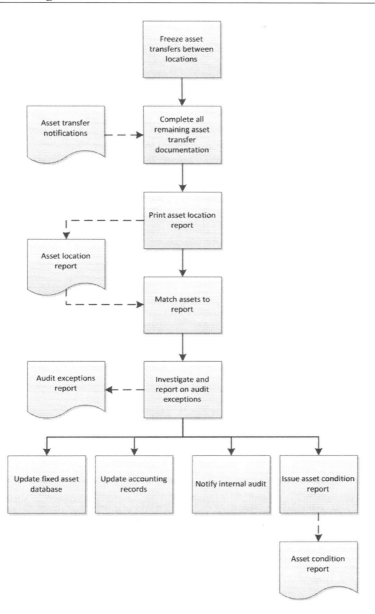

1. **Issue disposal form.** Upon notification that an asset is to be sold or otherwise disposed of, send an asset disposal form to the person responsible for that asset, with instructions for how to complete it. The form was described earlier in the Forms: Asset Disposal Form section.
   Responsible party: Fixed asset accountant

Control issues: It may be useful to include on the form a reminder to wipe all data from computer storage devices that are being disposed of.

2. **Verify approval of disposal.** When the responsible person returns the form, verify that all mandatory fields have been completed, and that a designated manager has signed the form to indicate approval of the proposed transaction.
    Responsible party: Fixed asset accountant and person responsible for the asset
    Control issues: Given the considerable resale value of some assets, it may make sense to be absolutely sure of the responsible person's approval by keeping signature copies on hand, and matching them against the signatures on approval forms.

3. **Forward to purchasing.** Forward the approved disposal form to the purchasing department, which handles the disposal. In reality, this could vary somewhat. For example, if the asset is to be scrapped, the disposal form could instead go to the shipping department, which may deal more directly with the local scrap dealer.
    Responsible party: Fixed asset accountant and purchasing manager
    Control issues: Consider having the shipping manager not allow any fixed assets to be shipped out of the building without a completed disposal form.

4. **Forward disposal notice.** Upon disposal of the asset, the purchasing manager signs the disposal form and returns it to the accounting department, along with a bill of sale and check payment (if sold), or a receipt from a charitable organization, or disclosure of any other disposal method.
    Responsible party: Purchasing manager
    Control issues: The purchasing department should retain a copy of these documents, which provides evidence in case someone subsequently intercepts the payment attached to the disposal form.

5. **Account for the disposal.** If the asset was sold, forward the check payment and bill of sale to the controller. The general ledger accountant removes the asset from the general ledger, along with all associated accumulated depreciation, and records a gain or loss on the sale. The controller also notifies the fixed asset clerk to note the disposal in the detail record for the asset, and forwards the check to the cashier for inclusion in the daily bank deposit.
    Responsible party: Controller, general ledger accountant, fixed asset accountant, cashier
    Control issues: If the payment is in cash, be sure to match the amount received to the amount stated on the bill of sale, and investigate any differences.

6. **File documentation.** The general ledger accountant files a copy of the journal entry and supporting documentation in the journal entry binder.
    Responsible party: General ledger accountant

The following exhibit shows a streamlined view of the asset disposal procedure.

Summary

This chapter contains what may appear to be an inordinate number of procedures. However, there are a number of very specific accounting rules governing the recordation of various aspects of fixed assets, and they must all be addressed. Also, the amounts of cash involved are so large that it only makes sense to impose a greater degree of control over this area. For these reasons, the fixed assets chapter is the largest chapter in the book.

This chapter has dealt with a number of detailed fixed asset accounting issues with which the reader may not be familiar. To learn more about fixed assets, see the author's *Fixed Asset Accounting* book, which is available at the accountingtools.com website.

Asset Disposal Process Flow

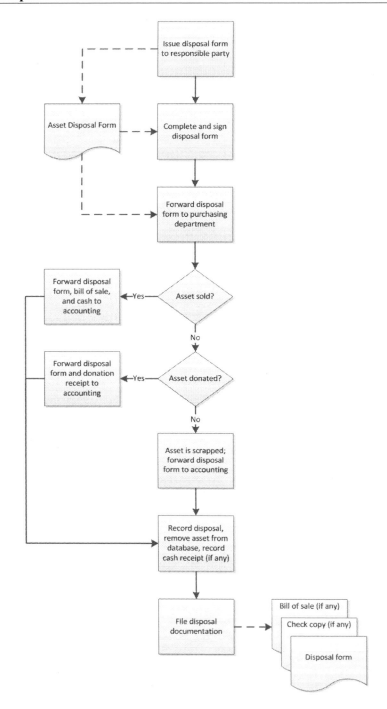

Chapter 17
Treasury Procedures

Introduction

In a larger company, there may be significant cash positions or cash flows that must be properly managed by the treasury department. These tasks include the forecasting of cash flows, investing excess funds, borrowing activities, and hedging foreign currency holdings. Without proper management of these areas, a company puts itself at risk of having sudden cash shortfalls, improperly investing funds, and incurring unexpected foreign exchange losses.

In this chapter, we provide examples of the forms resulting from or used in treasury processes, and then move on to the various treasury procedures. There are several types of treasury activities, so we provide separate procedures for:

- Cash forecasting
- Funds investment
- Cash concentration
- Line of credit borrowing
- Foreign exchange hedging

As usual, procedural improvement tips are provided throughout the text, as well as flowcharts showing a streamlined view of each procedure.

Forms: Cash Forecast

The cash forecast is used by the treasury staff to predict cash flows over the near term. It incorporates cash flow information from a variety of sources to show the most likely cash inflows and outflows. In the following cash forecast format, cash receipts are listed near the top, with detailed cash disbursements listed immediately below. The treasury staff then notes any expected changes in debt levels to arrive at the expected ending cash balance. The format also includes a borrowing base calculation, which is useful for determining the amount of debt available under a company's line of credit that may be used to fund any cash shortfalls indicated in the cash forecast.

Sample Cash Forecast Format

Cash Forecast						
Beginning Cash	Week 1	Week 2	Week 3	Week 4	Week 5	Week 6
Beginning cash:						
Cash Receipts: (+)						
Detailed receivables						
- Identified receivable						
- Identified receivable						
Remaining receivables						
Total cash receipts:						
Cash Disbursements: (-)						
Accounts payable						
Payroll						
Payroll taxes						
Dividends						
Capital purchases						
Total cash disbursements:						
Debt: (+/-):						
Additional debt						
Debt paybacks						
Net debt change:						
Ending cash:						
Borrowing Base:						
Estimated receivables						
80% of receivables < 90 days						
Borrowing base available:						

Forms: Investment Quote Sheet

If a company wants to obtain the best return on its invested funds, it should have a formal process for investigating the investment rates being offered. This is done with an investment quote sheet. The following sample shows that the form is divided into three parts. The top section states the amount of funds available and the targeted date range for the investment. The second section contains the various rate quotes for each type of investment considered acceptable under the company's investment policy. The final section contains the investment that was selected from the preceding quotes.

Sample Investment Quote Sheet

Investment Quote Sheet

Date	Funds Available	Required Investment Period

Quotes:	Approved Investment Vehicles				
Investment Entity	**Bankers' Acceptance**	**Cert. of Deposit**	**Term Deposit**	**Treasury Bills**	**Other** _____
Entity #1 Name	Rate Quote	Rate Quote	Rate Quote	Rate Quote	Rate Quote
Entity #2 Name	Rate Quote	Rate Quote	Rate Quote	Rate Quote	Rate Quote
Entity #3 Name	Rate Quote	Rate Quote	Rate Quote	Rate Quote	Rate Quote
Entity #4 Name	Rate Quote	Rate Quote	Rate Quote	Rate Quote	Rate Quote

Approved Investment:

Entity Name	Funds to Invest	Rate %	Maturity

Treasurer Approval: [signature]	Approval Date

The investment quote sheet is also useful as documentation that investments are being formally documented and approved.

Forms: Drawdown/Repayment Form

When a company accesses its line of credit for cash or pays back part of the outstanding balance, there is a potential for confusion with the lender regarding the specifics of the transactions. The following loan drawdown/repayment form is intended to clarify the terms of each transaction, as well as to require the approval of an authorized person.

The Cash Forecasting Procedure

A primary responsibility of the treasury staff is to project future cash flows, so that it can make better decisions regarding the investment and borrowing of funds in the near future. It is critical to have a consistently-applied process for generated a cash forecast, so that the department can develop reliable cash balance information. This calls for a procedure similar to the one shown below.

Sample Drawdown/Repayment Form

Loan Drawdown/Repayment Form

Customer Address Block	Lender Contact Information

Loan Drawdown/Repayment Information

Requested Transfer Date	Loan Identification Number

☐ Drawdown

☐ Repayment

Dollar Amount	From/To	Bank Account Number

Authorized By: [signature]	Title	Date

1. **Prepare forecast template.** Create a copy of the last cash forecast. Prepare the forecast with the following information:
   - Extend the forecast to cover the new forecast period
   - Delete from the forecast any dates that are now in the past
   - Label the spreadsheet with the forecasting date
   - Clear all numbers from the forecast line items

   A sample cash forecast was presented earlier in this chapter.
   Responsible party: Treasury staff

   > **Tip:** If you are calculating the cash forecast on an electronic spreadsheet, copy the most recent version of the forecast onto a new tab, and label the tab with the date of the forecast. This allows you to keep a historical record of all prior cash forecasts.

2. **Populate the template.** Enter the following information into the cash forecast template for each designated time bucket:
   - Current cash balance
   - The best estimate of cash receipts from open accounts receivable
   - The projected cash disbursements for payroll and payroll tax payments
   - The projected cash disbursements for accounts payable
   - The projected timing of expenditures for capital projects
   - The projected timing of dividend payments

- If the cash forecast extends beyond the period covered by the current group of accounts receivable, estimate the cash receipts from new sales that will arrive during the cash forecast period. The timing of these receipts will likely be based on the company's experience with the timing of cash receipts from the customers to whom sales are expected to be made.
- If the cash forecast extends beyond the period covered by the current group of accounts payable, estimate the cash disbursements related to the cost of goods sold and normal selling and administrative expenses during the relevant cash forecast periods.

Another use of cash that may be included in the cash forecast is that portion of an expected acquisition paid for with cash.

Responsible party: Treasury staff

> **Tip:** It can be very time-consuming to estimate cash receipts for all accounts receivable, so instead consider doing so individually only for the largest accounts receivable, and estimating receipt dates more generally for the remaining receivables.

> **Tip:** Compile a checklist of all the sources of information for the cash forecast and use it every time a new forecast version is compiled, to ensure that every issue impacting cash is included.

3. **Review and revise the forecast.** Print an initial copy of the forecast and review it for reasonableness. If any cash inflows or outflows appear to be unusual, confirm them with the person who compiled the information. It may be necessary to avoid funding shortfalls by shifting planned expenditures further into the future. This review and revision process can require several iterations.
Responsible party: Treasury staff

> **Tip:** A good way to detect flaws in a forecast is to compare the cash flow results for each forecast period to the results predicted for the same periods in the preceding cash forecast, and to investigate any differences.

4. **Adjust for funding changes.** If the cash forecast indicates that the company can invest funds or must borrow to meet expenditure requirements, discuss these issues with the treasurer. Incorporate into the forecast any cash withdrawals for new investments or the reduction of loans. Also make note of any loan drawdowns needed to fund forecasted cash requirements.
Responsible party: Treasury staff and treasurer

Control issues: Consider having the treasurer formally approve the final version of the cash forecast, since the treasurer will likely be held accountable if the forecast turns out to be flawed.

> **Tip:** It may be useful to note on the forecast the projected remaining borrowing base against which the company can draw down funds from its line of credit. This is useful for planning when to obtain additional debt.

5. **Distribute the forecast.** Send copies of the forecast to all parties on the distribution list, such as the controller and chief financial officer.
   Responsible party: Treasury staff
   Control issues: If the cash forecast is distributed by e-mail, consider issuing it as a locked spreadsheet or a PDF document, so the recipients do not make changes to the information. Also, lock down the spreadsheet model so that it is not inadvertently modified within the treasury department.

The following exhibit shows a streamlined view of the cash forecasting procedure.

The Funds Investment Procedure

The investment of funds is a minor issue for those businesses that are perpetually short on cash, since they merely park all available funds in their checking accounts. However, an organization with significant cash balances should consider a more methodical approach to investing, so that it can wring some additional interest income from its excess cash. The funds investment procedure is outlined below:

1. **Obtain cash forecast.** Obtain the most recent, finalized version of the cash forecast. See the preceding cash forecasting procedure for more information.
   Responsible party: Treasury staff
   Control issues: Be sure to obtain only the approved final version. There may be several earlier versions floating around in the department from one of the earlier iterations of the forecast.

2. **Calculate investable cash.** From the cash forecast, calculate the amount of cash available for investment purposes, as well as the time period over which the funds can be invested. Further, determine whether there is any cash being released from current investments that can be returned to an investment vehicle.
   Responsible party: Treasury staff

Cash Forecasting Process Flow

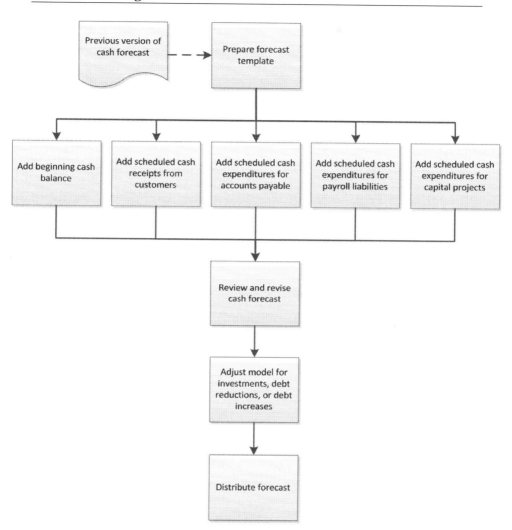

3. **Plan per investment guidelines.** Determine the best investment, based on the required liquidity level indicated by the cash forecast, and as allowed by the company's investment guidelines.

   Responsible party: Treasury staff

   Control issues: There should be investment guidelines approved by the chief financial officer that the treasury staff is required to follow when engaging in investing activities.

> **Tip:** Do not enter into an investment where funds cannot be liquidated until a date beyond the period of the cash forecast. If you were to do so, a sudden cash shortfall occurring just beyond the cash forecast period could place the company in severe financial straits until such time as the investment could be liquidated.

4. **Obtain quotes.** Contact the investment entities with which the company invests its funds, and obtain quotes from them for the best return on investment for the investment vehicle that the company plans to obtain. Summarize these quotes on a quote sheet. A sample investment quote sheet was presented earlier in this chapter.
   Responsible party: Treasury staff
   Control issues: The treasurer should periodically examine the quote sheets to ensure that the treasury staff is obtaining quotes, rather than investing solely with one entity. The internal audit staff may also want to review the quote sheets to ensure that the treasury staff is complying with the company's investment policy.

5. **Complete investment purchase form.** Based on the quotes listed on the quote sheet, select the best investment and document it on the investment purchase form. Have the treasurer review and approve the form.
   Responsible party: Treasury staff
   Control issues: The treasurer is ultimately responsible for the investments made by the company, and so should have the opportunity to review each one before it is finalized. The treasurer may also want to verify that the investment entities listed on the form are ones that the company has pre-approved.

6. **Make investments.** Send a copy of the investment form to the investment manager, who places the investment with the designated investment entity.
   Responsible party: Investment manager

7. **Record transaction.** Upon receipt of a confirmation from the investment entity, send a copy of the confirmation and the investment form to the general ledger accountant, who records the investment in the general ledger. This transaction is a debit to the investment account and a credit to the cash account. Another copy goes to the person responsible for the cash forecast, who needs to know if the invested cash will not be available during any portion of the forecasting period.
   Responsible party: Investment manager, general ledger accountant, and treasury staff
   Control issues: The confirmation is always retained as proof that the proper investment was made. Also, the general ledger accountant could send a copy of each investment-related journal entry to the treasurer; this practice may lead to the detection of incorrect investments.

8. **File documents.** Staple the confirmation to the investment form and file the documents by date. These documents are useful as a reference source, and may

be reviewed by the internal audit staff when they periodically investigate the treasury function.

Responsible party: Investment manager

Control issues: Someone could periodically match the interest rate stated on the confirmation to the amount indicated in the initial quote, to see if an investment entity is in fact paying out the interest rate that it quoted.

Tip: If an investment entity has a history of bidding one investment rate and paying a lower rate, that entity should be removed from the company's list of approved investment entities.

Tip: The treasury staff should reconcile the accounting records of investments at the end of each accounting period to their own records, and track down the reasons for any differences.

The following exhibit shows a streamlined view of the funds investment procedure.

The Cash Concentration Procedure

When a company has a number of subsidiaries, a common treasury activity is to periodically sweep all unneeded cash from the accounts of subsidiaries into a central concentration account that is used for investment purposes. Transferring funds in this way creates an intercompany loan from the subsidiaries to the parent company, on which the company should make inter-company interest payments. These actions are needed to derive the correct statement of financial position and profitability of each subsidiary. There may also be income tax implications at the subsidiary level. The procedure for cash concentration is outlined below:

Tip: Wherever possible, use automated cash sweeps into the concentration account. This eliminates all treasury staff time that would otherwise be needed to transfer funds. The following procedure assumes that automated sweeps are being used.

---

1. **Calculate inter-company loans.** At the end of each reporting period, use bank statements to determine the amount of cash that was swept from the various subsidiary cash accounts into the corporate parent's cash concentration account. Add to this amount the beginning balance of any inter-company loans from the subsidiaries. This information is needed to calculate the amount of interest to credit to each subsidiary.

   Responsible party: Treasury staff

   Control issues: Consider tracking cash sweeps from the bank statements for the bank accounts of the subsidiaries to the bank statement of the cash concentration account. If there is a difference between the two sets of information, contact the bank for an explanation.

Funds Investment Process Flow

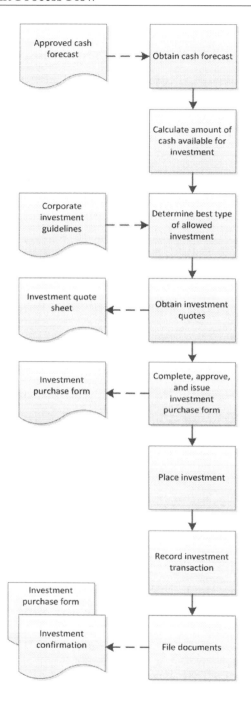

2. **Deduct debit balance replenishments.** The parent company may have issued funds to the subsidiary bank accounts during the period to offset debit balances. If so, deduct these amounts from the inter-company loans.
Responsible party: Treasury staff
Control issues: As was the case in the last step, consider tracking these replenishments through the bank statements of both the parent company *and* its subsidiaries. If there is a difference between the two sets of information, contact the bank for an explanation.

3. **Calculate average loan balance.** Calculate the average amount of inter-company loans outstanding during the period. The easiest approach is to add together the beginning and ending loan balances for the period and divide by two. An alternative is to determine the actual balance on each day of the month. Either approach is needed to derive the inter-company interest due to each subsidiary.
Responsible party: Treasury staff

4. **Determine interest rate.** Obtain the interest rate charged to the company by its primary lender for the company's outstanding debt as of the end of the reporting period. If there is no external debt outstanding, contact the lender to determine the rate that it would currently charge the company if there had been any debt.
Responsible party: Treasury staff
Control issues: Document the source of the interest rate, since this information may be reviewed by the company's auditors.

5. **Calculate inter-company interest.** Multiply the interest rate from the preceding step by the average loan balance for the month for each subsidiary.
Responsible party: Treasury staff
Control issues: Compare the amount of interest to be credited to each subsidiary to the amount calculated for them in each of the past few accounting periods, to see if the amount is reasonable.

6. **Record loans and interest.** Compile the incremental change in intercompany loans from subsidiaries and interest payable to subsidiaries, and record this information in a journal entry. Forward the journal entry, along with copies of supporting documentation, to the general ledger accountant for entry into the general ledger.
Responsible party: Treasury staff and general ledger accountant
Control issues: After the financial statements are released, the treasury staff can compare the intercompany loan balances and interest income listed in the financial statements to its own records, and bring any issues to the attention of the general ledger accountant.

7. **File documents.** Assemble the documentation of loan balances and allocated interest and file it by accounting period. This information may be needed as

backup for the amount of inter-company loans and interest recorded in the company's accounts.

Responsible party: Treasury staff

Control issues: Consider storing this information in three-ring binders, to make it easier to keep the information in order by date.

The following exhibit shows a streamlined view of the cash concentration procedure.

The Line of Credit Borrowing Procedure

One of the most common tasks for the treasury department is to borrow from the corporate line of credit. If the company has made the decision to maintain a low cash balance and fund most of its expenditures from a line of credit, shifting cash into and out of a line of credit may be a daily or weekly event. The procedure for borrowing from a line of credit is outlined below:

1. **Determine cash requirements.** Review the near-term cash forecast to estimate the amount of cash that must be borrowed from the line of credit.
    Responsible party: Treasury staff

    > **Tip:** The amount to borrow is based entirely on the accuracy of the cash forecast, so it is worthwhile to regularly evaluate the ability of the cash forecasting methodology to determine a projected cash balance, and adjust the forecasting system as necessary.

    > **Tip:** Evaluate any long-term investments to see if they will be liquidated in time to offset the required amount of cash indicated by the cash forecast.

2. **Calculate debt availability.** Calculate the amount of the borrowing base that can be applied to the line of credit. For example, a lender might allow a borrowing base of 80% of accounts receivable that are less than 90 days old. If the amount of the borrowing base is currently $500,000 and the amount of the line of credit already extended is $400,000, the amount of available debt is $100,000.
    Responsible party: Treasury staff

    > **Tip:** There is a certain amount of flex in the calculation of debt availability, since many businesses issue a large number of invoices at the end of each month, which creates a surge in the borrowing base and therefore the amount of available debt. Thus, it may be possible to borrow considerably more money a few days after month-end than a few days before month-end.

Cash Concentration Process Flow

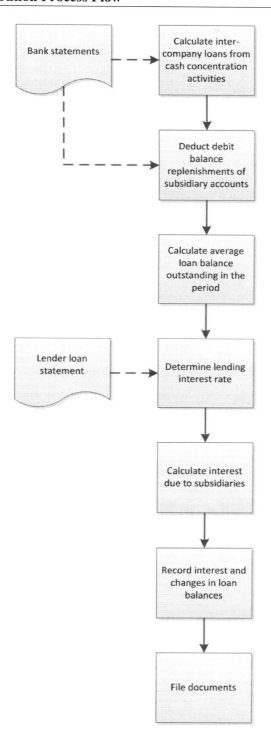

3. **Complete borrowing form.** Fill out a loan drawdown/repayment form that stipulates the amount of cash that the company needs, when the cash should be transferred, and the number of the account into which the funds should be deposited. A sample of the form was presented earlier in this chapter. Have an authorized person review and sign the form.
Responsible party: Treasury staff
Control issues: Keep a copy of each authorized drawdown/repayment form. The auditors may want to review these forms to see if all borrowings and repayments were authorized.

> **Tip:** The lender may be comfortable with increasing a line of credit with just a phone call from the treasury staff. However, it is better to document and authorize the approval of additional debt with a borrowing form.

4. **Deliver form to lender.** Either e-mail or fax the form to the lender. Contact the lender to confirm receipt of the document. Confirm that the cash has been transferred into the designated company bank account.
Responsible party: Treasury staff

5. **Record debt.** Send a copy of the drawdown/repayment form to the general ledger accountant, who records it in the general ledger.
Responsible party: Treasury staff and general ledger accountant
Control issues: The treasury staff may want to maintain its own informal reckoning of the outstanding amount of the line of credit, and compare it to the stated amount in the financial statements at the end of each month.

6. **File documents.** The lender should send a confirmation of any line of credit drawdown. Staple this confirmation to the department's copy of the drawdown/repayment form and file it.
Responsible party: Treasury staff

> **Tip:** The treasury staff should reconcile any differences between the company's record of a loan balance and the loan balance indicated by the lender.

The following exhibit shows a streamlined view of the line of credit borrowing procedure.

Borrowing Process Flow

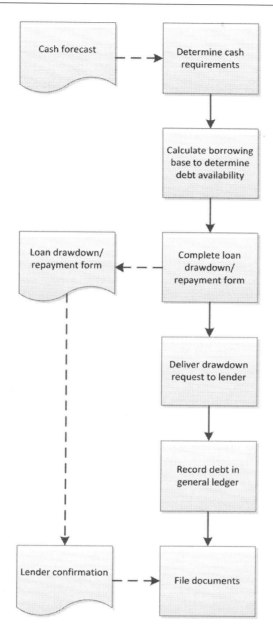

The Foreign Exchange Hedging Procedure

When a business has current or expected holdings or obligations involving foreign currencies, it may be prudent to create a hedging transaction to mitigate the company's potential losses arising from exchange rate fluctuations. A foreign exchange hedging procedure is outlined below:

1. **Calculate hedge requirements.** Based on the company's forecast of foreign currency holdings or obligations, determine the amount and duration of the hedging transaction needed to offset these holdings or obligations.
   Responsible party: Treasury staff

2. **Examine preliminary hedge.** Obtain information about the prospective hedge, and address the following issues:
   - Verify the sufficiency of the counterparty's credit rating
   - Determine the level of effectiveness of the hedging strategy
   - Review the proposed contract for legal issues
   - Obtain approval of the hedge

   Responsible party: Treasury staff, treasurer, and corporate counsel
   Control issues: It may be useful to use a proposed hedge signoff sheet, so that each person involved in a hedge can formally document that their assigned tasks were completed.

3. **Begin hedge.** Enter into the hedging transaction.
   Responsible party: Treasury staff
   Control issues: Be sure to confirm the details of the hedging transaction with the counterparty. Otherwise, you may find that the terms of the hedge do not meet the company's expectations, and may need to close out the transaction and start over.

Tip: An alternative to waiting for confirmation of a hedge from the other party is to issue your own confirmation. If the other party does not take issue with your confirmation, this can be taken as a form of agreement with the stated terms.

---

4. **Document the hedge.** Create all hedging documentation required under the applicable accounting standards. This includes documentation of:
   - How the company plans to measure the effectiveness of the hedging transaction
   - The relationship between the foreign exchange position and the hedging instrument
   - The risk management objectives of the company
   - The specifics of the hedging strategy

   This information is needed to properly account for the hedge.
   Responsible party: Treasury staff

Control issues: Be sure to confirm the details of the hedging transaction with the counterparty. Otherwise, you may find that the terms of the hedge do not meet the company's expectations.

5. **Account for the hedge.** At the end of each reporting period, charge to comprehensive income the effective portion of a hedge for any gains or losses resulting from having marked the hedge to market. Also, charge to profit or loss any ineffective portion of a hedge that is caused by having marked to market. If any hedge losses are considered to be non-recoverable and they have previously been recorded in other comprehensive income, shift them to earnings.
Responsible party: Accounting staff
Control issues: To ensure that this step is completed, include it in the list of period-end closing activities.

6. **Close out the hedge.** Once the hedging transaction has been completed and settled, move all gains and losses initially recorded in the other comprehensive income account to earnings.
Responsible party: Accounting staff
Control issues: Review the other comprehensive income account to ensure that all transactions related to a closed hedge have been removed from that account.

> **Tip:** There are onerous accounting standards for creating and maintaining an acceptable hedge. If the accounting requirements appear excessively oppressive for hedge documentation, consider not following the dictates of the accounting standards. Avoiding rule compliance only means that hedging results must be recorded as profits or losses at once, rather than being deferred.

The following exhibit shows a streamlined view of the foreign exchange hedging procedure.

Summary

The foundation of nearly all treasury department activities is the cash forecast. If it is inaccurate, a business cannot properly invest its funds in longer-term (and presumably higher-yielding) investments, nor can it reasonably estimate when it will need to access its line of credit. For these reasons, you should continually compare forecasted to actual results, determine the reasons for variances, and incorporate this information into the next forecast. In addition, it may be useful to experiment with longer-term cash forecasts, which allow the treasurer to plan further into the future for expected cash flows. Once a business has a more accurate and longer-term forecast, it becomes much easier to engage in the other procedures noted in this chapter.

Foreign Exchange Hedging Process Flow

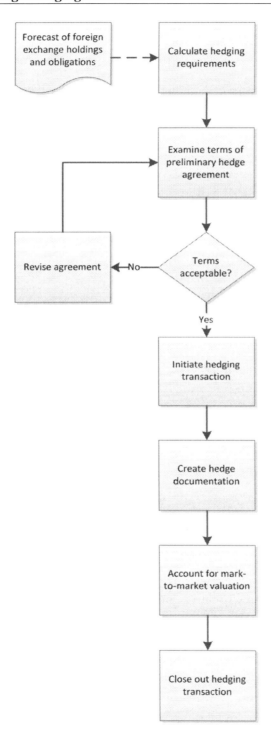

Chapter 18
Closing the Books Procedures

Introduction

The single most important work product of the accounting department is the financial statements. In this chapter, we make note of the various steps required to close the books. There are no forms involved in the closing process; instead, there are many work steps covering a multitude of functional areas. We provide separate procedures for:

- Closing the books – private company
- Closing the books – public company

As usual, procedural improvement tips are provided throughout the text. For a more comprehensive view of the closing process, see the latest edition of the author's *Closing the Books* book.

Related Podcast Episodes: Episodes 16 through 25 of the Accounting Best Practices Podcast discuss how to close the books. You can listen to them at: **accountingtools.com/podcasts** or **iTunes**

Closing the Books – Private Company

The closing process does not begin after a reporting period has been completed. Instead, the accounting staff begins to prepare for it well in advance. By doing so, a number of items can be completed in a leisurely manner before the end of the month, leaving fewer items for the busier period immediately following the end of the period. Accordingly, we have grouped closing steps into the following categories:

1. *Prior steps*. These are steps needed to complete the processing of the financial statements, and which can usually be completed before the end of the reporting period.
2. *Core steps*. These are the steps that are required for the creation of financial statements, and which cannot be completed prior to the end of the reporting period.
3. *Delayed steps*. These are the activities that can be safely delayed until after the issuance of the financial statements, but which are still part of the closing process.

The steps in this procedure do not necessarily represent the exact sequence of activities that a business will follow when closing the books, and so may be altered to fit the circumstances. The closing procedure for a private company is as follows:

1. **Prior step – update reserves**. Under the accrual basis of accounting, one should create a reserve in the expectation that expenses will be incurred in the future that are related to revenues generated now. Examples of these reserves are the allowance for doubtful accounts and the sales returns allowance.

Tip: There is no need to create a reserve if the balance in the account is going to be immaterial. Instead, many businesses can generate perfectly adequate financial statements that only have a few reserves, while charging all other expenditures to expense as incurred

---

2. **Core step – Issue customer invoices**. Part of the closing process nearly always includes the issuance of month-end invoices to customers, especially in situations (such as consulting) where billable hours are compiled throughout the month and then billed at one time, or where a company has a practice of shipping most of its products near the end of the month. In other cases, invoices may have been issued throughout the month, leaving only a residual number to be issued as part of the closing process. Irrespective of the number of invoices to be issued, invoices are always an important part of the closing process, because they are the primary method for recognizing revenue. Consequently, the billing staff normally spends a significant part of the closing process verifying that all possible invoices have, in fact, been created. This verification process may include a comparison of the shipping log to the invoice register, or a comparison of the shipping log to the timekeeping system where billable hours are stored or to a listing of open contracts. If some revenues are considered to not yet be billable, but to have been fully earned by the company, accrue the revenue with a journal entry.

3. **Core step – value inventory**. Potentially the most time-consuming activity in the closing process is valuing ending inventory. This involves the following steps:
   1. *Physical count*. Either conduct an ending inventory count or have an adequate perpetual inventory system in place that yields a verifiable ending inventory.
   2. *Determine the cost of the ending inventory*. There are several methods available for assigning a cost to the ending inventory, such as the first in first out method, the last in first out method, and standard costing.
   3. *Allocate overhead*. Aggregate overhead costs into cost pools and then allocate the amounts in these pools to ending inventory and the cost of goods sold.
   4. *Adjust the valuation*. It may be necessary to reduce the amount of ending inventory due to the lower of cost or market rule, or for the presence of obsolete inventory.

If there is a relatively small investment in inventory, it may not be so necessary to invest a large amount of time in closing inventory, since the size of potential errors is substantially reduced.

4. **Core step – calculate depreciation**. Once all fixed assets have been recorded in the accounting records for the month, calculate the amount of depreciation (for tangible assets) and amortization (for intangible assets). This is a significant issue for companies with a large investment in fixed assets, but may be so insignificant in other situations that it is sufficient to only record depreciation at the end of the year. If the company is constructing fixed assets (as would be the case for a factory or company headquarters) and have incurred debt to do so, it may be necessary to capitalize some interest expense into the cost of the fixed assets.

5. **Core step – accrue expenses**. It will probably be necessary to accrue expenses for some items as part of the closing process, usually because the company has not yet received supplier invoices as of the date when the financial statements are released, or because it has not recorded a payroll that spans the ending days of the month.

6. **Core step – consolidate division results**. If there are company divisions that forward their financial results to the parent company, the largest issue from the perspective of the close is simply obtaining the information in a timely manner. This information may be provided in the format of a trial balance. The accounting staff then inputs the summary totals for all accounts provided into the general ledger of the parent company. This process is repeated for all divisions. If the company uses the same accounting software throughout the business, it may be quite simple to consolidate the division results, but only if the software is networked together. Otherwise, it will be necessary to create a separate journal entry to record the results of each division.

> **Tip:** If you record division results with a journal entry, the transaction likely involves a large number of line items. To reduce the risk of recording this information incorrectly, create a journal entry template in the accounting software that includes only the relevant accounts. If the entries for the various divisions are substantially different, consider creating a separate template for each one.

7. **Core step – eliminate intercompany transactions**. If there are several divisions within a company for which accounting transactions are recorded separately, it is possible that they do business with each other. For example, if a company is vertically integrated, some subsidiaries may sell their output to other subsidiaries, which in turn sell their output to other subsidiaries. If this is the case, they are generating intercompany transactions to record the sales. Inter-company transactions must be eliminated from the consolidated financial statements of the business, since not doing so would artificially inflate the

revenue of the company as a whole. This elimination requires you to reverse the sale and offsetting account receivable for each such transaction.

8. **Core step – review journal entries**. It is entirely possible that some journal entries were made incorrectly, in duplicate, or not at all. Print the list of standard journal entries and compare it to the actual entries made in the general ledger, just to ensure that they were entered in the general ledger correctly. Another test is to have someone review the detailed calculations supporting each journal entry, and trace them through to the actual entries in the general ledger. This second approach takes more time, but is quite useful for ensuring that all necessary journal entries have been made correctly.

9. **Core step – reconcile accounts**. It is important to examine the contents of the balance sheet accounts to verify that the recorded assets and liabilities are supposed to be there. It is quite possible that some items are still listed in an account that should have been flushed out of the balance sheet a long time ago, which can be quite embarrassing if they are still on record when the auditors review the company's books at the end of the year. Here are several situations that a proper account reconciliation would have caught:

- *Prepaid assets.* A company issues a $10,000 bid bond to a local government. The company loses the bid, but is not repaid. The asset lingers on the books until year-end, when the auditors inquire about it, and the company then recovers the funds from the local government.
- *Accrued revenue.* A company accrues revenue of $50,000 for a services contract, but forgets to reverse the entry in the following month, when it invoices the full $50,000 to the customer. This results in the double re-cordation of revenue, which is not spotted until year-end. The controller then reverses the accrual, thereby unexpectedly reducing revenues for the full year by $50,000.
- *Depreciation.* A company calculates the depreciation on several hundred assets with an electronic spreadsheet, which unfortunately does not track when to stop depreciating assets. A year-end review finds that the company charged $40,000 of excess depreciation to expense.
- *Accumulated depreciation.* A company has been disposing of its assets for years, but has never bothered to eliminate the associated accumulated depreciation from its balance sheet. Doing so reduces both the fixed asset and accumulated depreciation accounts by 50%.
- *Accounts payable.* A company does not compare its accounts payable detail report to the general ledger account balance, which is $8,000 lower than the detail. The auditors spot the error and require a correcting entry at year-end, so that the account balance matches the detail report.

These issues and many more are common problems encountered at year-end. To prevent the extensive embarrassment and error corrections caused by these problems, conduct account reconciliations every month for the larger accounts, and occasionally review the detail for the smaller accounts, too. The following are some of the account reconciliations worth conducting, as well as the specific issues to look for:

Sample Account Reconciliation List

Account	Reconciliation Discussion
Cash	There can be a number of unrecorded checks, deposits, and bank fees that are only spotted with a bank reconciliation. It is permissible to do a partial bank reconciliation a day or two before the close, but completely ignoring it is not a good idea.
Accounts receivable, trade	The accounts receivable detail report should match the account balance. If not, there is likely to be a journal entry that should be eliminated from this account.
Accounts receivable, other	This account usually includes a large proportion of accounts receivable from employees, which are probably being deducted from their paychecks over time. This is a prime source of errors, since payroll deductions may not have been properly reflected in this account.
Accrued revenue	It is good practice to reverse all accrued revenue out of this account at the beginning of every period, so that you are forced to create new accruals every month. Thus, if there is a residual balance in the account, it probably should not be there.
Prepaid assets	This account may contain a variety of assets that will be charged to expense in the short term, so it may require frequent reviews to ensure that items have been flushed out in a timely manner.
Inventory	If the company is using a periodic inventory system, match the inventory account to the ending inventory balance, which calls for a monthly reconciliation. However, if a perpetual inventory system is being used, inadequate cycle counting can lead to incorrect inventory balances. Thus, the level of reconciliation work depends upon the quality of the supporting inventory tracking system.
Fixed assets	It is quite likely that fixed assets will initially be recorded in the wrong fixed asset account, or that they are disposed of incorrectly. Reconcile the account to the fixed asset detail report at least once a quarter to spot and correct these issues.
Accumulated depreciation	The balance in this account may not match the fixed asset detail if you have not removed the accumulated depreciation from the account upon the sale or disposal of an asset. This is not a critical issue, but still warrants an occasional review.
Accounts payable, trade	The accounts payable detail report should match the account balance. If not, you probably included a journal entry in the account, and should reverse the entry.
Accrued expenses	This account can include a large number of accruals for such expenses as wages, vacations, and benefits. It is good practice to reverse all of these expenses in the month following recordation. Thus, if there is a residual balance, there may be an excess accrual still on the books.

Account	Reconciliation Discussion
Sales taxes payable	If state and local governments mandate the forwarding of collected sales taxes every month, this means that beginning account balances should have been paid out during the subsequent month. Consequently, there should not be any residual balances from the preceding month, unless payment intervals are longer than one month.
Income taxes payable	The amount of income taxes paid on a quarterly basis does not have to match the accrued liability, so there can be a residual balance in the account. However, you should still examine the account, if only to verify that scheduled payments have been made.
Notes payable	The balance in this account should exactly match the account balance of the lender, barring any exceptions for in-transit payments to the lender.
Equity	In an active equity environment where there are frequent stock issuances or treasury stock purchases, these accounts may require considerable review to ensure that the account balances can be verified. However, if there is only sporadic account activity, it may be acceptable to reconcile at much longer intervals.

10. **Core step – close subsidiary ledgers**. Depending on the type of accounting software in use, it may be necessary to resolve any open issues in subsidiary ledgers, create a transaction to shift the totals in these balances to the general ledger (called *posting*), and then close the accounting periods within the subsidiary ledgers and open the next accounting period. This may involve ledgers for inventory, accounts receivable, and accounts payable. Other accounting software systems (typically those developed more recently) do not have subsidiary ledgers, or at least use ones that do not require posting, and so are essentially invisible from the perspective of closing the books.

11. **Core step – create financial statements**. When all of the preceding steps have been completed, print the financial statements, which include the income statement, balance sheet, and statement of cash flows. If the financial statements are only to be distributed internally, it may be acceptable to only issue the income statement and balance sheet, and dispense with the statement of cash flows. Reporting to people outside of the company generally calls for issuance of the complete set of financial statements.

12. **Core step – review financial statements**. Review the financial statements for errors. There are several ways to do so, including:
    - *Horizontal analysis*. Print reports that show the income statement, balance sheet, and statement of cash flows for the past twelve months on a rolling basis. Track across each line item to see if there are any unusual declines or spikes in comparison to the results of prior periods, and investigate those items. This is the best review technique.

- *Budget versus actual.* Print an income statement that shows budgeted versus actual results, and investigate any larger variances. This is a less effective review technique, because it assumes that the budget is realistic, and also because a budget is not usually available for the balance sheet or statement of cash flows.

Tip: There will almost always be problems with the first iteration of the financial statements. Expect to investigate and correct several items before issuing a satisfactory set of financials. To reduce the amount of time needed to review financial statement errors during the core closing period, consider doing so a few days prior to month-end; this may uncover a few errors, leaving a smaller number to investigate later on.

---

13. **Core step – accrue tax liabilities**. There may be a need to accrue an income tax liability based on the amount of net profit or loss reported in the financial statements. There are several issues to consider when creating this accrual:
    - *Income tax rate.* In most countries that impose an income tax, the tax rate begins at a low level and then gradually moves up to a higher tax rate that corresponds to higher levels of income. When accruing income taxes, use the average income tax rate that you expect to experience for the full year. Otherwise, the first quarter of the year will have a lower tax rate than later months, which is caused by the tax rate schedule, rather than any changes in company operational results.
    - *Losses.* If the company has earned a profit in a prior period of the year and has now generated a loss, accrue for a tax rebate, which will offset the tax expense that was recorded earlier. Doing so creates the correct amount of tax liability when you look at year-to-date results. If there was no prior profit and no reasonable prospect of one, then do not accrue for a tax rebate, since it is more likely than not that the company will not receive the rebate.
    - *Net operating loss carryforwards.* If the company has a net operating loss carryforward on its books, you may be able to use it to offset any income taxes in the current period. If so, there is no need to accrue for an income tax expense. A net operating loss (NOL) carryforward is a loss experienced in an earlier period that could not be completely offset against prior-period profits. This residual loss can be carried forward for up to 20 years, during which time it can be offset against any reported taxable income. If there is still an NOL remaining after 20 years have expired, it can no longer be used to offset profits.

14. **Core step – close the month**. Once all accounting transactions have been entered in the accounting system, you should close the month in the accounting software. This means prohibiting any further transactions in the general ledger in the old accounting period, as well as allowing the next accounting period to

accept transactions. These steps are important, so that the accounting staff does not inadvertently enter transactions into the wrong accounting periods.

15. **Core step – add disclosures**. If you are issuing financial statements to readers other than the management team, consider adding disclosures to the basic set of financial statements. There are many disclosures required under the various accounting standards. It is especially important to include a complete set of disclosures if the financial statements are being audited. If so, the company's auditors will offer advice regarding which disclosures to include. You should allocate a large amount of time to the proper construction and error-checking of disclosures, for they contain a number of references to the financial statements and subsets of financial information extracted from the statements, and this information could be wrong. Thus, every time you create a new iteration of the financial statements, update the disclosures as well.

16. **Core step – issue financial statements**. The final core step in closing the books is to issue the financial statements. There are several ways to do this. If you are interested in reducing the total time required for someone to receive the financial statements, convert the entire package to PDF documents and e-mail them to the recipients. Doing so eliminates the mail float that would otherwise be required. If you are incorporating a number of reports into the financial statement package, this may require the purchase of a document scanner.

17. **Delayed step – issue customer invoices**. From the perspective of closing the books, it is more important to formulate all customer invoices than it is to issue those invoices to customers. Consequently, issue the invoices immediately after the financial statements have been produced.

18. **Delayed step – closing metrics**. If you have an interest in closing the books more quickly, consider tracking a small set of metrics related to the close. The objective of having these metrics is not necessarily to attain a world-class closing speed, but rather to spot the bottleneck areas of the close that are preventing a more rapid issuance of the financial statements. Thus, you need to have a set of metrics that delve sufficiently far into the workings of the closing process to spot the bottlenecks. An example of such metrics follows. Note that the total time required to close the books and issue financial statements is six days, but that the closing time for most of the steps needed to close the books is substantially shorter. Only the valuation of inventory and the bank reconciliation metrics reveal long closing intervals. Thus, this type of metric measurement and presentation allows you to quickly spot where there are opportunities to compress the closing process.

Sample Metrics Report for Closing the Books

	Day 1	Day 2	Day 3	Day 4	Day 5	Day 6
Issue financials	xxx	xxx	xxx	xxx	xxx	**Done**
Supplier invoices	xxx	**Done**				
Customer invoices	xxx	xxx	**Done**			
Accrued expenses	xxx	xxx	**Done**			
Inventory valuation	xxx	xxx	xxx	xxx	**Done**	
Bank reconciliation	xxx	xxx	xxx	**Done**		
Fixed assets	xxx	**Done**				
Payroll	**Done**					

19. **Delayed step – document future closing changes**. After reviewing the closing metrics in the preceding step, you will likely want to make some improvements to the closing process. Incorporate these changes into a schedule of activities for the next close, and review any resulting changes in responsibility with the accounting staff. Do this as soon after the close as possible, since this is the time when any problems with the close will be fresh, and the accounting staff will be most interested in fixing them during the next close.

Closing the Books Procedure – Public Company

A publicly held company is required by the Securities and Exchange Commission (SEC) to file a large report concerning its financial condition at the end of each quarter. These are the Form 10-Q (for quarterly filings) and Form 10-K (for annual filings).

There are a number of time-consuming steps involved in the production of the Forms 10-Q and 10-K. In fact, though you may have an excellent system in place for producing reliable financial statements within a few days of month-end, the additional steps are so onerous that it may be difficult to file the reports with the SEC in a timely manner, even though the filing dates are a number of weeks later.

> **Tip:** If the company is a small one with a minimal public valuation, consider outsourcing the construction of the Forms 10-Q and 10-K to outside specialists. These reports require particular types of knowledge that the accounting staff of a small business is unlikely to have, which makes outsourcing a good option. However, since these specialists are overwhelmed with work from all of their clients following the end of each quarter, the company's reports may be filed near or on the last allowable date.

The additional steps needed to close the books for a publicly held company include all of the following:

1. **Auditor investigation**. The company's outside auditors must conduct a review of the company's financial statements and disclosures for its quarterly results, and a full audit of its annual results. A *review* is a service under which an auditor obtains limited assurance that there are no material modifications that

need to be made to an entity's financial statements for them to be in conformity with the applicable financial reporting framework. An *audit* is the review and verification of an entity's accounting records, as well as the physical inspection of its assets. The auditor then attests to the fairness of presentation of the financial statements and related disclosures. An audit is more time-consuming and expensive than a review. The auditor investigation is the most time-consuming of the public company requirements. The company can reduce the amount of time required for a review or audit by providing full staff support to the audit team, as well as by having all requested information available as of the beginning of the audit or review work.

2. **Legal review**. It would be extremely unwise to issue the financial statement package without first having legal counsel review the statements and (especially) the disclosures to ensure that all required disclosures have been made, and to verify that all statements made are correct and fully supportable. This review is usually completed near or after the end of the work done by the auditors, but can be scheduled slightly sooner if the disclosures are substantially complete at that time.

> **Tip:** The auditors can waste a considerable amount of time double-checking and triple-checking the accuracy of the disclosures that accompany the financial statements. Doing so delays the closing process, as well as increasing the fees charged by the auditors. To reduce the auditor time spent reviewing the disclosures, have one or more in-house personnel review them in advance.

3. **Officer certification**. Depending upon what type of form is being issued, different company officers are required to certify that the information in the financial statements presents fairly the financial condition and results of operations of the business. Since there are substantial penalties and jail time involved if an officer were to make a false certification, it should be no surprise that the signing officers will want to spend time reviewing the complete set of financial statements and disclosures. This review can be done before the auditors have completed their work, so officer certification does not usually increase the duration of the closing process.

4. **Audit committee and board approvals**. The audit committee must approve every Form 10-Q, and the board of directors must approve every Form 10-K. Given the number of people involved, schedule review and approval meetings well in advance, to be conducted a few days prior to the required filing date of the applicable form. Scheduling the review slightly early gives you time to make adjustments, in case anyone expresses concerns during the review, and wants changes to be made prior to filing.

Issue the complete set of financial statements and disclosures to the audit committee or board member at least one full day in advance of a review and approval meeting, so that they have sufficient time to examine the material.

5. **EDGARize and file**. Once the Form 10-Q or Form 10-K is complete and fully approved, file it with the SEC. The filing is done using the Electronic Data Gathering, Analysis, and Retrieval (EDGAR) system that is operated by the SEC. The company can submit this information in various formats, but you will almost certainly have to convert it from the format in which the documents were originally prepared. This means hiring someone to convert the reports to the applicable format, which is a process known as *EDGARizing*. Not only is the conversion specialist responsible for converting the financial statements, but this person also files the statements with the SEC on behalf of the company. The conversion process usually takes one or two days; also, factor in additional time for the auditors to review the converted format – the auditors must give their approval before you can file with the SEC.

> **Tip:** Spend as much time as possible reviewing the financial statement package in advance before sending it to the EDGARizing firm, because they charge significant fees if you want to make subsequent changes to the converted documents.

Of all the issues noted in this section, the largest factor standing in the way of closing the books is likely to be the work schedule of the auditors. If they have other clients scheduled ahead of the company, the review or audit work may not even begin until several weeks after you have closed the books in all other respects. Consequently, it is extremely useful to work with the audit partner to move the company to the head of the auditors' work queue. Of course, if the company is scheduled first by the auditors, this means that the financial statements and all supporting schedules must be prepared at a very early date – so be sure that you will be ready before lobbying for a scheduling change.

Summary

This chapter has outlined a large number of steps that are needed to close the books. You may feel that the level of organization required to close the books in this manner is overkill. However, consider that the primary work product of the accounting department is the financial statements. If the department can establish a reputation for consistently issuing high-quality financial statements within a reasonable period of time, this will likely be the basis for the company's view of the entire department.

It is likely that additional closing steps will be needed beyond the extensive list noted in this chapter. This is particularly common when a business has an unusual operating model, or operates in an industry with unique accounting rules. If so, you should certainly incorporate the additional closing steps into the list described in this chapter.

Glossary

A

Account reconciliation. The investigation and verification of the items stored in an account, sometimes based on information contained in a similar account maintained by a third party.

Accounts receivable aging report. A report that lists unpaid customer invoices and unused credit memos by date ranges. This report is the primary tool used by collections personnel to determine which invoices are overdue for payment.

Accretion expense. The expense arising from an increase in the carrying amount of the liability associated with an asset retirement obligation. It is not a form of interest expense. It is classified as an operating expense in the income statement.

Allowance for doubtful accounts. A reserve account that offsets the total amount of accounts receivable outstanding. The allowance represents management's best estimate of the amount of accounts receivable that will not be paid by customers.

Amortization. The write-off of an intangible asset in an orderly manner over its expected period of use. This is the same concept as depreciation for tangible assets.

Asset retirement obligation. A liability associated with the retirement of a fixed asset, such as the return of land in a quarry to its original surface condition.

B

Bad debts. Invoices not paid by customers.

Bank reconciliation. A comparison between the cash position recorded on an entity's books and the position noted on the records of its bank, usually resulting in some changes to the book balance to account for transactions that are recorded on the bank's records but not the entity's, such as bank fees and interest income.

Base unit. The unit of measure used to measure a fixed asset. It is essentially the corporate definition of what constitutes a fixed asset.

Bill of lading. A legal document between the shipper of goods and the carrier of those goods. The document describes the type, quantity, and destination of the goods that the carrier has agreed to transport. It is signed by the shipper, carrier, and receiving entity.

Bill of materials. The record of the materials used to construct a product. It can include raw materials, sub-assemblies, and supplies. It can be used to order parts from suppliers, and is a key part of the evaluated receipts system.

Blanket purchase order. A purchase order that covers a number of deliveries over multiple time periods. It is typically used for recurring purchases.

Borrowing base. The total amount of collateral against which a lender will lend funds to a business. A lender usually requires that a discount factor be multiplied by each type of asset used as collateral to arrive at the borrowing base.

C

Capital expenditure. A payment made to acquire or upgrade an asset. A capital expenditure is recorded as an asset, rather than charging it immediately to expense; it is depreciated over the useful life of the asset.

Capitalization limit. The amount paid for an asset, above which an entity records it as a fixed asset. If the entity pays less than the capitalization limit for an asset, it charges the asset to expense in the period incurred.

Commission. A fee paid to a salesperson in exchange for his or her services in facilitating or completing a sale transaction. The commission may be structured as a flat fee, or as a percentage of the revenue, gross margin, or profit generated by a sale.

Control. A means by which we gain a reasonable assurance that a business will operate as planned, that its financial results are fairly reported, and that it complies with laws and regulations.

Cost pool. A grouping of costs from which allocations are made to cost objects. The most common use of a cost pool is to accumulate overhead costs that are then allocated to manufactured goods.

Credit application. A standard form sent to customers, on which they enter information needed by a company's credit department to determine the amount of credit to grant customers.

Credit insurance. A guarantee by a third party against non-payment of an invoice by a customer.

Credit memo. A credit memo is a contraction of the term "credit memorandum," which is a document issued by the seller of goods or services to the buyer, reducing the amount that the buyer owes to the seller under the terms of an earlier invoice.

Customer purchase order. A document that a customer may submit to the receiving company, in which it authorizes the purchase of specific items or services.

Cycle counting. The process of counting a small proportion of total inventory on a daily basis. A key aspect of cycle counting is to investigate and correct the reasons for any errors found, rather than merely adjusting the inventory records when an error is found.

D

Deduction. An amount that an employer withholds from the earnings of an employee. Examples of deductions are for payments into a pension plan, or for the employee-paid share of medical insurance, or for child support garnishments.

Depreciation. The gradual charging to expense of a fixed asset's cost over its expected useful life.

Derecognition. The process of removing a transaction from the accounting records of an entity. For a fixed asset, this is the removal of the asset and any accumulated depreciation from the accounting records, as well as the recognition of any associated gain or loss.

Drop shipping. The practice of having suppliers ship directly to a company's customers, bypassing the company itself.

E

Evaluated receipts. A system of paying suppliers based on a combination of goods or services received and the authorizing purchase order. There is no need for a supplier invoice.

Expense report. A form completed by an employee, with attached receipts, stating the expenses that he or she paid on behalf of the company. A business uses this report as the basis for reimbursement payments to employees.

F

Financial statements. A collection of reports about an organization's financial condition, which typically include the income statement, balance sheet, and statement of cash flows.

Fixed asset. An expenditure that generates economic benefits over a long period of time. It is also known as property, plant, and equipment.

Foreign exchange hedge. A transaction in which the parties exchange different currencies in amounts and on dates specified in the contract.

G

Garnishment. The withholding of a specified amount from a person's wages in order to satisfy a legal claim or an obligation to a creditor. Garnishments are common for spousal support, child support, and paying for unpaid taxes.

General ledger. The master set of accounts that summarize all transactions occurring within an entity.

Generally Accepted Accounting Principles. A set of authoritative accounting standards issued by several standard-setting bodies, which entities should follow in preparing their financial statements.

Gross earnings. The total amount of an employee's earnings, including regular and overtime pay, and before any deductions.

I

Impairment. When the carrying amount of a fixed asset exceeds its fair value. The amount of the impairment is the difference between the two values.

Income tax. A government tax on the taxable profit earned by an individual or corporation.

Intangible asset. An identifiable, non-monetary asset that has no physical substance. Examples of intangible assets are copyrights, patents, and taxi licenses.

International Financial Reporting Standards. A set of authoritative standards set by the International Accounting Standards Board, which an entity must comply with if it wishes to create financial statements that are accepted in those countries mandating the use of IFRS.

Invoice. A document submitted to a customer, identifying a transaction for which the customer owes payment to the issuer.

L

Line of credit. A commitment from a lender to pay a company whenever it needs cash up to a pre-set maximum level.

Lockbox. A mail box operated by a bank, to which the customers of a company send their payments. The bank deposits all payments received into the company's bank account, and posts scanned images of all payments on a secure website, which the company can access.

M

Mark to market. The adjustment of the recorded value of an asset to its current market value.

Master purchase order. An agreement between a company and its supplier, under which the company commits to a certain purchase quantity within a designated period of time, usually in exchange for reduced pricing.

N

Negative approval. An approval technique where authorizers only notify the accounts payable department if they do not approve of the payment of a supplier invoice.

Net pay. The amount that an employee is paid after all taxes and other deductions have been withheld from his or her pay.

Not sufficient funds check. A check issued for which there are not sufficient funds in the issuer's bank account.

O

Overtime. A premium wage paid that is calculated at 1 ½ times the regular wage rate, multiplied by those hours classified as overtime.

P

Packing slip. An itemization of the goods included in a shipment. This typically includes the description, part number, and quantity of each item. This document is prepared by the shipper, and is attached to the outside of a delivery container. It is used by the recipient as evidence of the contents of a shipment.

Payroll cycle. The length of time between payrolls. Thus, if an employer pays employees once a month, the payroll cycle is one month.

Payroll register. A summarization of the payments made to each employee in a payroll, including gross pay, deductions, and net pay.

Petty cash. A small amount of cash that is kept on the company premises for the purpose of paying for small, incidental expenditures.

Petty cash book. A ledger book in which are detailed all disbursements from and replenishments of a petty cash fund. It contains a running total of the actual cash balance in the fund.

Petty cash reimbursement voucher. A form used as a receipt whenever someone withdraws cash from a petty cash fund. The voucher is used as evidence for recording expenses, as well as for reconciling the cash balance in a petty cash fund.

Picking ticket. A printed list of items to be picked for a customer order.

Positive pay. An anti-fraud measure whereby a company issuing checks notifies its bank of all checks it has issued. The bank then compares this information to checks being presented for payment, and refuses to accept any checks for which it has not received prior notification from the company.

Prepaid expense. An expenditure that is paid for in one accounting period, but for which the underlying asset will not be entirely consumed until a future period.

Procedure. A series of actionable steps designed to complete a business transaction, under the guidelines set by one or more policies.

Procurement card. A credit card used to make small-dollar purchases for a business.

Procurement card reconciliation. The review of variances between the monthly statement issued by a card provider and the receipts associated with the procurement card linked to that statement.

Purchase order. A document authorizing the purchase of goods from a supplier.

Purchase requisition. A form filled out by someone requisitioning goods or services, stating the items needed. The purchasing department uses this form as the basis for its purchasing activities.

R

Receipt. A document used as evidence of an expenditure. Examples of receipts are hotel bills and air travel invoices.

Regular hours. The first 40 hours that an employee works in a designated work week. All additional hours worked in the same work week are categorized as overtime.

Glossary

Remittance advice. An attachment to a check payment, detailing the contents of the payment.

Remote deposit capture. The use of a scanning device to create a legal, scanned image of both sides of a check, which is then uploaded to a bank as a valid deposit.

Return merchandise authorization. An authorization granted by a seller for a buyer to return goods to it.

Reversing entry. A journal entry made at the beginning of an accounting period, which reverses selected entries made in the immediately preceding accounting period.

S

Salary. A fixed amount paid to an employee for services performed, irrespective of the actual hours worked during a time period.

Sales order. An internal document used to specify the details of a customer order. It may be derived from a customer purchase order or some less-formal type of communication.

Sales tax. A tax imposed by the government of a city, county, or state on the retail price of a product or service.

Salvage value. The estimated amount that would be currently obtained upon the disposal of a fixed asset at the end of its estimated useful life. It is also known as residual value.

Shift differential. Extra pay earned by employees who work a less than desirable shift, such as the evening, night, or weekend shifts.

Shipping log. A summary of shipments issued by the shipping department, usually organized by day.

Statement. A summary of all outstanding invoices that a customer has not yet paid.

Suspense account. An account in which transactions are recorded for which final disposition has not yet been determined.

T

Three-way matching. The comparison of a supplier invoice and related purchase order and receiving document by the accounts payable staff prior to payment.

Throughput. Revenues minus all totally variable expenses. This is a key factor in constraint analysis.

Timecard. A standard form on which an employee records time worked, or on which a time clock stamps the individual's start and stop times.

Trade accounts receivable. Amounts billed by a business to its customers when it delivers goods or services to them in the ordinary course of business.

U

Useful life. The estimated lifespan of a depreciable fixed asset, during which it can be expected to contribute to company operations.

V

Vendor master file. A computer file in which is stored the key information for all suppliers with which a company has business transactions.

W

Wage. An amount paid to an employee that is based on time worked or units produced.

Withholding. The portion of an employee's wages that an employer holds back and then forwards to the government as payment for the taxes owed by the employee.

Index